ZIGZAG

ZIGZAG

Reversal and Paradox in Human Personality

Michael J. Apter

Matador
9 Priory Business Park,
Wistow Road, Kibworth Beauchamp,
Leicestershire. LE8 0RX
Tel: 0116 279 2299
Email: books@troubador.co.uk
Web: www.troubador.co.uk/matador
Twitter: @matadorbooks

ISBN 978 1788038 867

British Library Cataloguing in Publication Data.
A catalogue record for this book is available from the British Library.

Printed and bound by CPI Group (UK) Ltd, Croydon, CR0 4YY
Typeset in 11pt Minion Pro by Troubador Publishing Ltd, Leicester, UK

Matador is an imprint of Troubador Publishing Ltd

To Mark Denneen –
Without you, I might never have written this book, or any other book
for that matter

"When we dismiss as absurd that which does not seem to us to be logical, we merely prove that we know nothing about nature."

Marc Chagall.

(Cited in "Chagall" by Jacques Damase, New York: Barnes and Noble, 1963.)

"A zigzag can be the shortest distance between two points."

Anon.

CONTENTS

Four self-contradictory people, illustrating the four basic pairs of contradictory motivational states that underlie personality.

How reversals occur between opposite motivational states, with examples from everyday life. All about you.

The need to go beyond both trait and situational theories of personality: understanding people in their full complexity.

REVERSALS BETWEEN OPPOSITE MOTIVATIONAL STATES

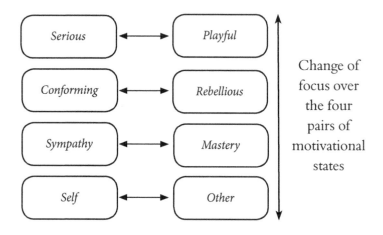

Serious	Playful
Conforming	Rebellious
Sympathy	Mastery
Self	Other

Change of focus over the four pairs of motivational states

Frontispiece

ACKNOWLEDGMENTS

"No man is an island," and this is particularly true of an author, who must remain open to every possible source of information and inspiration during the writing of his or her book. There are more people, therefore, than I can possibly acknowledge here for their help. But I would at least like to place on record my gratitude to Robert Blackstock, Thea Edwards and Mary Margaret Livingston, all of Louisiana Tech University, for their expert advice. I am also most appreciative of feedback from Gareth Lewis, Jennifer Tucker, Jay Lee, Jolena Juers, Brandon Moore, Brian Hindman, James Tornabene, Ann-Marie Rabalais, Christophe Lunacek, Eugénie Rambaud. I would also like to thank Jean Rambaud who, in the course of translating this book into French for publication in France by Dunod InterEditions, made mwany useful suggestions. I also profited from the creative collaboration on the concept of Motivational Intelligence with Tim Routledge, Danielle Swain, and their colleagues at Experience Insight Ltd, and with James Parker of Trent University, Canada.

My thanks are due to the South Carolina Department of Public Safety, Office of Highway Safety, for allowing me to cite some of the Apter International findings on seat belt usage and driving under the influence of alcohol, and for sponsoring this research.

My special thanks are with Joe Shillito, Hannah Dakin and their colleagues at Troubador Publishing.

It goes without saying, but I am pleased to say it anyway, that my major indebtedness, both personal and professional, is to my wife Mitzi Desselles.

PREFACE

If you are like me, you rarely open a nonfiction book and start reading at chapter one. Personally, I try to get an impression of what a book is about by flicking through the pages and seeing what catches my eye. I also turn to the end to see what final conclusions are provided. If all this looks interesting, then I turn to the first chapter (and perhaps buy the book). I do essentially the same with an electronic book.

In case you have started here rather than at the end, I can tell you that this book is centred on the idea that human personality is essentially dynamic and changing, and that the trait concept, which is at the basis of nearly all personality research, tends to be simplistic and limiting. After all, if you tell someone "This is how you are," you restrict, at the outset, their possibilities for change. You also in some sense restrict them to less than they could be.

Looking at human personality in this more dynamic way can open up new vistas for research and be liberating to patients and clients. It can also explain various paradoxes that arise in everyday behavior. This is not to deny that there are some kinds of consistency, but these consistencies tell only part of the story, and, I believe, in many ways, the less interesting part. We change from day to day, hour to hour, even minute to minute. The engine for this change is motivation: Now you want this, now you want that. As our motives change, so we see the world from different perspectives and become different kinds of people. Indeed, we can even, in short order, contradict ourselves. Well-being involves, among other things, our ability to navigate through such innate contradictions and turn them to our advantage.

The theme of the book is not just the limitation of trait theory. More positively, it provides an alternative way of looking at things by arguing that there is a structure underlying everyday behavior. There may be inconsistency but there is also pattern underlying this inconsistency. Specifically, I suggest that there are four pairs of contradictory motivations. This structure will inform the organisation of the book. We shall look at these contradictions and see how they play out in peoples' lives, sometimes helpfully and sometimes harmfully, often producing paradoxes and anomalies. In doing this I shall draw particular attention to these paradoxes, since they are overlooked or downplayed in modern personality research. In this way I hope to provide a more realistic account of what it means to be human – not to say a more colourful and surprising one.

The book is organised in three sections. In the first, I introduce the basic ideas, all of which derive from "Reversal Theory." These include such ideas as "reversal" and "motivational state." In the second part I take each of the four pairs of motivational states separately and show examples of the paradoxes that they generate. In the third section I apply the ideas generated in the first two sections to our understanding of economic behaviour, and to the nature of happiness. Finally, I relate all this to some fundamental biological processes. There are also some Appendices which provide background information.(1)

Reports on psychological studies will jostle alongside historical and biographical accounts, and both will be supplemented with personal reminiscences. The psychological studies will include some well-known experiments, such as Zimbardo's prison experiment and Milgram's shocking study of obediance. The aim in presenting them again here will *not* be to rehearse their already widely known results, but to provide them with a new interpretation – to see them afresh and from a different angle. My personal reminiscences, while being trivial in themselves (and in some cases embarrassing), may serve to illustrate, and hopefully to illuminate, whatever point I am trying to make. Since I was born and raised in England, but spent a large part of my later adult life in America, my personal anecdotes will involve both cultures.

While there will be a unity of theory, and the integration that comes with this, there will be a diversity of illustration, including material that is aesthetic, domestic, organisational, economic, educational, and sexual. In each of the central chapters of the book I will focus on one particular kind of paradox. I hope that all this, taken together, will produce a rich stew rather than a dog's dinner.

As we go along, we shall see that there are some common patterns underlying a huge diversity of seemingly unrelated behaviours and experiences. This book is therefore for people who like making connections between ideas, especially when they result in novel ways of seeing the world. The interest will be in two directions. One is trying to understand certain phenomena that are interesting in themselves. The other is seeing how explanations of these phenomena can be fitted together to support a cohesive general model of human motivation and personality – and one that has practical applications. In the process we find that we are adding a whole new principle of individual psychological change – reversal – to the two which have historically been the mainspring of psychological theorising about change – namely learning and maturation.

In summary, there are three intertwined themes, each supporting the other two. The first has it that the trait concept is inadequate on its own, since we are all changing all the time. The second argues that underlying this changeability is a structure of motivational states that oppose each other. The third is that using this structure, and the dynamics that go with it, allows us to provide new explanations of various intriguing puzzles and paradoxes that have never before been satisfactorily accounted for.

INTRODUCTION:
THE LOGIC OF DESIRE

"Watch the paradoxes fizz." (1)

He was a likeable and modest young man, with a sweet face, and here are some of the things that witnesses attested to in court. He never uttered an offensive word about anyone. He was always well behaved and polite. He helped an old woman whose windows broke by paying for the repairs himself. He saved the life of a friend's son who needed an emergency operation by taking him to hospital, and even covered all the expenses. He liked nothing better than to spend the day quietly fishing. As one witness said, he "would not hurt a fly." And yet this young Bosnian Serb was convicted at the War Crimes Tribunal in The Hague of executing thirteen Muslim prisoners during the wars in Yugoslavia. It seems that in fact he personally executed more than a hundred people, but the prosecution focused on these thirteen. He would enter the area where the prisoners were held and summon victims at random. Often he would beat them. He would then make each victim kneel down, give him a couple of minutes to plead for his life, and then shoot him in the back of the head. He is quoted as saying to a victim: "I can see you are scared. It is nice to kill people this way." (2)

How often do we read some similar contradiction in the newspapers? It seems that whenever someone is convicted of a murder, especially if it is gruesome or multiple or serial, friends and neighbours are reported as being mystified. "He could not possibly have done it," they say, "He is such a nice man." "There must be some mistake." "He does charity work." "He loves children." "He teaches Sunday School."

Now consider this man. He was called "the mass murderer of Steinhof," which was a mental hospital near Vienna. It was in this hospital that Nazi medical officers systematically killed patients, some of whom were mentally ill and some handicapped. It is reported, in fact, that they killed more than 7,500 patients, including over 800 children who were in a children's wing of the hospital, some suffering from as little as stuttering or having their eyes too far apart. The children were killed by injection, starvation or exposure. Their brains were then removed for examination and were still being stored years after the war ended. (3) The doctor in question, who was a senior doctor at Steinhof, was captured by the Soviets at the end of the war, and imprisoned in the notorious Lubianka prison in Moscow run by the KGB. A fellow prisoner reports that this doctor died there of cancer at the age of 40. But he added that "Before he died … he showed himself to be the best comrade you can imagine! He gave consolation to everybody. He lived up to the highest conceivable moral standard. He was the best friend I ever met during my long years in prison." (4)

Motivational Patterns

This book is not about murder, mass or otherwise. It is centrally about what I shall call 'human paradox,' including the paradox of self-contradiction. I have started with these war crime examples, because they demonstrate in a particularly dramatic fashion that people can contain contradictions within themselves – that they can embody opposites and switch between them at a moment's notice. And these contradictions are not just petty ones, like preference for one brand of beer over another, but go down to the very depths of our being and to our fundamental values and motives. They go to the very things that make us a person. These anomalies are not only intriguing in themselves, but important for another reason: anomalies often open the way to fruitful new directions for exploration in science.

When we look at people behaving in the real world rather than the laboratory, we observe great complexity, and continual movement. We observe a kind of dance. But, as with a dance, there is structure as well as complexity. Surface confusion can be anchored in an underlying pattern, just as all the complexity of chemical processes can be reduced to the structure of the Periodic Table, or the complexities of chess can be reduced to a handful of pieces and some movement rules. What I want to show is that there is a pattern of motivational opposites, and reversals between them, underlying the variety of behaviours that we see in everyday life. Knowledge of these polarities, and alternations between them, can help us to understand various behaviours that would otherwise remain puzzling. This understanding can provide insights not only into other people, but also into ourselves. Wherever we look such knowledge helps us to make sense of things.

Of course psychology, like all science, is a search for pattern. But on the whole, psychological theorising in recent times has been about specific processes such as decision-making, language learning, and pattern recognition. My rather ambitious aim in the present book is to look for patterns that relate to the person as a whole. And in order to do this we have, more than anything, to start from motivation, because this is what drives and organises everything else, and acts as the coordinator that allows a person to act, at a given time, in an integrated way.

The analysis derives from a theory with a strange name: Reversal Theory (5). This theory has been used in the elucidation of many different topics in psychology (6), and my aim here will be to take advantage of its generality in attempting to make sense of a diverse range of perplexing behaviours. Each paradox, like 'inoffensive people who do terrible things,' will present us with a kind of detective mystery: what is going on, and why? In investigating these paradoxes, I shall extend reversal theory by adding some new and previously unpublished concepts.

Human Paradox

I shall be using the term "paradox" quite often in this book. (See p. 109 for example.) I must admit straight away that I shall be using the term in a rather special sense. In logic, a paradox is strictly a statement that contradicts itself, so that its truth cannot be decided. A good example is the famous Liar Paradox which consists of the assertion: "This statement is false" when referring to itself. If it is true that this statement is false, then it must be false. But if it is false, then it must be true, because this is exactly what the statement says. So which is it? True or false? (7) But in fact the term 'paradox' has been used in many different ways over the centuries and in different subjects, and need not be restricted to self-referential paradoxes such as the type represented by the Liar Paradox (8).

The term 'human paradox' here will refer to those things about human behavior that appear to make little or no sense in terms of reasonable common sense assumptions, such as the assumption that people want to survive, avoid pain, do what is worthwhile, be happy, and be self-consistent. When such common sense assumptions are violated, the result seems to be absurd and to call out for explanation.

I want to make clear at the outset that paradox is not a quality of things themselves but of how they are seen. Each paradox will involve the relationships between an observer and something observed. Typically the observer will be you and I, so that the paradox is in the way that *we* see things. An example would be our enjoyment of bad emotions at the movies, which appears to be almost universal. But sometimes it will be necessary to make reference to other observers and their interpretations of what is going on, since the paradoxes will be special to these particular observers. (For example, the people who panicked on hearing "The War of the Worlds" radio broadcast to be discussed in a later chapter.)

I should add that my emphasis will be on human paradoxes that are widespread and part of everyday life, rather than psychiatric abnormalities in need of therapy, although we shall touch on some of these too. Some human paradoxes are already recognized in psychology and even have names: the Franklin paradox, the Abilene paradox, and so on. Others are paradoxes that I shall be bringing to light for the first time in this book.

While we shall often be looking at dramatic and extreme examples, such as the behaviour of the Bosnian Serb war criminal referred to at the start of this chapter, our examples will generally be recognisable as exaggerations of more normal ways of being. They will involve processes that we can all identify with at some level, and recognise in our own behaviour. So we shall be asking ourselves such questions as: "Why do people sometimes take risks that they do not have to take?" "Why do people sometimes work less hard at something when they get to be rewarded for it?" "Why is persuasion sometimes counterproductive?" "Why do people sometimes go out of their way to help their enemies?" "Why is it difficult to remain happy for very long?" Just listing some of these questions reminds us how strange and enigmatic our species is. In the exasperated words of the poet Alexander Pope: "Good God! What an incongruous animal is man." (9)

Of course people can be irrational in all kinds of ways. These include making such mistakes as stereotyping, confusing correlation with cause-and-effect, and arguing tautologically. But this is not what we shall be concerned with here. In this book I shall be dealing with a different logic: the logic of desire rather than the logic of truth. Contradictions make no sense in 'truth-logic,' but, as we shall see, they are of the essence in 'desire-logic,' which has its own kind of rationality. For instance, one of the paradoxes that we shall look at is the way in which people seek out bad feelings, as they do when they go to the movies and willingly experience such emotions as anxiety, disgust and grief. This is perplexing, because these are emotions that in other circumstances people would go out of their way to avoid. It goes against the assumption that such emotions are, by definition, unpleasant. And it shows people being self-contradictory over time, sometimes trying to avoid or escape from such emotions and sometimes seeking them out and embracing them. This may seem irrational, but it will make sense when we understand the motivational processes underlying these changes, including the process of reversal. As we shall see, they have their own kind of logic.

PART ONE

FOUNDATIONS

CHAPTER 1

FOUR LIVES

Four Americans, four lives, four kinds of puzzling self-contradiction and paradox, four enigmas... these will be the topics of this chapter. A politician, a businessman, a soldier, a scientist, all of them inconsistent with themselves in fundamental ways. Let's start with the politician, Eliot Spitzer.

ELIOT SPITZER: MAN OF RECTITUDE?

Eliot L. Spitzer was Governor of the State of New York. He made his name known nationally for his toughness on crime, first as the state's Attorney General and then as Governor. Seen as a vigorous fighter against corruption and fraud, especially on Wall Street,(1) *Time* magazine named him "Crusader of the Year" for 2002. He was also known as "The Sheriff of Wall Street," and was seen as a potential Presidential contender. In the process, this tall, skeletal figure had made himself much hated in some quarters, many seeing him as going beyond toughness to vindictiveness. But in his attempts at enforcing regulations, he can be seen as having been prescient and doing no more than was necessary to deal with some of the excesses and greed that would lead to the financial meltdown in 2008. In any case, he was highly aggressive in his pursuit of those he saw as being less than fully honest in their financial dealings, and he brought a number of major Wall Street figures to book.

Among various high-profile campaigns as state Attorney General, he had also crusaded against prostitution rings, bringing two prosecutions. One of these, for a travel agency arranging "sex tours" was dismissed. But in the other, an "escort agency" in New York, the proprietor was convicted. Later, as Governor, he advanced legislation increasing the maximum sentence for patronising a prostitute from six months to one year. At that time he described prostitution and human trafficking as "among the most repugnant crimes." (2) In doing all this, he presented himself as a figure of great rectitude.

Imagine (or remember) the universal shock when, in early 2008, it was discovered that this puritanical figure, this paragon of integrity, had himself been a client of just such a ring – the Emperors Club VIP, a high-priced 'escort agency' based in New York. It was disclosed that, identified as "Client-9," he had met with one of their prostitutes in the Mayflower Hotel in Washington DC and paid several thousand dollars for her services. In fact, Spitzer appears to have been a regular client of the agency, both while Attorney General and more frequently as Governor. (3) Ironically, he was tracked down by the FBI through their use of some of the very same wiretap techniques that he had himself developed in the pursuit of prostitution. Not long after this disclosure he went through the American resignation ritual of standing in front of a row of microphones, his ashen-faced wife by his side, to resign his office. In fact he was never charged for anything, but the damage to his life and work was done. Among other things, he could no longer be realistically seen as a future candidate for the Presidency.

HALO AND HORNS
_____

Spitzer's case is arresting, because we are confronted by someone whose personality is, as it were, split down the middle. It has two opposing halves: the good guy and the bad guy, Dr. Jekyll and Mr. Hyde. How is it that they can co-exist? And which is the *real* Eliot Spitzer?

We see that on the one side, the 'good guy,' there is the desire to be dutiful, to support certain moral principles, and to do what society needs and expects. A book written about him before the scandal broke, makes much of his emphasis on ethics. (4) On the other side, there is a desire to be personally free, to do what one wants without let or hindrance, to 'be oneself.' These two contradictory principles can become a particular problem when they are tied to the very same thing – in this case prostitution. Then we are particularly struck by the self-contradictory nature of Spitzer's personality as it moves to and fro between these opposite ways of being.

These two principles are very basic. On the one hand we have the principle of duty. On the other we have the principle of freedom. Speaking psychologically, rather than morally, it is not that one of these is desirable and the other not. As values, they are both desirable. We all want to fit in and be respected and approved, but we also want to be able to 'do our own thing,' and 'be ourselves,' even, on occasion, in defiance of others. Spitzer himself described his transgressions as a kind of 'outlet.' (5) Rule-following and rule-breaking can each have their own special uses in life and their own special satisfactions. And these come into focus for most of us at different times and places. But trying to satisfy both can lead to problems.

You may have noticed that I have just slipped into talking about 'us' rather than Spitzer, by talking about people in general, including ourselves. This is what we must do if we are better to understand Spitzer's puzzling behaviour. This is because we can see it as an exaggerated version of something that applies to all of us, and that enters into all our lives – namely the push and pull between the desire to conform and the desire to be free, between the wish to do the right thing and the wish – yes – to do the wrong thing, if this means escaping from the tyranny of other peoples' expectations.

I want to suggest that most of us experience both of these desires at different times, and switch – reverse – between them from time to time. On the conformity side, there are groups that we are pleased or proud to belong to – family, community, work organisations, clubs – and we feel satisfaction when we fit in and do the right thing and provide them with what they expect of us. On the rebellious side, we feel impatient with the need to fit in. We feel restless and discontented with our lot, looking for something different. These feelings can even rise to the level of anger, which is the quintessential rebellious emotion. In anger we want to swear, be impolite, break something or even hurt someone – all things we know are wrong, but do temporarily very much want to do in the face of unfairness and constraint. Carrying out such actions may even give us momentary pleasure. There are also situations where we are, as it seems to us, unfairly prevented from doing something, and this very prohibition makes it more desirable to do that very thing, precisely because it is not allowed, as in certain kinds of sexual behaviour. The "Prohibition Era" in American history is a dramatic lesson in this respect.

Sometimes we prohibit ourselves. When I go on a diet and hold myself back from eating a certain kind of food, then this is the very food that I particularly crave – and when in a rebellious state this is what I am particularly liable to eat. This is why it is so difficult to diet, or to give up smoking or drinking. Think again of Governor Spitzer. The prohibition against doing the very things that he devoted himself to prosecuting must, in rebellious moments, have made those things seem especially attractive. What could be more restricting than something that one has publicly committed oneself to opposing? And what could give a greater feeling of freedom than reacting against exactly this? This would seem to be all part of this particular paradox.

In any case, whichever principle applies, it takes over our whole being at that moment. It engenders a kind of mini-personality. When you are rebellious, everything is seen through this particular lens. This doesn't mean that you are unaware of the rules, and of what you should do. Rather, these rules come to be seen, at that moment, as constraints – even unbearable constraints – that have to be broken. So we may assume that Eliot Spitzer, in his 'bad' moments, assumed a rebellious personality, which is the one that led to his subsequent problems.

Unfortunately, you cannot mix these two motivational opposites – they are not quantities that can be run together in different proportions, like hot and cold water making warm water. Rather they are alternative ways of making sense of the world, each complete in itself. They are like different television channels: you cannot mix channels, but have to receive one channel or another. For this reason, in what follows in this book I am going to call them 'motivational *states*' rather than just motivations. Each state is an orientation to the world based on a value, like freedom or duty. They are not so much about what we look *at*, as where we look *from*.

In Spitzer's case the rebellious state results in a very human paradox, and one that is far from unique. We think of political leaders committing fraud, preachers found with prostitutes in sordid motels, priests molesting little boys behind the confessional. Why would people whose lives are dedicated to doing good allow themselves to commit acts of questionable morality – acts that they may well themselves condemn and judge to be evil? This does not necessarily mean that they are being hypocritical, but rather that they want opposite things at different times.

Going back to my earlier question: "Which is the real Eliot Spitzer?" I have to answer: "Both" – which is to say that both sides of his personality, both motivational states, can be seen as equally genuine parts of who he is. Concluding that he is *really* a hypocrite and a cheat may only be half true. The other half would be that he is also *really* a reformer and champion of justice, that he really wants the best for society.

Here's another interesting thing that we need to bear in mind. This is that we cannot say that the conformist state is always desirable, and the rebellious undesirable. After all, in the conformist state we may fail to point out problems that need attention. On the other hand, rebelliousness can lead to innovation and change. A man in a temper can, in a burst of energy, do essential things that other people are afraid to do. A stubborn dissenter can draw attention to real problems that need to be dealt with. An innovator can get outside the box by destroying it. But clearly in Spitzer's case it worked out that for him, being rebellious in the way that he was rebellious, was a negative rather than a positive. It did not exactly work for him.

What I have done here is to identify a kind of self-contradiction, in this case a contradiction between a *conforming* and a *rebellious state of mind*. In fact it is possible to identify three other basic kinds of motivational contradiction and we shall look at these in the rest of this chapter. (6) In discussing each I shall, again, illustrate the self-contradiction in question through the life of a particular well-known person in whom the contradiction can be discerned particularly clearly.

JOHN ROCKEFELLER: BRUTAL PHILANTHROPY

John Rockefeller, owner of Standard Oil, was one of the great "robber barons" of the nineteenth century. He was a pinched and mean-looking man – the phrase 'dessicated calculating machine" comes to mind. (7) But he was reputed during his lifetime to be the richest man in the world. He started his company in the 1870s, and it quickly grew through his purchase of other companies, so that within ten years he controlled an amazing 90% of America's refining capacity. By 1882 (after he had converted the company into a trust) he owned a near monopoly of all the oil business in the U.S. This was a phenomenal business success, of a scale and kind that had never been seen before, and it constituted a threat to free market activity. In order to return the oil industry to some semblance of competitiveness, in 1911 the Supreme Court split Standard Oil into 38 separate companies. (8)

As with all large scale financial dealings, the reasons for Rockefeller's success were complex. But one key component was the deal that he made with the major railroads so that they would give Standard Oil, and Standard Oil alone, special rebates. This gave him a major advantage over his competitors, who he then offered to buy out on terms highly favourable to himself. Under this threat, these smaller operators largely buckled and sold out, in some cases for a major loss and with the ruination of their owners, who he regarded with contempt.

"He was willing to strain every nerve to obtain for himself special and unjust privileges from the railroads which were bound to ruin every man in the oil business not sharing them with him," wrote Ida Tarbell. (9) Ida Tarbell plays an interesting part in the Rockefeller story. She was an investigative journalist – what at the time they called a 'muckraker' – who devoted much of her life to exposing and documenting the abuses of Rockefeller and Standard Oil. She became a perpetual thorn in his side, and through her writings, which exposed some of his shadier dealings; she helped to make him a symbol of corporate greed and personal ruthlessness.

When the railroad owners started to unite against him, he outsmarted them by building pipelines to carry his oil. Once again he beat the competition and his corporate empire grew once more. The result is that commercial failure was suffered by others on such a grand scale that a financial depression was experienced across the country.

But now we come to the psychologically intriguing part of the story. As he started to make money, so he started to give it away. This calculating machine turned out to have a heart after all. Initially, as a Baptist, he gave unostentatiously to Baptist causes, and even before he started his spectacular career in oil, when he was still a clerk earning only $3 a week, he had his income tithed. (10) But as he earned more, so he gave more away. It is told how, at church, he would awkwardly slip small envelopes, carrying money, into the hands of less well off parishioners as they shook hands and said good-bye. (11) (In later life he would give dimes to children and nickels to adults wherever he went.) In these and other ways he donated to charitable causes increasingly large amounts of what he had so brutally acquired. Eventually he was making so much money that it became impossible even for him to give it away fast enough. At this point he felt compelled to set up major philanthropic institutions that could deal with his largesse in a more systematic and professional way. In this manner he founded the Rockefeller Foundation, The General Education Board and the Institute for Medical Research – some of the first and finest major philanthropic foundations in the history of the United States. Being particularly interested in education, he also founded the University of Chicago. However you look at it, these are historic acts of generosity and social responsibility

Rockefeller's major modern biographer writes that "… his good side was every bit as good as his bad side was bad. Seldom has history produced such a contradictory figure. We are almost forced to posit, in helpless confusion, at least two Rockefellers: the good, religious man and the renegade businessman, driven by baser motives."(12) William James the great Harvard psychologist, who knew Rockefeller socially, was intrigued by the way that he could be "…so complex, subtle, oily, fierce, strongly bad and strongly good a human being." (13)

Strongly bad and strongly good! Two Rockefellers! Just as in the case of Eliot Spitzer, we are confronted by someone whose personality is split down the middle – and there is no reason to assume that both sides of the split are not equally authentic. And although the opposing motivations involved are different from those of Spitzer, we see the same phenomenon of opposition, and of switching back and forth from one way of being – one motivational state – to the other. Again we are led to the conclusion that there are innate contradictions in human nature which play themselves out over time. In the case of Rockefeller we see particularly clearly an opposition between a *self-oriented* and an *other-oriented* *motivational state* – one concerned primarily with personal gain and the other with the needs of other people.

Which of us is not concerned with our own needs and desires, and who among us does not often put these ahead of the needs and desires or others? It is "only human," so to speak. Indeed, many of us are fiercely competitive at times, and at these times enjoy overcoming and dominating other people. In this, Rockefeller was not so different from the rest of us – only spectacularly more successful. But at the same time, who among us is not, at times, genuinely concerned with the needs of others, with whom we identify and help if we can – as parents, spouses, teachers, friends or neighbours?

We also identify with causes greater than ourselves, from following a local football team to sending money to a political campaign, to – well, like the young Rockefeller – supporting our local church. In this respect we all contain contradictions within us.

We have now seen two dimensions of self-contradiction: conformist versus rebellious and self-oriented versus other-oriented states of mind. Let us look at a third.

ULYSSES GRANT: COMPASSION AT COLD HARBOR

The Battle of Cold Harbor in 1864 was a particularly brutal one, even for the American Civil War. Early in the battle General Ulysses S. Grant ordered what turned out to be a suicidal frontal assault by 40,000 of his Unionist troops against fortified Confederate positions. The charge turned into a slaughter, and it is estimated that some 7,000 Union troops were killed or wounded in the first half hour of the attack. To put this in perspective, it was not until the First World War, half a century later, that there would again be such a high casualty rate in battle.

Survivors of the ill-advised charge scrambled back and dug themselves into the earth, the battle settling into trench warfare. But the terrible thing, horrifying to contemplate, is that thousands of wounded soldiers lay dying in agony between the lines, moaning and pleading for help, with no food, water, or medical attention. Grant waited two days before he got around to sending a message to Robert E. Lee, the Commander of the Confederate forces, requesting a two hour cessation of hostilities to attend to the wounded on both sides who had fallen within what was called the "slaughter pen." Since they could not agree on some details, it was a day later again – four days after the charge – that stretcher bearers were finally able to enter the no-man's-land and witness the horror of what had happened. But it was, tragically, too late to do anything: all but two of the survivors of the charge had died.

Clearly part of Grant's success as a military leader was his steely ability to turn off any caring feelings he might have had towards either the enemy or even his own men, in order to be able to make the dispassionate decisions that were needed to achieve victory. Grant had a reputation for being hard-hearted and cold – he was known by some as the "fumbling butcher." His view was that if you do have to fight a battle, then you must be committed to doing whatever is necessary to win, however repugnant. War was simple: it was about killing the other side, and killing them in greater numbers than they could kill you. This calculus made him what one writer called "a frighteningly effective warrior." (14)

But here is the strange thing: on the way to the battle, Grant had passed a teamster whipping a horse about the head. Upset at what he saw, and in a rage, he ordered that the man be tied to a post for six hours as punishment (15). As at least one observer has pointed out, "…it was the plight of a horse that drew his anger at Cold Harbor, not the plight of the men." (16) It seems that he could be caring as well as calculating, although in this instance it certainly seems odd that his focus of concern seemed to invert what we would normally expect. Most of us would be more concerned about the well-being of humans than we would about the well-being of horses.

Here is another strange thing. While the wounded were dying in the 'slaughter pen,' and begging for help, he wrote an affectionate letter to his daughter Nellie, telling her that he would get her a buggy to go with the family pony. (17) In fact, as we know from his autobiography, he was highly sensitive to the carnage caused by battle. In the photographs we see of him (and there are not many), there is a kind of wistful sadness. As he admitted: "While a battle is raging one can see his enemy mowed down by the thousand, or the ten thousand, with great composure, but after the battle these scenes are distressing, and one is naturally disposed to do as much to alleviate the suffering of an enemy as a friend." (18) There are many accounts of his kindness to wounded men after a battle, and in one of these it is reported that he was crying. (19) After the battle of Shilo, the battle from which the 'butcher' epithet derived, it is reported that he spent the night sleeping under an oak tree in the rain because he could not bear to hear the moans of the wounded in the camp. When the principal Confederate forces finally surrendered to him at Appomattox Court House he commanded that they be treated with respect, and he prohibited celebration in front of them. So we do indeed see someone who, while steeling himself for battle, allowed himself feelings of compassion outside of battle.

Going even further, if we make Grant's acquaintance altogether outside the military context, we find a man of fine sensitivity and generosity. The heartless commander was, in his private life, devoted to his wife and children. Before the civil war he farmed for a time, and reportedly knowingly overpaid his hired hands. He bought a slave and gave him his freedom a few months later even though he was in dire financial trouble at the time. He disliked the cruelty of hunting and was horrified by a bull fight that he was taken to see in Mexico.

As with Spitzer and Rockefeller we see someone made up of two opposing halves. In Grant's case, one half is toughness and the other is tenderness. If we are to put this in terms of motivational states, we could say that he seems to have experienced both what I shall call a 'mastery state' and a 'sympathy state' at different times. It is interesting that we can observe in him a regular reversal during campaigns from the mastery state during combat itself, to the sympathy state afterwards.

Just as with Rockefeller, the reversals – and contradictions – are ones that we can discern in our own lives. Most of us switch backwards and forwards between a task-oriented attempt to control people and things, often associated with what we do at work, to a more caring and even loving state, frequently when we are with our families and friends. In the one case we want power, even if this means distancing ourselves from, or manipulating, others; in the reverse case we long for closeness and intimacy, even if this means making ourselves vulnerable. These alternative feelings come and go in the course of daily life in all kinds of shifting and nuanced circumstances, so that there may well be moments on any given day when we feel periods of sympathy even though at work and mastery even though at home. We can also experience these states in ways that are not necessarily obvious to others: we can hide our feelings. The point of choosing Grant as an example of all this was to show these states, and reversals between them, in as clear a way as possible.

This mastery/sympathy contradiction is different from the 'Rockefeller contradiction' between self-oriented and other-oriented states – even if, at first sight, they seem to be similar. A moment's thought will show us that sympathy is not necessarily about helping others – it can also be about the desire to be cared for *by* others, and therefore self-oriented. For instance, when I am ill in bed I am much of the time in the self-oriented and sympathy states. Likewise, the mastery state is not necessarily about having power for oneself. It can also be about the desire for others to have some kind of power, like the football team that one supports, or the child one is teaching. In this case it is the mastery and other-oriented states that would be combined.

ALFRED KINSEY: SEX REVELATION AND REVOLUTION

The name of Alfred C. Kinsey is synonymous with sex. When Philip Larkin (20) wrote:

Sexual intercourse began
In nineteen sixty three

he was really referring to the effects of the sexual revolution brought about largely by Kinsey – although Kinsey's two weighty tomes on sexual behaviour were published in the late forties *(The Sexual Behaviour of the Human Male)* (21) and the early fifties *(The Sexual Behaviour of the Human Female).* (22) Both these "Kinsey Reports" became huge best-sellers, and shocked the world by showing that people had more sex, of more kinds, under more different circumstances, and breaking more taboos, than had previously been suspected in peoples' wildest imagination. Premarital sex was widespread, as was adultery and homosexuality. So, too, were various actions that were regarded as 'perversions.' The effect of the reports appears to have been to free people from feelings of guilt about sex. It would not be too much to say that this liberating effect set off a revolution in sexual attitudes – the revolution of the 'swinging sixties' referred to in Larkin's poem.

The popular image of Kinsey was that of a serious scientist who was studying sexual behaviour in a properly detached and emotionally uninvolved manner, as one might dispassionately observe and record the activities of some insect species. In fact, it is not without relevance here that until he started his research on sexual behaviour, Kinsey, a Zoologist by profession, had in fact devoted his career to insects, specifically to the detailed study of gall wasps. His dedication – even obsessionality – was shown by the fact that he personally collected and catalogued some 100,000 specimens, over twenty odd years. (23) His scientific credentials were therefore impeccable, and he was indeed, by any standard, a serious researcher.

His reason for discarding all this, and moving on to the study of sex, was his dawning realisation that there was a widespread ignorance and even desperate misunderstanding about sexual functions (an ignorance from which he had himself suffered as a young man). There was clearly an enormous need, especially because of unwanted pregnancies and sexually unfulfilled marriages, to educate young people in these matters. But when he came to look at the scientific literature, which he had to do in writing a course preparing students for marriage (a course required by students of his university), he was amazed to discover how little was actually known about human sexual behaviour. He pointed out that considerably more was known about sexuality in barnyard animals. He therefore determined to find out as much as he could, and in this he was supported steadfastly by his University, Indiana University, where he was able to set up the research institute that came later to be called the 'Kinsey Institute.' (Incidentally, the institute was supported by the Rockefeller Foundation.)

The research that he carried out was based on a meticulous and detailed "Sex Interview" that could take as much as two hours to complete with each interviewee. His aim was simply to uncover the facts, and he and his co-workers took care to remain morally neutral and emotionally unengaged. The same applied to the movies he made of people having intercourse, which he never published in any form and which anticipated the later research of Masters & Johnson.

It seems clear that Kinsey was a driven scientist. He worked long hours, set the highest standards for himself and others, and was utterly devoted to his pursuit of data. Between them, he and his colleagues interviewed thousands of people from all walks of life. In motivational terms, we can say that, in pursuing this mission, he displayed a *serious motivational state*. That is, the overriding value that he expressed in this work was that of achievement and he was attempting to do something that would be highly consequential for society. He was therefore willing to forego the pleasures of the moment in order to move towards significant long-term goals. Indeed, he was prepared to put up with fatigue, stress and vociferous opposition from colleagues and others, in order to accomplish these goals. 'Serious' does not necessarily mean 'solemn' or 'grave.' It means being aware of long-term consequences.

Now we come to the surprising part. A biographical study of Kinsey, based on twenty five years of research, has brought to light the unexpected fact that this is only a partial picture. (24) Interviews with friends and colleagues disclosed that, at least some of the time, he did in fact throw himself into the study of sex in a more recreational and participative way. At these times, sex became for him fun rather than work. We should perhaps not be surprised, given his curiosity, that he displayed tendencies towards voyeurism – this would be of a piece with his scientific work. But more surprisingly, he seems also to have enjoyed exhibitionism and was notorious to his neighbours for his near nudity while gardening. Worse, he also went out of his way to break conventional taboos, not only by engaging in oral and anal sex, but by means of various sadomasochistic practices, such as tugging at his testicles with a length of rope. And he fostered an open situation in which those working with him at the institute were encouraged to have intercourse with each other as well as each other's wives. He was himself involved with his wife in a threesome with one of his institute colleagues. In this way he "endeavoured to create his own sexual utopia". (25) Furthermore, throughout his life he experimented with homosexual behaviours, and was clearly bisexual. He also developed a network of individuals in half a dozen cities who were willing to perform sex acts while others watched. In sum, these new disclosures show that he was passionate as well as dispassionate. As one colleague later put it, he was "orthogonal ... high on the scientific-objective and high on the prurient". (26) Clearly this personal sexual experimentation was highly risky for his career. He was lucky to get away with it.

At least some of the time, then, he was shockingly fun-seeking rather than serious in his reaction to sex. By 'fun-seeking' here I mean that he was at these times more concerned with immediate pleasure and sensation than with long-term significant goals, such as those of science. As a result he allowed himself to take various kinds of playful risk and 'hang the consequences.' Of course none of this came out at the time, and if it had it would have given powerful ammunition to those who opposed his research, especially those who wished to ban it on moral or religious grounds. What a field day his opponents would have had if they had known!

In any case, we can say that Kinsey displayed both *serious* and *playful motivational states* at different times, moving between them without difficulty. Which was the real Alfred Kinsey? The serious scientist or the sexual adventurer? The far-sighted researcher, or the joyful libertine? As with Spitzer, Grant, and Rockefeller, we can answer that he spent periods of time in each of two opposing motivational states. So again, the answer is: "Both." And again we see an example of someone whose personality cannot be pinned down in terms of simple fixed traits. We see him in our mind's eye wearing a smart suit and his signature bow tie, giving a professional presentation to a large audience at a conference. And then we see him later at night, on the prowl around the bars, looking furtive, perhaps, for all I know, even wearing a grubby raincoat.

The larger point here is that we are, all of us, both serious and playful at different times in our daily lives. This seems to be a universal human characteristic. Examples hardly seem to be needed. Most of us enjoy watching television, having a nice meal, a good laugh, an intense orgasm. We might enjoy taking risks by gambling. But most of us also get satisfaction out of making solid progress in our careers, gradually paying off our mortgages, and increasing our status at work. I do not think that it is too much to claim that this difference between serious and playful states is one of fundamental importance in understanding human behaviour, whether there is an alternation between extremes, as in the case of Kinsey, or between more everyday versions of these two motivational states as is probably the case with most of us.

SIDE BY SIDE

A general point that has emerged for all four of our 'case histories' is that, where there is contradiction in a personality, we are not necessarily faced with a true self and an apparent self. Rather, we are faced with two 'true' selves.

The spirit of this point is captured by Richard Sale in his book on traitors, when he says that "We say of (Bob Hanssen, the spy)… that he lived a double life. But what if, in fact, he led several lives lying side by side, just as layers of different species of rock peacefully adjoining each other… Perhaps the self that denounced communism was just as earnest as the one that served it. Perhaps the loving husband was just as sincere as the husband who disliked his wife and felt revengeful satisfaction by displaying her nude on the internet or allowing his friend to watch her performing sex." (27)

The same point is well put by Walter Langer, a psychologist who was employed during the Second World War by the American government to diagnose Hitler. He argued that Hitler had different personalities, but that they were all equally genuine. "As one surveys Hitler's behaviour patterns, as his close associates observe them, one gets the impression that this is not a single personality, but two that inhabit the same body and alternate back and forth… It is a kind of Dr. Jekyll and Mr. Hyde personality structure in which two wholly different personalities oscillate back and forth." As he describes them, we can recognise in Hitler the sympathy state – in which he "wants nothing quite so much as to be amused, liked and looked after." – and the mastery state in which we see a "hard, cruel and decisive person." (28)

WE ARE DANCERS NOT STATUES

How does all this relate to ourselves and our own behaviour? How do these four motivational oppositions play out in our own lives? It will be clear that the simple trait view of personality – the basis of psychological testing which has it that we have fixed personality characteristics – just will not do as a full explanation when it comes to the complexities of real life. How could we describe Spitzer in purely trait terms? Was Kinsey a cautious and serious person or playful and risk-taking? How could we place Rockefeller on a selfish-to-altruistic dimension? What would Grant's traits be? No: we are dynamic not static, fluid not fixed, dancers not statues. These cases alone are enough to raise problems for trait theory, but we shall see that the psychological principles involved are not restricted to the rich and famous but are in the very air that we breathe.

CHAPTER 2

INVITATION TO THE DANCE

In the previous chapter I made a large claim. This was that we all embody contradictions, even if we usually do so in considerably less dramatic forms than Rockefeller and the others whose lives we looked at. Such contradiction is paradoxical since it is reasonable to assume that most people would want to be consistent, and not do things at one time that might work against the things they do at another time. Why, as it were, build a sandcastle only to knock it down?

Montaigne, the great French essayist of the sixteenth century (he invented the whole idea of an 'essay'), was particularly aware of such inconsistency. "There is as much difference between us and ourselves as between us and others" he writes. (1) "We float between different states of mind." (2) We are "Nothing but oscillation and inconsistency." (3) "Some imagine that we have two souls" (4) "We are, I know not how, double within ourselves." (5) He cites an earlier writer to the effect that, of a given tribe, they "abandoned themselves to pleasures as if they were to die on the morrow, and built as if they were never to die" (6). This insight concerning inconsistency seems to have been downplayed by psychologists – or if noticed, systematically overlooked. Montaigne is clearly not the patron saint of trait theory.

In this book, I shall be going further than simply putting forward the rather vague view that inconsistency is part of human make-up: I shall argue that there is pattern in these inconsistencies. There is not just an ever-changing collection of contradictions, but a basic and universal set of eight states, arranged in four pairs of opposites, which provide some structure to what would otherwise be chaotic. These states make up a key group that, in the normal way of things, are universal in the sense that we all experience them and we experience them all. (I have described their individual characteristics in Appendix One.) I used each of the four personalities we looked at in the previous chapter, to illustrate each of these four fundamental kinds of contradiction.

To summarize, here are the four pairs:
- Serious versus Playful (e.g. Kinsey)
- Conforming versus Rebellious (e.g. Spitzer)
- Mastery versus Sympathy (e.g. Grant)
- Self-oriented versus Other-oriented (e.g. Rockefeller)

I want to suggest that each state (e.g. serious, or mastery) represents a complete 'way of being' that sees the world in a particular manner, acts in it with a particular style, has a particular perspective and is able to experience certain emotions rather than others. Each state contains its own affirmations and joys, but also its own dreads and despairs. This complexity is why I call them motivational *states*. But each state is defined by, and anchored in, its underlying desire. That is why I call them *motivational* states. Everything stems from the motivation. (7) A consequence of all this is that every time that you reverse between opposite motivational states, you change the world you live in, in the sense that you see it in a completely new way. We might almost say that you are a different person.

To take an everyday example, when I am googling for a

piece of information that I need for something I am writing to a deadline, I judge each piece of information I get in terms of whether it is what I need, or at least leads towards what I need. In this case I am in the serious state, and my primary aim is therefore not so much to enjoy myself as to achieve something, whether I happen to enjoy what I am doing or not at that time. My world is focused, and I am willing to tolerate the problems I have to deal with for the sake of the consequences of success, even if this entails some degree of anxiety. This means that I am looking at the world in a particular way. But when I am googling in the opposite, playful, state I am looking at it in a very different fashion. Now I am open to enjoying what in the serious state would have been experienced as distractions. Now I am looking for information that I may not need, but that I am curious about, and if the search leads in unexpected but interesting directions, so much the better! I am now in a very different world from that of the serious state, and one in which I make different choices.

Multiple Contradictions

I may have given a wrong impression in the last chapter, namely an idea that every person embodies a single contradiction. Certainly we looked at only one contradiction in the case of each of the four lives we examined, such as Kinsey and his serious-playful contradiction. The reason that I presented things in this overly simple form is that I wanted to adopt a method rather like that of teaching wine appreciation – starting with wines that have exaggerated flavours – a kind of 'method of extremes.' In this fashion it is possible to establish a set of recognisable qualities that can be used as points of reference in more subtle, nuanced and mixed cases. So I chose to focus on just those contradictions that were particularly clear-cut in the four people we looked at. What I *am* suggesting now is in fact that we are *all* characterised by *all* four kinds of contradictions, although each one will be more or less important in each of our lives, and this is one of the ways that we differ from each other and express our personalities. So for Rockefeller, the most striking contradiction was that of being self-oriented versus being other-oriented, but this certainly did not preclude him experiencing other states and other contradictions, and we may suppose that he did so frequently. Likewise, your own most characteristic contradiction might be between the serious and playful states, but you will experience the other three forms of inconsistency too at different times. This represents a critical aspect of human complexity.

In fact, in the normal way of things, there is a sense in which we experience all four dimensions all the time, just as we experience four physical dimensions all the time. These four are the psychological dimensions in which we live our lives and have our being. They are as inescapable as the multiple physical dimensions in which we also live.

There is another point here. This is that each of the motivational states can be experienced and expressed in many different concrete ways, and in relation to many different kinds of situation. I don't want to give the impression that each state is attached to just one activity. Ulysses Grant might have expressed his mastery motivation by, among very many other things, leading men in battle. You, on the other hand, might express it by playing video games, arguing, or driving a car too fast, among many other things. Kinsey might have expressed his playful needs through, among other things, taking an active part in sexual activities. You, on the other hand, might express them through watching television, eating a good meal, or drinking with friends (as well as engaging in sexual activities). A state may express varied behaviour, and involve feelings that are more or less intense, more or less extreme, more or less unusual, but with a basic motive that holds everything together and defines the state. (See Appendix 1.) Each state has its own voice, whether whispered or shouted, spoken or sung. It has a distinctive style.

To make these ideas more personal, you might ask yourself: What are the things that are most important to me in my life? Family? Career? Church? Friends? Golf? Drinking? Charity work? Whatever they are, if you think about them you should be able to see which, or which combination, of the eight motivational states you satisfy – or hope to satisfy – in each. Which motivational states are invested, and to what extent, in which of your major life activities? Perhaps you tend to invest conforming in going to church, seriousness and mastery in your career, and so on. If you watch yourself carefully, you will probably find that you invest a variety of states, including opposing states, in each of these, but in less frequent and more subtle ways. How you distribute your motivational states is an important part of your personality.

THE TWO ANGELS OF FLORENCE NIGHTINGALE

Tempting as it might be, we *cannnot* assume that, for each dimension, one end is always desirable and the other undesirable – that, for example, it is always good to be serious and never good to be playful, or vice-versa. But in different people and different circumstances, calling on different skills, and subject to different strengths and weaknesses, each state can be played out in a way that is positive or negative, fertile or futile, appropriate or inappropriate. (8) The point here is that there are opposite motivations, not that each motivation always has either good or bad consequences. Among other things, this means that a given person might even display a polarity in which *both* opposites are in some sense good for much of the time.

To illustrate the last point, about a double-benefit, take the case of Florence Nightingale, the English nineteenth century nurse. She is famously known to history as "The lady with the lamp." She revolutionised the way that wounded soldiers were treated and then went on to revolutionise the way that civilian hospitals were run, and have been ever since. In both cases, military and civilian, she argued that patients should be seen as people with feelings and emotional needs, and that they should have access to good food, clean sheets, comfortable beds, hygienic toilets, regular washing, and good books to read, not to mention a little care and consideration. This seems obvious now, but at the time it was all rather strange, even outlandish. In the military case she faced stiff opposition from those who could see no earthly reason to change traditional ways of doing things that had worked for hundreds of years, and no good reason to treat soldiers in a 'namby-pamby' manner by coddling them. Weren't they supposed to be tough and courageous?

Her response to all this was twofold. On one hand she led by example, which is where the "lady with the lamp" sobriquet came from. In the Crimean War (1853-6) between Russia and an alliance of countries including Britain, she organised a large hospital at Scutari, where she mothered the wounded, getting to know personally as many as she could, and she would wander the wards at night, with her oil lamp, giving comfort where it was needed and reassurance to all. In the terms that I have introduced, it seems clear that this involved the sympathy state. But in dealing with those who opposed her – doctors, administrators, military officers, bureaucrats, politicians – she made very good use of the mastery state. She confronted, faced down, manipulated, cajoled, scolded. After she returned to England from the Crimea, she never gave up, and did whatever seemed to be necessary to get her way. Her determination became legendary, and she was feared especially by politicians and government officials. But it worked. The hospital system in England, and then in other countries taking heed of the British example, became changed for the better and for good. Here we are faced with someone who took opposite tacks with different people, utilising both the mastery and the sympathy states where each could best serve its purpose. (9) Her contradiction was a kind of *'virtuous contradiction,'* a spiraling upwards.

What about someone with a pair of opposite states both of which are expressed in ways that are problematic – a kind of *malevolent contradiction*? Here is a case, again a medical one, even if the medicine was perverted. Josef Mengele was both a doctor and an SS officer at Auschwitz, where he was known as the "Angel of Death" and where he carried out his notorious and horrifying medical experiments on living prisoners, including children. In order to do this work, he must have been in the mastery state of mind, since he was able to treat people as objects, and use them in a detached way for his own deranged purposes. But there were also moments when he appears to have been in the sympathy state. In particular he seems to have been genuinely fond of the children of the Gypsies in the camp, and he would do them small favours, bringing them candy and little toys, and even taking them for outings. They would greet him warmly when he turned up, and called him "uncle." This sounds unproblematic, except that on at least one occasion he transported some of them to the gas chamber in his own car, drawing on their trusting relationship, and talking to them tenderly, so that they arrived without fuss or fear. Now he may well have been in the mastery state when actually doing this, disguising his true feelings, but it was only possible because of the sympathy relationship that he had previously established with these children.(10)

PERSONALITY IN MOTION

So we have four pairs of motivational states. Put them together and what do we get? We get a model of personality that can be represented in the way depicted in the Frontispiece. (You may wish to refer to the Frontispiece from time to time as you read this book, as well as Appendix One.) The Frontispiece shows us four pairs of opposing motivational states with horizontal arrows representing the possibility of reversals between them. We can think of these as twin states. On the top row, we see the serious and playful states, the two-way arrow representing the possibility of switching backwards and forwards between them. Below that, the other three pairs of states are also represented, and again the possibility of reversal is shown, in each case again by means of a two-way arrow. At any one time, one of each pair on each row will be 'active,' making a kind of 'chord.' For example: when I am at a game of football, I am usually for much of the time in the playful, conforming, mastery and other-oriented states (the latter because I am emotionally invested in the team I support). But it is also possible for a switch to occur from one to the other on any row. (This means that these pairs are like pairs of toggle switches.) For example, at the football game, I may switch to the sympathy state if a player has been injured. All this highlights the idea that there is a continually changing pattern of active motivational states, a kind of kaleidoscope, that shifts around during our waking life, endlessly making new patterns. (11) In this respect, personality is a moving target.

Every time that a reversal occurs there is a complete switch from one way of seeing things to another. We find a good analogy to such reversals in a kind of figure that has been much studied in the psychology of perception, and is called a Necker cube. Look at Figure 1, where you will see a line drawing of an open lattice cube. If you look at it for long

Perceptual Reversal

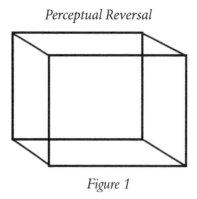

Figure 1

enough, something surprising will happen: it will jump from one orientation to another. The front face becomes the back face and vice versa. In one case you seem to be looking at the cube from slightly below and in the other from slightly above. In other words, a perceptual reversal has taken place. This is like the reversals discussed in the present book. For one thing, when the switch takes place it does so instantaneously: Now it is this, now it is that. For another, you do not see intermediate positions: it is completely one thing or the other. Also, you have to see it one way or the other the whole time you are looking at the cube, so that the two views are exhaustive. All of these apply to both perceptual and motivational reversals. A science fiction novelist has suggested that we use the word "necker" as a verb to mean switching from one psychological perspective to another. (12) That is a fun idea, but I shall stick here to "reversal."

Frequent Reversals: The Dance Tempo

This brings us to another interesting point, which is that the frequency of reversals that a person experiences can vary. A given state can be prolonged for many hours – the duration of a battle, a business meeting, a sexual encounter – and sometimes even longer. Some people can get 'stuck' in a state for days. Alternatively, states can also change relatively frequently.

Let me illustrate frequent reversals with an example of how a typical sequence might play out in the everyday activity of driving. I come up to a red traffic light. At this moment I am experiencing the serious state (I am aware that not stopping can have serious consequences, such as sudden death), the conformist state (I am inclined on this occasion to do what I am supposed to do and stop), the mastery state (I want to be in control of my own car) and the self-oriented state (I have to confess that I am mostly concerned about myself here).

So what I am experiencing at that moment is a combination of the following four states (in representing this I have put the active state in each pair in capital letters):

SERIOUS/playful
CONFORMIST/rebellious
MASTERY/sympathy
SELF-ORIENTED/other-oriented

As the light changes and I drive off, I reverse to the playful state and turn on the car radio. Now I am:

Serious/PLAYFUL
CONFORMIST/rebellious
MASTERY/sympathy
SELF-ORIENTED/other-oriented

I see someone on the sidewalk who looks as if he might be about to step into the road without looking. This produces a reversal in me from the playful to the serious state and from the self-oriented to the other-oriented state:

SERIOUS/playful
CONFORMIST/rebellious
MASTERY/sympathy
Self-oriented/OTHER-ORIENTED

As I drive on (he did not walk into the road) I continue to

move between different states. I do a kind of motivational dance.

FOCUS ON FOCUS

Looking at the Frontispiece diagram again, you may notice that there is also, up and down on the right-hand side, a vertical arrow representing movement between rows. This is intended to represent the idea that *one* of the four rows will, at a given time, be particularly important in the sense that it is the dimension that I am most aware of at that moment. It is the dimension I am focused on. In the example just given of the experience of driving, the conforming state may be focal if what I am most aware of is the desire to follow a rule, namely the rule not to go through a red light. A few moments later, when I have to slow down because someone might jump into the road, the other-oriented state might come to the fore and be focal. One or another state is in a sense privileged over all the others at a given moment. It is foreground rather than background. And this kind of shifting of focus may occur in the complete absence of reversals. It is up and down rather than side to side in the diagram in the frontispiece.

This simple-seeming model will run through the whole book and turn out to be rich in its implications. To understand a given person – like you – we have to take into account all four pairs, and how often each is at the focus of attention. So we see that Kinsey will have spent a lot of time focused on the top row, moving backwards and forwards between serious and playful states. Someone like Ulysses Grant might have spent much time in the mastery and sympathy states. In any case, most people will spend time in all the states, over time, during daily life. Doubtless Kinsey also spent time in the mastery and sympathy states, Grant in the self-oriented and other-oriented states, and so on. But people will spend more time in one state than its opposite, and more time focused on one pair of states than the others. In this way different motivational states will have different degrees of importance in a person's life.

Active motivational states within an individual can also of course combine in their effects: When Grant felt sympathetic for the mistreated horse, he was probably not only in the sympathy motivational state but also other-oriented and, as evidenced by his anger, rebellious. Kinsey's sexual recreation was probably not only playful, but also rebellious against the Victorian prudery that still lingered in the nineteen forties. Spitzer's sexual recreation was probably not only rebellious against his publically stated views, but playful in its risk-taking. Rockefeller, in his ruthless pursuit of profit, was probably combining the self-centred with the mastery motivational state.

Extrapolating from this, when I talk about a particular state being active, I do not wish to imply that it is the only active state at that moment, but simply that it is the state that is of interest to use at that point in the discussion, and that may be playing a particularly important part in what is going on.

AGASSI'S INTERESTING DAY

Early in his autobiography (13), Andre Agassi the great tennis player takes us through a day on which he plays an important match, so that we can live it with him. This match, at the US Open in 2006, is crucial to the rest of his career because he has decided that if he loses he will retire. (He is 36 years old and feels that he is running out of steam.) He describes in vivid detail his feelings before, during and after the game. In doing so, he provides a wonderful illustration of the ebb and flow of motivational states. As we follow him through his day, and the evening of the match itself, we shall see different motivational states come and go. I will note in parentheses the particular states that seem to be active and focal in his experience of different episodes. As we shall see, things finish in an unusual way.

He wakes in discomfort and pain, having spent the night on the floor of his New York hotel suite because of problems with his back. He feels too weak to get up. But he hears the voices of his children and wife, the tennis player Stefanie Graf, in another part of the suite. This makes him want to get up and see them, which he manages to do after a struggle with his own body. (Getting up is therefore a serious act, not enjoyable in itself but done for a future purpose; it is also a sympathy state act – it is about love.)

After breakfast and after his family have gone out, he takes a shower even though still in pain (*serious*) and then lounges around for the rest of the morning, reading, watching television and dozing (*playful*). His back is feeling better. He enjoys his family looking in (*sympathy*). In the afternoon he takes a long shower, and suddenly feels very sorry for himself, finding himself crying uncontrollably as the water pours over him (*self-oriented sympathy*). After a while he reverses back into the mastery state. "Control what you can control" he tells himself, thinking of his much younger opponent the Greek Marcos Baghdatis. He says it again and "This makes me feel brave" (*mastery*). (14)

With his two children he mixes the concoction that he will drink at the game. They have fun doing this (*playful*) but then his coach and his manager arrive to pick him up and take him to the stadium, and he feels a burst of energy and power (*mastery*). In the car they assess his opponent, and he feels nervous butterflies (*serious*), noting that he experiences such butterflies in different ways at different times.

In the locker room at the stadium he occupies himself with preparing his bag. This is an obsessive ritual – everything has to be just right and in the right place, and in particular his eight rackets have to be in the correct order (*conforming*). Going through the ritual calms him down (*serious*). Then he goes with his coach to the practice court, signing some autographs on the way (*other-oriented*). He practices with his coach for nearly half an hour (*mastery, serious*), and notes that his back now feels normal. The cortisone shot he had the day before must be working.

Yet another shower, then a quick meeting with Stefanie and the children outside the locker room (*sympathy*). Back in the locker room his vulnerable feet are taped up by a trainer (*self-oriented*). Across the locker room he sees his opponent doing some daunting stretching exercises. He goes over to him and they wish each other good luck (a *conforming* courtesy).

He finds Stefanie and embraces her again (*sympathy*), then he is off to the tunnel with an entourage of officials and others. He lets Baghdatis enter the court first and take the cheers. Then he enters and the cheers triple in intensity, as he thought they would because the word had got around about his potential retirement. Baghdatis looks around and realises that the louder cheers are for his opponent, not for him or even for both of them. This is a psychological blow by Agassi, a "trick of the trade" (15) (*self-oriented, mastery, rebelliousness*).

Once the match has started it goes without saying that it all becomes a matter of dominating and imposing (*self-oriented mastery*). Agassi wins the first two sets, but then Baghdatis takes the third. Agassi feels himself beginning to tire, and is aware that his opponent is only 21 and likely to get stronger than him as the game goes on. Indeed, Baghdatis wins the fourth set to make it 2-2. What is worse for Agassi is that he wrenches his spine and every shot becomes agony. He sees the game slipping away, but then Baghadatis falls to the ground writhing, suffering from leg cramps. They are now both injured and the result of the match is going to be a question of who can deal with pain the better, who can remain standing upright longer, who can just hold on (*self-oriented, mastery*). In fact, Agassi prevails through his pain, but with some desperation, and finally wins the match.

By the time Agassi reaches the locker room he can no longer walk or stand, and has to be carried and lifted onto a table. Not only is he in great pain, but he finds that he is having difficulty breathing, and a doctor is called. Stefanie is there briefly (*self-oriented sympathy*). Someone turns on a TV over the table to distract him while waiting, and they leave.

Agassi hears moans to his left, and on turning his head he sees Baghdatis on the next table being worked on by his team. Whatever they do seems to hurt Baghdatis and make matters worse. Baghdatis begs his team to leave, and everyone clears out, leaving him and Agassi alone on the neighbouring tables. They catch each other's eyes and smile (*other-oriented sympathy*). Then on television come the highlights of their match, which the commentator calls a classic. Agassi turns to see Baghdatis extend his hand, as if to say "we did that" (*other-oriented mastery*). "I reach out, take his hand, and we remain this way, holding hands, as the TV flickers with scenes of our savage battle" (*other-oriented sympathy*). (16)

This highly personal account is not only enthralling in its own rights, but illustrates that it is very possible to experience opposing needs at different moments, with each of the eight states occurring at different points in the narrative. Some of the reversals and changes of focus have obvious causes while others just seem to come and go, but in any case, the changes in this account occur relatively frequently.

TRACKING INCONSISTENCY

One way in which inconsistency has been documented is by means of a questionnaire that I devised with colleagues and that allows us to measure how much time respondents spend in daily life in each of the four pairs of motivational states that have been identified here. Very few people respond with 'never' to any of the items representing the different states, which means that for most people all eight states are experienced at different times. If we look at the data from over 8,000 men and women we find that most of these states are reported as being experienced somewhere in frequency between 'sometimes' and 'often.' The rebellious state is rated as the least frequent, with an average response between 'rarely' and 'sometimes.' But even here most people 'confess' to experiencing the state from time to time – in other words, rebelliousness is part of their complete motivational repertoire. In general, then, most people experience opposite motivational states in their daily lives. And since they experience opposites, they must also experience reversals between them and the possibility of self-contradiction. But within each pair a given person may well spend more time in one than the other. One person may spend more time in the serious than the playful state, another may spend more time in the mastery than the sympathy state, and so on. This 'dominance' of one state over its opposite is a measurable aspect of their personalities. (17)

Research of various kinds has followed people in their lives and recorded their patterns of change over time with respect to these states. People have been interviewed at regular intervals, answered questionnaires administered by means of hand-held computers, written diary accounts, and so on. And all of these studies have shown people reversing between states during the course of their everyday lives. (18) For example, office workers were tested every quarter of an hour through the working day, and it was found that, even though they were at work, they reversed from time to time into the playful state. (19) In another study, students were given the choice of playing video games or studying statistics by video over a two hour period, and most of them spontaneously reversed from time to time from one to the other. (It had previously been ascertained that the video games were experienced as fun and the statistics programs as serious). (20) Nurses switched between a combination of self-oriented mastery (when having to carry out medical procedures like giving injections) and other-oriented sympathy (when caring for their patients and their comfort). (21)

If we observe ourselves in everyday life, it is easy to see that we frequently switch between states. This happens when we change situations, from getting dressed in the morning to arriving at work, to having lunch. But it can also happen even in the same situation. Here is a personal example, again from driving: When I drive long distance, I take a motorway if I can. This is boring but practical. But then I occasionally go off the motorway to take a more scenic route. If my aim is to get to my destination as soon as possible, taking the scenic route does not make much sense. But if I want to enjoy the drive it does not make much sense to go on the motorway. These strategies are contradictory. But each serves its own purpose at the appropriate time, one serious (getting there quickly) and one playful (enjoying the drive).

The experience of reversals in our lives is part of what makes us fully human. But how can people be said to have personalities at all if they are changing all the time, especially if this change leads to contradiction and paradox? This challenging question leads us naturally into the next chapter.

Chapter 3

GOING BEYOND TRAITS

There are obviously many characteristics in terms of which people differ from each other. Take any dictionary and starting at "A" you might find, among others: abusive, adjusted, adventurous, aggressive, aggravating, angelic, antisocial, artistic, appalling, appealing, awesome, awful, awkward, etc. Gordon Allport, regarded by many as the father of personality research, identified as many as eighteen thousand adjectives that could be used to describe people's personalities. (1) The point about the four dimensions being presented here – only four! – is that they are specifically about motivation. They are grounded in the key psychological needs that drive people rather than the seemingly endless ways that their behaviour can be described and evaluated from the outside.

Needs, if described in rather concrete terms, are also numerous. One could identify many specific things that you or I might want: a haircut, a warm bath, a cigarette, a smile, to get to bed, and so on. But if we drill down, and examine the motives that underlie this huge diversity of particular human needs, it seems that they reduce at the psychological level to the four pairs presented here. A haircut might be self-oriented, a cigarette playful, a smile sympathetic. Even biological needs can be assimilated to them. I might eat not only because I am hungry but also because it is the time and place to eat (conforming), because I enjoy the taste (playful), because I want to please my host (other-oriented) and so on for all eight states.

In due course, we may need to add further pairs to these four in order to gain a fuller understanding of human personality. But for the moment, and on the basis of research and practice over more than thirty years, this set of four pairs seems adequate to account for the general ebb and flow of experience. After all, we want to explain the most with the least – this is the scientific principle of 'parsimony.' So we must resist adding concepts unless we are really forced to do so. (2)

How does present-day personality psychology deal with the kinds of reversals and contradictions discussed here? The answer has to be: miserably. Indeed, they have hardly been recognised at all.

To put this in context: there have been two broad tendencies in research on personality over the years, both of them allowing certain predictions to be made. In one, the central concept is that of trait. (3) In the other it is that of situation. What has been called the 'personality paradox' is that people seem to have enduring traits, yet these tend not to show up across situations. (4) Most psychometric work – work involving the development and use of tests – involves the concept of a trait. Since most research in personality is psychometric, this means that most personality research as also based on the trait concept. In contrast, the alternative situational perspective comes out more from social psychology, sociology, and the psychology of learning. And this view is becoming increasingly influential.

TRAITS

There are many definitions of traits, but trait researchers all more or less agree to define them as enduring personality dispositions that allow us to predict how particular people will behave over time, or across different situations. The key word is 'enduring.' In this respect, peoples' personalities are seen as relatively frozen in time, petrified. The best known example of a trait dimension on which people can have fixed positions is probably that of extraversion-introversion. (See Appendix Two.) This is one of the so-called 'Big Five' personality traits that are the object of much contemporary research. My point is not that there are no consistencies – and there may be many kinds, including consistencies in habits (like smoking) and attitudes (like political orientation). It is rather that focusing on them to the extent that personality psychologists have done, can be limiting and misleading.

According to the trait perspective, if Anne is highly sociable in one situation, she will be likely to be highly sociable in other situations (compared to other people). Anne would in this case be expected to have a high sociability score on a test for this trait. The whole emphasis here is on consistency. Such consistency is difficult to reconcile with the kinds of changes that are the centre of interest in reversal theory. Certainly a given person might spend more time in, say, the sympathy state than the mastery state. This is a kind of tendency that is trait-like on the surface. But that person is still likely to spend periods of time in the opposite mastery state, and to be as fully into the spirit of mastery when in that state as someone who spends considerably more of their time in it. I would bet that Anne, even though sociable, is not particularly sociable when doing her taxes, taking a bath, or in the toilet. So is she sociable or isn't she? She is both. If this is a trait, it is an odd kind of trait. Could we say that Rockefeller was high on caring for others, or low? Was Kinsey high on seriousness, or low? Just asking such questions reveals that there is a whole fluid level of personality that is missed by trait approaches.

The conceptual difference between reversal theory states and traditional traits is clarified in Figure 2. The horizontal axis represents the passage of time, and the vertical represents the degree of some personality variable. The variable marked with an X is essentially a straight line, and is what a trait theorist would expect, or hope, to see if the same individual was tested repeatedly over time. There would be some slight variation, since measurement is never perfect, but the line would indicate that the trait is basically unchanging. Contrast this with variables A and B that represent what a variable that reverses might look like. In this case sometimes the individual being tested would respond as if his personality was at level A, and sometimes at B. For example, sometimes he would report being serious and sometimes playful. This is obviously quite

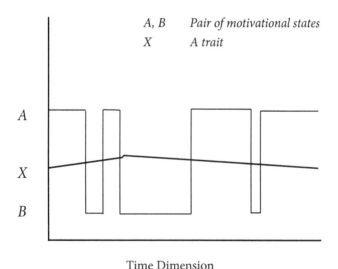

Time Dimension

Figure 2

a different pattern over time. It is a kind of graphical zigzag rather than a straight line, and comes out of a whole different notion of what personality is 'all about.'

Now it remains the case that for a pair of states like the serious and playful states, some people will spend more time in one state than the other. This *dominance* of one state over the other could be seen as a kind of trait. But if so, it is a very different kind of trait from the usual trait conceptualised in personality testing.

As I mentioned, it must be allowed that trait theorists do recognise that some inconsistencies will occur between measurements of a given trait in a given person at different times. What is seen as 'reliability,' to use the technical term, is rarely perfect. The problem is dealt with by aggregating readings from each respondent over time in order to produce an average for each trait being measured in relation to that respondent. In this way 'error' can be, if not entirely eliminated, at least much reduced, and the respondent's personality treated as a kind of constant. Unfortunately, this is rather like trying to understand a Mozart symphony by averaging all the notes. The message can be in the variation.

Self-Labelling: For Eternity?

Some people, and you may be one of them, resist this whole trait-measurement process and feel uncomfortable about being reduced to a set of numbers or a category. I have heard people bitterly complain after they have received the results of testing that in reality sometimes they are (let's say) extravert and sometimes introvert, and this is annoyingly not reflected in what they are being told about themselves by the scale.

But for many others there seems to be a thirst for self-labelling. All personality tests play into this desire, especially the

'Myers-Briggs Type Indicator,' that sells in millions of copies every year, mainly to training or development programs, and is known around the world fondly as the "MBTI." In the Myers Briggs the reduction is even greater than in most personality tests because the person finishes up in one of sixteen 'boxes,' this characterisation being typically represented to respondents as permanent. Many people seem to love this, and wear badges, baseball caps and tee-shirts proudly declaiming their type.

Is it pushing things too far to speculate that this need to label oneself derives in part from the idea that goes back to the beginnings of philosophy and religion – namely that we each have an eternal and unchanging soul? Such permanence gives us fundamental reassurance in the face of death. Personality tests seem to support this idea, albeit rather superficially. They supposedly tell us what is 'essentially us.' They are therefore comforting. We all want to know "who we really are," and tests like the MBTI purport to tell us. Presumably if we are extravert on earth, we shall be extravert in heaven too – and for eternity.

SITUATIONS: CHANGING ROLES

In the contrasting, situationist, view, the assumption is that people will behave in the same way in the same situation, when they encounter it on different occasions, but *differently* in *different* situations, so that there is some change in people as they move between different situations. This concept comes in part out of social psychology and sociology, based on a theatrical metaphor that people play different roles or follow different scripts under different circumstances. (5) So a given person may have the boss role at work, and the wife role at home, a customer's role in a shop and a patient's role in hospital. The situationist view also comes out of "Learning

Theory" in psychology, particularly the phenomenon that is referred to as 'discriminant conditioning.' This has it that specific behaviours become likely in the presence of given specific stimuli. One eats in the presence of a plate of food, one stops the car in the presence of a red light, and so on. In other words, certain contexts become the occasion for certain behaviours.

Situationists draw attention to data showing that situations often predict behaviour better than traits do. (6) Someone might be sociable in one situation – in a bar, say – but not in another, like the library. This means that we can predict that they will be sociable on other occasions in which they are in a bar, and not sociable on other occasions when they are in the library. Thus there is consistency, but not necessarily across different kinds of situation. The consistency only applies across repeats of the very same situation: from one time in the bar to another time in the bar, and so on. (It should be noted that there is some looseness in the concept of situation: it can be a place, a task to be performed, a social setting, and so on.)

The situationist view is closer to the reversal theory perspective adopted in this book, since it admits of psychological change. But it is still rather different. After all, in some examples I gave in the opening chapter, the *same* situation was reacted to very differently at different times by the same person – prostitution for Spitzer, money for Rockefeller, and so on. The view that I am presenting here is that people may be different *even in the same situation* at different times. This is radically different from situationism which requires that the same situation calls forth the same response. According to reversal theory there is an internal instability that keeps people 'on the move' and complicates the matching of person and situation. Recognising this is crucial to understanding the complexities of human behaviour. As a case in point, I know that in a library I am sometimes serious, and sometimes playful. Sometimes I am self-oriented in a bar and sometimes other-oriented. So my behaviour is far from predictable on the basis of situation alone. I might even change in the course of the very same action, for example in putting a recalcitrant child to bed switching back and forth between concern for the child and determination to be in control of the situation and suffer "no nonsense" (thus reversing between the twin sympathy and mastery states).

A further problem for the situationist view is that it is confronted by the fact that people choose and even *create* the situations that they afterwards respond to, so it is not helpful to see people as simply responding passively to situations in which they happen to find themselves. Indeed, we actively set up elaborate spaces for ourselves, full of chosen objects that we interact with as and when we please – chairs and television sets and suitcases. (7) It is me that has chosen to be in the library, and therefore I have myself chosen my situation, at least at that moment. In this respect there is a kind of two-way process between me and the setting. This kind of reciprocal action has been recognised by some researchers (8), but it is difficult to reconcile completely with either the situationist or the trait position. (See Appendix Three.)

INHERENT INSTABILITY: DANCING TO YOUR OWN MUSIC

Here we come to the crux: I would argue that a reason for inconsistency in a given situation may be that people follow *internal* rhythms that do not necessarily correspond with the environments that they find themselves in. Often they dance to their own music. Although generally high in the trait for sociability, one could be at a party and not happen to be feeling at all sociable at that moment. Or one could be looking after someone but not feeling particularly caring at that moment. The existence of such mismatches does not fit easily into either the trait or the situationist approach, but it surely happens. In other words, we have changing internal as well as external environments that influence our feelings and actions. We cannot say that Eliot Spitzer had a single enduring trait of some kind, such as ambition or dishonesty, but rather that he alternated between different motives at different times, generating different internal contexts – what we might call 'intexts' for his actions – and therefore different actions. (9)

Clearly reversals can occur in response to changing situations and events, and this would be consistent with situationist views. We shall see many examples in the course of this book. My point is that reversals can also occur in response to some kind of internal rhythm which eventually brings about reversal if nothing else does. This is the most important thing that is missing from both the trait and situationist perspectives.

It is rather like the alternation between sleeping and waking. If nothing occurs to wake you up, then eventually you will wake up anyway. And if nothing happens to put you to sleep, you will in due course drop off. There is a kind of *satiation* of sleep and satiation of wakefulness, each of which eventually leads to a reversal from one to the other, if it has not occurred already for some other reason, like a loud noise waking you up. Likewise, there seems to be a satiation process for motivational states. This means that once you have been serious for long enough you will feel the need for recreation. Once you have been playful for long enough you will feel the need to do something significant and stop 'messing around.' Similar considerations apply to the other pairs of states. It may be that this satiation process is not as evident in a complex culture such as our own as it would be in a more primitive culture, because reversals are continually being induced by endlessly changing circumstances in our information-rich surroundings. For this reason, satiation may not have the time to build up sufficiently to induce a reversal before a reversal is induced for other reasons. But this idea of satiation, that sooner or later a reversal will occur anyway if nothing else happens to bring it about, is central to reversal theory. It argues that we are inherently unstable and reversal-prone. Sooner or later the tide always turns.

The thrust of this chapter has been that neither of the general approaches in traditional personality theory – neither the trait nor the situationist approach – is perfectly suited to deal with motivational states and reversals between states. I would even go further than this and argue that trait approaches involving personality *testing* are not only inadequate as complete and general accounts of personality, they also risk being counterproductive, and even dangerous, when used in practice because they imply that personality is already determined. Suppose you want to help someone to change – and after all, change is the aim of every kind of treatment or intervention, otherwise why bother? Then telling people that this is "how they are," and perhaps reinforcing this with the results of a personality test, implies that change is not possible. What is more, it provides them with an excuse not to try to change. Also, when personality tests are used for selection purposes in an organisation – for choosing the person for the job – it implies that there is no room for growth into the job. It also implies that there is only one way of doing the job successfully. And it implies that you know what it is.

The situationist side also has its problems. The idea that people can be totally controlled from the outside, through conditioning and in other ways, surely encourages us to try to manipulate and control other people and may even lead us to treat them (and perhaps ourselves) as less than fully human. There are large issues here. At the conceptual level, it could be argued that the situationist viewpoint is a reflection of post-modernism, one of whose characteristic views is that everyone is essentially constructed by culture and society, so that a self-determining self is an illusion. Reversal theory, in contrast, argues that internal contexts – intexts – are as important and determining as external, and that selfhood is a thoroughly meaningful concept.

THE PLACE OF INSTINCTS

I am sometimes asked if reversal theory is a form of instinct theory. The answer is that it depends on what is meant by 'instinct.' The term has been defined in dozens of different ways in the history of psychology, but all the definitions have in common the idea that there are forms of response that a particular species of animal does not have to learn, but that are biologically built in, and emerge as it were in full bloom at the first touch of rain. Everything innate in this sense – from coughing and scratching an itch to fearing the dark and falling in love – would count as an instinct. We know how to do these things without being taught. Over the years, numerous lists were compiled of such innate behaviours in many animals and especially the human animal, and many of them were long. (10) But eventually it became evident that they explained little, just redescribing what was already known in a new language. So instinct explanations of this kind went out of style in psychology for much of the last century. However, the study of instinct was kept alive in the considerably more insightful and sophisticated work of 'ethologists' – zoologists like Konrad Lorenz – who systematically observe animal behaviour in its natural habitat. And instincts, in the sense of innate capabilities, have been making a big comeback in the last few decades, especially following the surge of interest that there has been in language learning as a preprogrammed human capacity based on innate cognitive structures. (11)

If we regard instincts as concrete behaviours, we do not seem to see much in the way of oppositions or reversals. There is no real opposite to salivating to food or to blinking in bright light. But if we add motivation into the mix, and define instincts as motives, together with the ability to behave in such a way as to attempt to satisfy such motives, then we begin to see oppositions emerge.

British social scientist Colin Talbot in his book "The Paradoxical Primate" (12), defines instincts in this way, as including motivation, and argues that human instinctive behaviours, especially social behaviours, come in opposites. Indeed, it is even possible to see a resemblance between the set of contradictory instincts proposed by Talbot and the set of contradictory motivational states proposed here. Talbot's set are: Peace-making versus aggression, cooperation versus competition, conformity versus autonomy, and selfishness versus altruism. All of these can be observed in different species, including humans. These are similar to the reversal theory set, although the serious-playful dimension is notably absent.

However, we should remember that motivational states, as defined in reversal theory, are more than instinctive-motivations-plus-behaviour. As we have seen, a motivational state combines in itself certain values, motives, ways of seeing, families of related emotions and styles of interacting with the world – as well as a flexible range of behaviours that can result – and integrates these into a coherent whole, a kind of mini-personality that takes over at a given time. Reversal arises from the fact that each motivational state either functions as a whole or does not function at all at a given time, but cannot be 'mixed' with its opposite. The result is that we see things in alternative ways as our lives unfold over time.

We should bear in mind, too, that different motivational states can each respond in their own way to the very same situation, interpreting it in their own way. This is an idea which does not have much place in instinct theories, since in these theories fixed stimuli (like predators) elicit fixed responses (like fleeing): One stimulus, one unvarying response. All the same, there is no reason why complex and flexible motivational states may not have evolved from simpler and more automatic instinctive behaviours.

THE CONSISTENCY OF INCONSISTENCY

A series of rifts run through the human psyche. In the outsize characters we looked at in the first chapter, the rifts threatened to tear apart the surface of their personalities. But I hope that I have begun to convince you that the same rifts run through all of us, if usually in ways that are less immediately apparent. It is interesting that biographers frequently talk about the self-contradictions in their subjects without realising that such contradictions are not special to the particular people about whom they have chosen to write. (13) They are true of all of us, if usually not so blatantly. The implications of all this for personality research are enormous. (14)

So if we ask again the question "Why do people sometimes act in ways that are self-contradictory?" the preliminary answer is that it is because everyone has self-contradictory desires, and the same basic set of innate contradictory desires to boot. These are programmed into all of us, as a birthright, together with the tendency to switch back and forth between them. This naturally leads to the question of why we should be gifted with these innate contradictions, given the inconsistencies and paradoxes that they generate. This most basic question is one to which we shall return towards the end of the book. But until then, in the chapters that follow, I shall use this structure of motivational states, and the dynamics of movement between them, to make sense of a variety of perplexing psychological phenomena. We start in the next chapter by asking why people go out of their way to do dangerous things that they could so easily avoid: The paradox of voluntary risk-taking. Why in the world would anyone climb a high mountain or dive to the depths of the ocean if they did not have to?

PART TWO

PARADOXES

CHAPTER 4

THE PROTECTIVE FRAME

"Why do people take unnecessary risks?"

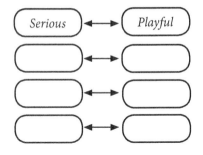

Over six thousand climbers have attempted to scale Mount Everest since it was first conquered in 1953, littering the route to the summit with oxygen tanks, frozen garbage, human excrement and even bodies. (1) Hundreds of people have chased tornadoes in the American Midwest, clogging up the roads so that emergency teams could not get to the survivors. (2) Large cruise ships have regularly deposited thousands of tourists on the pristine snow of the Antarctic. Where Scott and Shackleton once heroically challenged the elements, people now buy souvenirs, and even skydive and scuba dive. (3) These are examples of a far-reaching paradox of human nature. Biologically, our fundamental need is to survive. This is what we might call the 'Biological Imperitive.' And yet many of us – more and more of us, it would seem – take risks that we do not need to take and that may even jeopardise the very existence of ourselves and other people, not to mention causing enormous damage to the environment. (4)

Why do we do this? Why do we ever seek out danger that could be avoided? Such behaviour is paradoxical because it has the opposite effect to that which, from a biological and evolutionary point of view, one would expect behaviour to have: it threatens rather than protects.

There are of course situations in which risk is unavoidable, when desperate actions are called for. A melodramatic example would be the response to someone crying out for help from a burning building. But that is not what I am referring to here. I am referring here to situations where danger, which could have been utterly avoided, is instead deliberately sought out, cultivated and even celebrated. Here's what I have in mind. I am thinking particularly about dangerous sports like bungee jumping, skydiving, mountain climbing, potholing, ocean rowing and base jumping. (5) But I am also thinking about those minor forms of risk-taking that most of us indulge in as part of our daily lives, such as driving too fast, running red lights, swimming in high waves, or gambling for small stakes.

We can start to make sense of all of this if we see that the risk-taking in these cases is essentially playful. For the risk to be enjoyed, the activity must be about the pleasures of the moment, about enjoying the activity in itself, rather than about the consequences – be they good or bad. One way of putting this is to say that in the playful state of mind, we experience a *protective frame* around ourselves and what we are doing, putting it in a kind of bubble. In this way we experience the activity as being cut off from consequences, so that it can be relished in itself. When a child plays on a swing, the activity is carried out for its own sake, not to achieve some consequence beyond the swinging. When you or I go to a bar for a drink, we are normally looking for immediate gratification rather than a

Nobel prize. If there turns out to be a loss as a result of taking risks, then it is a manageable loss. As long as the protective frame prevails, one feels that everything will be OK. So taking risks is OK too, because failure, if it occurs, will not really matter.

When the frame dissolves, so we become vulnerable again – we become aware that bad things *can* happen – *really* bad things. This, in turn, is another way of saying that we are in the serious state of mind – that we *are* aware of consequences and that anything is possible. We really can get injured, or lose a pile of money, or fail in our careers. We can humiliate, embarrass and upset ourselves as well as causing physical harm. As we move through our daily lives, and the protective frame comes and goes, so we reverse backwards and forwards between the playful and serious states of mind, now doing things for their own sake, now doing them for the sake of advantages that we hope will accrue in the future.

THE TIGER IN THE CAGE

Here is a little 'thought experiment.' Imagine that you are at a zoo and that you find yourself looking at an empty cage. My guess is that you would find this pretty boring, and after a while the arousal you experience (how worked up you feel) would be pretty negligible. But now suppose that, as you are about to move on and look for something more interesting elsewhere, a tiger slinks menacingly into view from a tunnel that you had not noticed in the dark recesses of the cage. At this point things become considerably more interesting, and you feel some degree of excitement as your arousal increases. Since there are bars between you and the beast, you feel safe. Because of this you may well move right up to the bars to see the tiger as closely as you can, and in this way increase your excitement. But now suppose that the bars at the front of the cage are suddenly hauled up by some pulley hidden in the ceiling, and you find yourself face to face with the tiger with no protection at all. I have no doubt that your arousal would immediately turn to anxiety, even panic. But then the bars of the cage crash back down again between you and the tiger, and the tiger is ushered back out of the cage, so that once more you are observing an empty cage. Now you have feelings of relief as arousal returns to the low level it was at when everything started.(6)

The most interesting thing to notice about this is that while both anxiety and excitement are high arousal emotions, one turns instantly into the other as the protective frame comes and goes – in our imaginary example, as the bars of the cage are raised or lowered. So it is not that one thing is replaced by something quite different. It is rather that the anxiety and the excitement are the same thing, namely high arousal, but high arousal experienced in diametrically opposite ways. To use an obvious metaphor: These two emotions are like the two sides of the very same coin.

You will have realised that there is a general formula here that runs something like this:

High arousal and no protective frame: anxiety
High arousal and protective frame: excitement
Low arousal and no protective frame: relaxation
Low arousal and protective frame: boredom

We move from one emotion in this set to another either by experiencing changes in arousal level, or by experiencing the protective frame coming and going. This will be true whatever particular form that the protective frame takes and whatever the source of the arousal. (7) To take another example, imagine that you are walking along the edge of a cliff. If there is a railing, this can act as a protective frame. In this case you can enjoy the walk and be stimulated by the proximity of danger. You might even lean over the railing to get more excitement. Take the railing away, so that one slip can lead to oblivion, and you will instead feel terror. You are in the same place, but the presence or absence of the protective frame makes all the difference to the experience of this place. Now imagine that you are at a football game and the game has become monotonous and predictable. Then suddenly a brilliant goal is scored. Your boredom turns to excitement. In this case the protective frame has been there all the time, but it is your arousal level that has changed from low to high.

In a classic study, a developmental psychologist reported the following observation of a little experiment he did with a child of nearly one year old. (8) He showed her a pair of opera glasses, and when she touched them he blew a loud whistle. She was not startled at all, but did look around with interest to see where the noise was coming from. Then he showed her a caterpillar – something she had never seen before. She 'waggled' her hand at it from the wrist and turned away with a shudder. When she turned back to look at it again, he blew the whistle once more. This time her reaction was very different: she gave a loud shriek. He concludes that sometimes it can need two things to cause fear, in this case the caterpillar and the whistle. In this he is surely right, but with the idea of protective frames we can better understand what is happening. One of the two things has to induce the serious state (in this case the threat of a caterpillar), and the other to increase arousal (in this case the sound of the whistle). In contrast, the opera glasses did not induce the serious state and so there was no anxiety in response to the whistle. In a second case, the psychologist crawled towards her with his head down. She retreated, whimpering and waggling her hands at him. But then she was hauled onto her mother's lap and here she showed no signs of distress but a lively curiosity, leaning forward to see him when he approached right up to her. (9) Being put on her mother's lap induced the protective frame and resulted in her becoming interested in, rather than fearful of, the strange psychologist crawling oddly towards her.

The moral of all this is that a great way of experiencing things is to experience them not only as arousing but also within a protective frame. The trick of getting to experience excitement is, paradoxically, to take risks without really taking risks. This is why, to respond to the questions asked at the beginning of the chapter, people take unnecessary risks: they do so for the very pleasant high arousal – the excitement that they experience when, paradoxically, they feel safe in the face of danger. (10) In this case, danger is not just tolerated, it is attractive and wonderfully desirable, and even exerts a kind of pull. A witness to the twin towers collapsing on 9/11, who was watching through a viewfinder that made what she saw seem like a movie, admitted that she felt *drawn towards* what was happening and part of her wanted to be there. (11)

Some Exciting Studies of Arousal

Let's look at an actual study rather than a thought experiment. The study asks: Why do people jump out of aircraft in flight, with nothing but a patch of canvas to protect them from certain death – and do so without being pushed? A colleague and I put these questions to over sixty sports parachutists in the American Midwest, using a detailed questionnaire that we devised to look at every aspect of the sport. (12) Some of the items dealt with risk and arousal. One of these asked them to indicate where they felt the point of greatest danger to be. Most frequently and not surprisingly, the point of maximum danger was indicated as occurring during the few seconds of gut-wrenching free fall, somewhere between stepping out of the plane into open space and the parachute deploying. One set of items asked people to mark on a straight line representing time, from ten minutes before to ten minutes after their point of maximum perceived danger, where they would place the point of their greatest anxiety and where they would place the point of their greatest excitement. The point of greatest anxiety was most frequently placed as being immediately *before* the point of maximum danger, in other words while waiting in the plane to make one's jump and then stepping out of the plane. The point of greatest excitement was most often shown as immediately *after* the parachute opened.

This all makes sense in terms of the model that has been described here. Being faced with the possibility of a horrible death is liable to induce or maintain the serious state of mind in most people: after all, jumping from a plane can have far-reaching consequences (to put it mildly) if things do not go well. For the same reason, making a jump is also likely to induce a high level of arousal. Together, this combination spells high anxiety. But once the parachute has opened, then one knows that one is safe, meaning that a protective frame is now being experienced and the situation has become playful. But the arousal is still pounding around. The upshot is a strong feeling of excitement in the immediate aftermath, and continuing, if milder, excitement for a prolonged period afterwards. (13)

We can now begin to understand why people would willingly perform such a crazy-seeming stunt. What they do is to face real danger, which raises their arousal levels. Then they master the situation in such a way that the danger is overcome, but the arousal is still there and takes time to dissipate. The effect is that excitement, even euphoria, is felt for a goodly period. If the anxiety can be tolerated, then they are able to achieve wonderful feelings of 'being fully alive,' and intensely 'in the moment.' This is possible because of the reversal phenomenon, the serious to playful reversal causing a switch from anxiety to excitement. One 'buys' excitement with anxiety in a transaction that people who engage in such activities find worthwhile. And this activity is a model for many similar dangerous activities like bungee jumping, skydiving, free diving, hang-gliding, and base jumping. In all such activities there is real physical danger, resulting in anxiety, but when the danger is overcome, the anxiety is replaced by excitement – which is another way of saying that the same arousal is experienced, in sequence, in two opposite ways, one pleasant and one unpleasant. It's the same coin, but it flips onto its other side.

This experimental design has been repeated in a very different situation: with Japanese dance performers. For these dancers, the maximum point of danger is when the curtain first rises. Before it rises they report experiencing some degree or another of stage fright, but, once it has risen and they have started to perform, the anxiety turns to excitement.(14) In this case the danger is psychological rather than physical, but the effect is the same and due to the arrival of a protective frame.

Here is a rather different study that bears on the relationship of anxiety to excitement. In this case the setting was a suspension bridge slung high above a rocky gorge in the mountains near Vancouver. Most tourists crossing this narrow shaky bridge, made up of wooden slats, feel highly anxious. But the experimenters arranged for unaccompanied males crossing the bridge to be approached individually, while still on the bridge, by an attractive young female who asked to interview them, ostensibly under the guise of a study of tourists' reactions to the beauties of British Columbia. Included in the interview was a test which allowed the experimenters to measure subjects' emotions and feelings at the time. These were compared with those of subjects who had been tested in the same way, again by an attractive female, but this time on a low solid bridge nearby. It was found that those on the high suspension bridge showed much more in the way of sexual thoughts and feelings than those on the low bridge. What seems to have happened is that the intense arousal on the high bridge was converted from anxiety to excitement by the presence of the charming interviewer. In other words, in redefining the situation as a sexual one, a protective frame was set up that converted the arousal from anxiety about falling to (in this case erotic) excitement. Where there was low anxiety, on the low bridge, there was little sexual excitement because there was comparatively little arousal to convert. (15)

THREE TYPES OF PROTECTIVE FRAME

An experienced mountain climber, climbing with trustworthy companions, and using well-tested equipment, might well feel confident that he has what is needed to deal with the challenges that they will have to meet. Under these conditions he should experience much excitement in confronting the rigors of the climb. This is a particular kind of frame that we can call the *confidence frame*, which is about feeling that one has what it takes to meet prospective challenges. Of course, such confidence may or may not be justified, but it is what the climber feels at the time. It is the kind of frame needed by people who actually face real dangers, if they are to enjoy the confrontation: soldiers, test-pilots, bull-fighters, explorers, stunt men, men of action in general. Nor need the risk be physical. It could be financial in the case of stock brokers, about reputation in the case of surgeons, a loss of face in the case of public speakers (or performers as in the example of dancers just given), a lack of audience laughter for comedians, and so on. In all such cases there is danger, but the danger is what these people need to thrive on.

Let me give a personal example of a non-physical kind of

risk. I was attending a small one-day psychology conference in France, and found that I was the last speaker of the day. Since I knew none of the participants, and was in a foreign country, I did not feel that my professional reputation was much at stake. I was therefore experiencing the confidence frame. I was in the playful state of mind looking for stimulation. But as the morning wore on I became increasingly bored and restless. To try to make things more interesting, I decided to challenge myself by writing a new paper that would incorporate much of the material that I was hearing, and show how it might fit together. When the time came, this was the paper that I actually gave. I am sure now that it was less good than the paper that I would have given, and the response was not particularly warm. What I intended to be a bravura performance fell rather flat. But at least I got away with it (I think). The point is that there was no reason for me to do this, since I was taking a quite unnecessary and foolish risk and one that required a lot of unnecessary effort. I only did it because I was in the playful state, desperately bored, and in need of something to engage me fully.

But there is a second kind of frame beyond the confidence frame. We can think of this one as a *safety-zone frame*. Here one is far from actual danger, but still aware of danger. Imagine someone in a gym, practicing climbing on a climbing frame. Here any dangers are more or less imaginary, although the climber may play on these in order to make the situation as life-like as possible in his or her 'minds' eye.' To the extent that he or she succeeds in raising arousal in this way, some degree of excitement will be felt. People playing video games may experience something similar, especially with military combat games that are full of violence.

In the safety zone there are, of course, other possible sources of arousal and interest than danger, or imagined danger, and this is the area in which most of us spend much of our recreational time. We play sports, listen to music, and so on. (16) Sometimes there is an actual framed-off area that helps in establishing this zone as a real physical area – for example the playground, the tennis court, the bar, the casino, the bedroom, the golf course, the swimming pool, the football stadium, the fairground, the cruise ship. This obvious physical framing means that people entering this area are induced into the playful state, and then tools for achieving excitement are made available, such as the necessary sports equipment.

At other times the safety-zone frame is more notional than physical, though none the less psychologically real – for example, hearing a good joke may establish a protective frame, as may being on vacation, or knowing that it is Christmas day, or just hanging out with friends.

You might object that there are in fact consequences in sports competition, namely the consequences of winning or losing. But if the sport is played in the playful state of mind, then the goal of winning is not really about future consequences. Rather the goal of winning is the principle way of making the game interesting and arousing at that time. In other words it is a means – a means of having fun – rather than an end. In amateur sport, winning or losing is secondary to having a good time, which is what the real goal is. If this is not the case, if it is not primarily about fun, then the game is being played seriously rather than playfully. (Presumably this is the way that most professional athletes play the game.) So we have the paradox in the playful state that the goal is really only a means – a means to help enjoy the activity more.

When you were imagining the tiger in the cage, which of these forms of protective frame were you experiencing in reality? It could not have been the confidence frame, because there was no real danger to be confronted while you were doing the imagining. It was also not really the safety zone frame either, because you were not doing anything. You were probably experiencing the *detachment zone frame,* which is a third type of protective frame. This is the safest zone of all. In this zone you are observing something that causes arousal, such as danger, but you are not directly involved. So you might be watching someone else do something risky, such as performing a high-wire trapeze act, or driving in a Nascar event, or bull riding, and you might empathise with the danger that they are in; but it is all at a distance as far as you personally are concerned.

What you are 'observing' may be completely imaginary, as is the case when you are watching a thriller movie. And indeed, everything might be imaginary, as in your experience of the tiger in the cage. But it might also be real. A particularly self-observant and honest reporter who was at the scene of Ground Zero on 9/11, admitted to a kind of 'exaltation' as he observed and wrote about the events of the day. (17) The fact that he was an observer and not a participant meant that he could enjoy his arousal, and he was courageous enough to admit it.

Even more cut off from reality and consequences is the world of fantasy and imagination. This explains why sexual behaviour of a kind that one would definitely not enjoy in real life can be attractive in sexual fantasy, because it is highly arousing and not about to happen in reality. For example, being raped is a frequent fantasy in women.(18)

Despite their differences, all three kinds of protective frame – confidence, safety-zone and detachment – operate in such a way that they convert anxiety to excitement.

THE FALLACIOUS FRAME

One problem that arises for the individual is that the protective frame may not really be protective at all. Indeed the protection it offers may be a total illusion. In the case of the confidence frame, this illusion might lead you to be over-confident and to overrate your skills and your luck. Perhaps you have performed some superstitious ritual and feel that this confers on you complete immunity from danger. In the safety-zone you may misunderstand just how safe you really are, and in the detachment frame you may discover that you are, after all, and perhaps to your horror, not just an observer but a full participant.

We can think straight away of the example of Kinsey who we have already discussed, and of the risks he took to his career and reputation by indulging in various risky sexual practices. He clearly felt that he was in some kind of safety-zone which was cut off from his professional and academic life. And in fact he did get away with it at the time. But his safety frame was probably more precarious than he realised, and his risks could have resulted in disaster for his career.

Some criminals admit to experiencing what they are doing as fun. They commit their crimes within a protective frame – probably a confidence frame – that tells them, erroneously, that what they are doing is safe and that they are bound to get away with it. A case in point is the notorious bank robber and jailbreaker Willie Sutton. He is famous for responding to the question "Why do you rob banks?" with the answer "Because that is where the money is." (Actually, he denies ever having said this. In his autobiography he gives the following answer to the same question: "Why did I rob banks? Because I enjoyed it. I loved it. I was more alive when I was inside a bank, robbing it, than at any other time in my life. I enjoyed everything about it so much that one or two weeks later I'd be out looking for the next job. But to me the money was the chips, that's all. The winnings. I kept robbing banks when, by all logic, it was foolish. When it could cost me far more than I could possibly gain." (19)

A mass version of the fallacious protective frame can be discerned at the first battle of the American Civil War – the Battle of Manassas, which is some thirty miles from Washington. Crowds of people made the trip from the capital, with an air of gaiety, to view what was widely believed would be an easy victory for the North. Out they came in all their finery, on horseback and in phaeton, bearing picnic hampers and other comforts. But before the end of the day they would find themselves part of a frenzied retreat by a beaten army, their smart phaetons becoming caught up with artillery and drums and wagons, as panicking soldiers pushed past them in the race to safety.

The existence of such a 'fallacious frame' helps us to understand another paradox: why people do not in fact always flee to safety when faced with some devastating threat. For example, why did everyone not rush directly to the lifeboats when the Titanic was sinking? (There were about 500 empty places in the lifeboats after they had been launched.) It has been suggested (20) that many people did not do this because they felt safer on board a big ship than a small boat, however irrational that might seem since it was the big ship that was sinking. "We are safer here than in that little boat" J.J. Astor, the millionaire, is reputed to have said (he drowned). Passengers preferred not to leave their "well-ordered haven". (21) In fact, after the ship hit the iceberg, most cabin passengers returned to their state rooms, and stewards had to plead with them to come out. (22)

Why did people not flee from Pompeii in 79 AD? Earthquakes began four to five days before Vesuvius erupted, and the eruption went on for nearly two days. There was plenty of time for them to escape. We can only imagine what their fear must have been. And yet they felt safer in their homes, and they died in their thousands in these familiar surroundings. (23)

Why did so many people not evacuate when ordered to do so after Hurricane Katrina, but remained in their homes, eventually finishing up on their rooftops or in the water, waving desperately to helicopters? Again, home feels safer than anywhere else, even when, objectively, it is not. Why did so many German Jewish families in the nineteen thirties choose not to emigrate when they had the opportunity to do so, and the threat was clear, but stayed at home and were eventually killed in Nazi concentration camps? The reason, again, is that nowhere feels safer than home. Why do fighter pilots often fail to bail out of a disabled plane? One reason is that they hold on to "the cocoon of the cockpit."(24) In all these cases we see the impact of a protective frame, albeit a misleading and, in any event, tragic one. (25)

THE INVISIBLE FRAME

There is an opposite to the fallacious frame. This is what we might think of as 'the invisible frame.' By this I mean that there really is safety, but it is not seen for what it is. There is a frame, but one looks right through it and therefore misses it. The result is that one is in the serious state when one should, or could, be in the playful state, meaning that one is experiencing some degree of anxiety rather than excitement. (Compare this with the fallacious frame, which has the opposite outcome in that we are playful when we should be serious.) Here's a case in point, I start to feel a small pain in my ankle while playing tennis. Instead of continuing to focus on and enjoy the game, I start wondering if I have done something serious and need to see a doctor. Have I broken my ankle? Will I ever walk again? Do I have cancer of the ankle? In any case, my protective frame feels as if it is now shot, and I can no longer enjoy the game.

Usually we can tell the difference between fact and fiction.

We know when we are reading a novel or watching a movie, and this knowledge provides a protective frame, so that we enjoy our emotions, safe in the belief that nothing bad could happen. But suppose people do not pick up on the cues and think that what they are attending to is real rather than make-believe? Then the protective frame that should be there becomes invisible, and psychological trauma can result. An amazing example is that of the radio broadcast of a play based on H.G. Wells's science fiction novel "The War of the Worlds," which tells the story of the invasion of Earth by monsters from Mars. (26) The play was broadcast in the U.S. in 1938, on the night before Hallowe'en, and produced by the then up-and-coming twenty-three year old Orson Welles. The problem was that the drama was presented as if it was real. A music program was apparently interrupted increasingly frequently, by breaking news reports of strange capsules that had landed in or around Grovers Mill in New Jersey. A terrified running account was given by a CBS 'news correspondent' who was an eye witness to a large squid-like Martian emerging from one of the space ships, and aiming a heat ray at the crowd that was gathering, and then at him – in a further touch of realism, the broadcast went temporarily, but ominously, off the air. When it continued, the Martians were reported as increasing in number and marching towards New York. The invasion continued to escalate as the broadcast continued. The "Secretary of the Interior" was interviewed and asked people not to panic.

In fact, believing that their lives were under threat, panic is exactly what many people did, especially those near Grovers Mill. People ran into the streets, drove their cars around at high speed not exactly sure where to go, and jammed telephone lines trying to get through to their loved ones. According to a survey conducted shortly after, over a quarter of the six million listeners took the play to be factual, and the majority of those who did so finished by panicking. (27) In fact, when it was realised what was happening, a special announcement was hastily inserted during the broadcast to reassure people that what they were hearing was fictional – in other words, to re-establish their protective frames. Just how fragile the protective frame can be is shown by the fact that people overlooked an announcement at the start of the broadcast saying that it was a play, and people did not think to check their radio listing, where they would have seen it listed as a play. A lot of people were shame-faced the next day. Life magazine printed a staged cover photograph of a farmer with a pitchfork ready to fight the aliens.

It might seem that we are much more sophisticated these days and that this kind of thing could never happen again. But two examples occurred while I was writing these very pages. A newspaper in Jordan, Al-Ghad, ran a front page story saying that 10-foot aliens had landed in flying saucers in a desert town in Eastern Jordan. It was an April fool's joke, but caused great commotion and upset. Security authorities were sent out to chase the Aliens down.(28) In Georgia, a television channel, Imedi, broadcast a fiction about being invaded by Russia. Just like the "War of the Worlds" situation, people did not recognise that it was indeed fiction and ran into the streets in terror. Apparently cellphone networks crashed, cinemas closed and fugitives had heart attacks. (29)

THE BROKEN FRAME

It sometimes happens that a traumatic experience will damage a protective frame, making it more difficult for a person to avoid anxiety in related situations in the future, even the distant future.

A well-known psychologist (30) tells how he was watching

television when the news of Martin Luther King's assassination was announced. He was upset and decided to have a walk. In doing so he passed a cinema showing the film "Bonnie and Clyde" and thought that this might help to distract him. But when it came to the final scene in which these two bandits are killed in a hail of police bullets, he felt faint, and got as far as the lobby where he collapsed and remained unconscious for a few minutes. Here we see the effect of a temporary loss of protective frame due to the shock of the assassination, meaning that the scene in the film felt real and was difficult for him to cope with.

I personally experienced something similar, although in a much milder way, with the explosions at the end of the Boston Marathon (April 15, 2012) in which three spectators were killed and nearly two hundred injured. One of the two explosions occurred across the street from the Boston Public Library. Much of the book that you are reading at this moment was written sitting at a large table in this beautiful library, looking out over the area where the explosion took place. I was not there at the time, but the damage to my protective frame over the next few days was noticeable. In particular, I was more anxious than usual and had trouble sleeping. The library no longer seemed such a safe place to be, or to have been. Nor, by extension, did any library.

A more generic and long-term example of the protective frame being broken, occurs in sexual dysfunction. If any threat or obligation leads to a reversal to the serious state in a sexual situation, then, as we have seen, anxiety will be felt rather than excitement. Indeed, the anxiety *is* the sexual excitement, but now experienced in the serious state. The paradox is that the greater the arousal, and therefore the greater the pleasure in the playful state, the worse the feelings in the serious state when a reversal occurs to this state. It follows that the greater the arousal in the telic state, the greater the inhibition of sexual performance and the less the ability to perform after a reversal.

It is amazing how many things in a sexual situation can lead to a reversal into the serious state. (31) Research has shown that these include fear of pregnancy, fear of being infected by AIDS or some other sexual disease, fear of being discovered or observed, fear of inadequate performance (especially by the man), fear of being forced to indulge in a kind of sexual act that one finds disgusting or degrading, fear of being seen to be 'easy' (by the woman), fear of loss of control, fear of doing something immoral, fear of subsequent practical or emotional entanglements, fear of accusations of harassment, fear of not being desirable. It is a wonder that sexual activity ever takes place at all. It does in any case explain why sexual behaviour in many married couples tends to be repetitive, since in this way couples stay where they know they have been safe before. But the main point here is that once the protective frame has become damaged in relation to sex – perhaps through a single unfortunate incident – it will be likely to cause recurring problems until the protective frame heals.

There can be a positive side to temporarily losing the protective frame in relation to sexuality. For instance, avoiding an unwanted sexual response can be achieved by deliberately thinking about something worrying and in this way entering the serious state. A male massage patient reports that to make a regularly occurring, and embarrassing, erection go away during therapy, he thinks of something serious, like retirement planning. "It's a constant source of concern in my life right now, so thinking about it usually makes (my erection) go away quickly." (32)

Here is a serious example of the undesired loss of protective frame, this one concerning a skydiver. As we have seen, a protective frame slots into place when the parachute opens, converting intense anxiety into intense excitement.

Presumably, each time this happens, this particular protective frame is strengthened. But one serious fright can destroy the frame, making it difficult or impossible to obtain excitement thereafter from the activity concerned. In one reported case history a female skydiver gave up skydiving when a close friend died following an accident. His chute had got tangled up on exiting the aircraft, so that he hit the tail section which broke off, and he fell to the ground with it. (The others in the plane, and the pilot, were able to parachute out of the plane safely before it crashed.) A week after the accident she jumped again, but that was the last time. It had become too "scary" for her. (33) But not only did she give up skydiving, the loss of a skydiving protective frame generalised to other parts of her life. She was off sick from work for a month, and then resigned from her job; she was depressed and considered suicide; and she felt anxious much of the time. In other words, she lost the capacity to maintain a protective frame across large swathes of her life.

This is an example of a phenomenon that has recently become widely referred in the mass media: Post Traumatic Stress Disorder, or PTSD. By this is meant that some terrifying event or ordeal brings about psychological changes that persist, or recur, long after the original event is over. Symptoms include anxiety, depression, insomnia, anger and flashbacks to the traumatic event. As is well known, this illness was identified in the mid nineteen seventies following the Vietnam War, although it had long been known under other names from earlier wars, such as 'shell shock' or 'battle fatigue'. But the term PTSD generalised it to traumas of all kinds, not just military. It can be seen that it is an extreme example of what happens when the protective frame is lost and remains that way for an extended period of time.

Wherever anxiety enters into a problem of mental health, be it in the form of PTSD, depression, obsessive-compulsive disorder, phobia, sexual dysfunction, or in any other way, the assumption of most therapists is that they should find a way to reduce arousal – whether this be through meditation, or medication, or in some other way. Whatever the technique, the aim is to replace the anxiety by relaxation. But the approach that I have adopted here – the reversal theory approach – suggests as an alternative that a radically different strategy may be used: Namely to cause a reversal, so that anxiety is replaced not by relaxation but by excitement. This can be accomplished in various ways such as the playful use of humour, stories and metaphor, all of which can help induce a protective frame.

One way that seems to be particularly effective is the technique known as 'paradoxical intention,' which was invented by Viktor Frankl. (34) The idea here is to get sufferers to exaggerate their symptoms rather than trying to remove them. For example, an obsessive compulsive individual who is fixated on cleanliness and washes frequently might be encouraged to wash even more frequently during his or her daily life, and avoid touching anything at all if they can help it. They might also carry a bottle of water around with them, for immediate washing in case they do touch something. In this way, the whole thing becomes a farce. In reversal theory terms, the exaggeration induces the playful state, which means that real anxiety can now no longer be felt. Another way of saying this is that the symptoms are being play-acted in a ridiculous way, so that they can hardly be taken seriously any more by the patient.

In one case history written about by a colleague of Frankl, the patient – a thirty year old mother of four – suffered from feelings of imminent death, and spent much of her time convinced that she was about to have a heart attack. Instead of being sympathetic, or trying to persuade her that her feelings were irrational since she had no medical problems (which was in fact the case), the psychiatrist told her that she should go downtown with her husband and pick out her coffin. Meanwhile they should decide on a suitable colour for the inside of the coffin. He also told her that she should try as hard as she could to die instantly from a heart attack. Immediately she started to feel better, had a good laugh, and eventually, after more sessions, was completely cured. (35)

In another case by a different psychiatrist using Frankl's methods, the patient, a 25 year old woman, had the compulsion to look at the genital region of the men she met, and was so embarrassed by this that she wore dark glasses whenever she went out, in order to conceal her direction of gaze. She was persuaded by the psychiatrist to remove her glasses on her excursions, and to look impudently at the crotch of any man she met. After a few days she no longer felt the need to do this and in two weeks the compulsion had completely disappeared. A paradox indeed! (36)

CHAPTER 5

PARADOXICAL EMOTIONS

"Why do people enjoy bad emotions?"

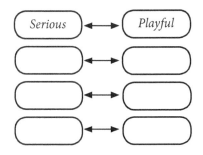

This way of looking at the experience of arousal has an implication that is both surprising and counter-intuitive. I pointed out that in the playful state people enjoy high arousal which they experience as excitement. But if this is true, then *any* high arousal emotion must be experienced as desirable in the playful state, not just excitement or other closely related emotions like thrill and ecstasy and euphoria. This would have to mean that we enjoy *unpleasant* emotions too – emotions like rage, horror, disgust or grief – to the extent that they are also intense. And the more intense they become, the more we should enjoy them. At first blush, it would seem that this is ridiculous, and that it thoroughly disproves the approach described in the previous chapter. How can we possibly enjoy bad emotions? That would be absurd.

But it does not take much self-observation to see that this is exactly what does happen. We can, and *do,* take pleasure from such emotions. If you think about it, most of us spend some hours every day trying to do precisely this: to experience bad emotions. One of the most common ways that we go about this is by watching movies on television. After all, what we want in a thriller movie is suspense, what we want in a horror movie is horror, and maybe some disgust and dread thrown in, what we want in a tragedy is sadness and even grief, what we want in a romantic movie is… well, you get the idea. These are typically mixed in with good emotions, like triumph and love, but the bad emotions are desirable too. Would you really want to see a thriller that had no tension, or a horror movie with no horror, or a romantic movie where everything went exactly according to plan? The same of course applies to novels, plays, or any kind of fiction. In one form or another, fiction plays an important role in most of our lives, meaning that these kinds of enjoyable emotions must play an important part too. The house lights dim and the curtain goes up, or we hear the words "Once Upon a Time," and a world of paradoxical enchantment magically opens up before us – a world in which emotions are turned upside down.

This is not confined to fiction: Such enjoyment arises in non-fiction as well. Any kind of arousing narrative can produce this same effect. Biography and autobiography, documentary television, political speeches, personal anecdotes, gossip, even the TV evening news – they can all be the source of gratifyingly pleasant emotions. This is often not owned up to, and may be disguised by the fact that we continue to use 'bad' emotion words to describe our experiences. So when we say that learning from the television news about the effects of a tornado is horrifying, this implies that we did not take pleasure from learning about it. We do not admit that we actually enjoyed looking at the amateur video of the devastated trailer park.

Nor are such pleasantly 'bad' emotions restricted to narrative but can arise in many different ways. The mild fear that one might experience on a Ghost Train at an amusement park is enjoyable, even if this consists of little more than a tingle of apprehension. The momentary astonishment that one experiences in watching a conjuror remove a rabbit from his top hat is an enjoyable kind of mystification – at least the first time that we see it. The concern that one might feel in passing a car wreck may well, if one is being really truthful, be somewhat agreeable: all those flashing lights, and policemen annoyingly waving you on when you want to see what happened.

I am going to call these good/bad emotions *'paradoxical emotions.'* (1) Then in watching a thriller movie we could be said to experience paradoxical anxiety, in telling a story against oneself at a dinner party one might experience paradoxical embarrassment. In the example just given of learning about a tornado, one might experience paradoxical horror or even paradoxical grief while watching the news item. In all these cases the emotion is paradoxical because we have enjoyed it, despite its supposedly negative quality. (2)

We need to remember that to experience the enjoyment that comes with high arousal, we have to remain in the playful state. This means that we have to continue to experience things within a protective frame. Without this frame there is no playful state, and paradoxical emotions cannot occur. Suppose, to continue the tornado example, that we are watching a television weather channel, which is talking about tornadoes in some neighbouring state, and showing pictures of the devastation. But then we learn that there is a tornado warning for our own area, and that the tornadoes are heading directly our way. It may well happen that this new information destroys our protective frame. The pleasant paradoxical anxiety and concern that we were experiencing before, now become real anxiety and real concern. Good arousal is turned back into bad arousal.

Another example: You pass on some gossip, feeling deliciously – paradoxically – guilty about doing so because you are enjoying the moment, and not thinking of consequences. Then you realise that the person to whom you have entrusted this information is in fact a good friend of the person you were gossiping about, and that it will probably get back to her. Say goodbye to the protective frame and cue in real guilt.

One thing that should be pretty evident at this point is that the protective frame can come in many different shapes and forms, be prompted in different ways, and is necessarily in the eye of the beholder. A cup of tea, a locked door, a particular piece of music, a walking stick, a blanket – these may all be protective frames for some people but not for others. All that frames have in common is that they represent safety and are therefore reassuring. But what reassures one person may not do so to another and may even be threatening. A gun to one person is a mortal danger, to another the guarantee of safety. Being naked may represent vulnerability and shame to one person, but feelings of rejuvenation and joy to a nudist in the safety zone of a nudist beach.

The key part played by the protective frame has been demonstrated experimentally. The experimenters showed participants a clip from a horror film. Some of the participants were not partial to horror films and would not willingly go and see such a film at the cinema if left to their own devices. The other participants reported that they were fans. As expected, the non-partial group, on the whole, did not enjoy the film clip while the fans did. Three experiments with similar designs (but different actual subjects) showed this in different ways. In a fourth experiment, a protective frame was ingeniously introduced for both sets of viewers, emphasising the artificial nature of the movie. Participants were informed about the actors' biographies before the video clip was shown, and during the showing pictures of the actors were displayed next to the screen. In this way, a detachment frame was set up, allowing the viewers to distance themselves from what was happening on screen and recognise that it was only a story. In this case, both groups reported enjoying the film. It seems reasonable to infer that the difference between the two sets of subjects in the earlier studies was due to a lack of protective frame in the case of the subjects who did not normally enjoy such films. When such a frame was introduced, they enjoyed it too. (3)

A point that arises from all this is that paradoxical emotions are not feigned. They are not pretense. They are genuine emotions, but emotions in which the pleasant/unpleasant dimension has become inverted, so that what felt bad comes to feel good. One might say: "Where the undesirable is, there the desirable can be."

The previous chapter was all about a special case of this. In exposing oneself to risk within a protective frame one is enjoying the anxiety and fear that the risk has called up. This is why we enjoy riding the swings and roundabouts that we find in amusement parks, why we enjoy the archetypal fears that Edgar Allan Poe summons up for our delectation (such as being buried alive, or cut in half), why children delight in dinosaurs and fantastical monsters. In this respect, 'excitement' is a way of saying 'paradoxical anxiety.' But in this chapter we are going beyond both excitement and anxiety to look at a wider range of emotions and feelings.

Pleasurable stress

It is generally assumed that stress is a negative experience. But if by 'stress' we mean becoming worked up and engaged in meeting challenges, then clearly we can enjoy stress. It becomes paradoxical stress. This is exactly what we do in sport, for example. We confront the challenge of competition. But the point is that such stress is only enjoyable if it is experienced from within a protective frame. For genuine amateurs, winning or losing has no consequences outside the game itself, so they can willingly take on the challenge for the fun that the competition itself can provide. But for professional athletes, winning or losing has real, and long-term, consequences. For them, the stress will indeed be stressful, at least while they are aware of the consequences of their success or failure.

It is also possible to enjoy the challenge of learning some new skill – playing the piano, let's say. This will require time and effort, and difficulties will have to be faced and overcome. But if the learning can be engaged in for fun, and nothing serious depends on it, then the challenge will be all part of the fun. If, on the other hand, one's progress has consequences – perhaps there is an exam to be taken, and a career to be considered – then the situation may indeed call up genuinely stressful feelings, together with exasperation at the difficulties that arise.

The paradox here is that someone who is in the playful state, within a protective frame, will in fact experience a *'lack of stress'* as 'stressful.' They will feel unstimulated, restless and bored. They will feel that they are no longer fully 'alive,' and will therefore seek out, rather than avoid, challenges, problems and confrontations. All of us, in the normal way of things, experience such 'lack of stress' distress from time to time. An example would be the experience of waiting in a long line, with no distractions, no friends to talk to, no magazine to read. Another would be attending a dinner party when you have nothing in common with anyone, and your host has made it disappointingly clear that discussing politics and religion is out of bounds. I have my own particular list of things that I find particularly boring when I am subjected to them for too long: music by Wagner, Lacanian psychoanalysis, church services, most speeches, low-scoring baseball games when nobody seems to be able to hit the ball (actually, now I come to think of it, high-scoring games are pretty boring too). What would be at the top of your own personal list of boredom infamy? Whatever it is, I feel sure you will experience it as a kind of stress.

If it is true that lack of stimulation is disagreeable in the playful state, then we may expect someone who is often in the playful state and lacking the stimulation of stress to report being generally unhappy. In fact, research shows this to be exactly the case.

In one study (4), students were given a questionnaire in the form of a list of stressful events, and asked to check off those events that they had had to put up with in the previous year. They were also asked to complete a scale of positive or negative mood, and a scale measuring how frequently they were in the serious or playful states. For students who reported being frequently in the serious state, the more their stress then the more negative their mood. This was of course just as would be expected. But the interesting finding is that for students who reported being frequently in the *playful* state, the more the stressful events that they reported, the *better* they felt! (5) The relationship of stress to mood was inverted compared to the more serious group. When the study was completed with a different stress questionnaire, this time one that measured "hassles" experienced during the previous month, the same set of relationships were found.

In another study, students were asked to provide a written description of their most stressful experience in the past month and were also asked to complete questionnaires to measure depression and how frequently they were in the serious and playful states. It was found that for stress that was still ongoing in these students' lives, the more often they were in the serious state the more depressed they felt. This would make sense in common-sense terms: the more frequent the stress the greater the depression. But with stressors that were reported as *being resolved*, the opposite turned out to be the case. Now it was students who were frequently in the playful state who were more depressed, presumably because they lacked challenge in their lives compared to those who still had significant problems to kick around. When the study was repeated using a biochemical measure of stress in place of the depression scale, essentially the same result was found.

These studies on stress are not only interesting in themselves, but they also throw a question mark over the whole field of stress research, because, taking the field as a whole, the distinction is rarely made between good and bad stress, and good stress is rarely recognised. So the results of many studies that have assumed that all subjects were having bad feelings when exposed to arousing situations may be misleading.

PLEASURABLE SADNESS

The most obvious kind of pleasurable grief is experienced when we go to the theatre to see a tragedy, or when we read a tear-jerker novel. From the ancient Greek tragedian Euripides to the contemporary novelist Judy Picoult, works of fiction have caused tears to flow joyfully. But it is not only in fiction that we can enjoy bad things happening to other people, and the Germans even have a word for it: *schadenfreude*. This is the momentary pleasure that one can have on first hearing that a friend has had bad luck, for example losing his job or having an accident. Clearly we can willingly enter into, and enjoy, the landscape of loss, however fleetingly. In this respect such an emotion is paradoxical.

A less obvious way that we enjoy sadness is through what has been called 'dark tourism,' which means visiting places where historically bad things have happened. Taking myself as an example, I can think of at least the following 'dark' places that I have enjoyed visiting over the years: Buchenwald, Omaha beach, Dunkirk, Verdun, The Tower of London, Ground Zero, New Orleans just after Katrina, Pompeii, Gettysburg, Antietam, Salem, Ford's Theatre in Washington DC, and the infamous book depository in Dallas, not to mention numerous cemeteries, especially military cemeteries and certain museums, like the Holocaust Museum in Washington. Taken together, this long litany of places representing desolation and cruelty gives a good idea of what is meant by dark tourism, and there must be few people who have not engaged in it to some extent or another. You may want to pause here and think of your own examples.

This is not to say that paradoxical sadness is the only emotion that one is likely to feel in such places, or that the feeling of such emotions is the only reason for going to see them. For one thing, it is possible to feel 'real' sadness, and perhaps to reverse backwards and forwards between these two types of sadness, during the same visit. For another there is obviously the intellectual interest that one might have in the historical events that took place there. But paradoxical sadness is a phenomenon to be recognised and catered to – as indeed it is by tour companies, travel agents, hoteliers, guides, and all the others who make a living out of it.

Pleasurable Anger

In fiction, we enjoy being angry at the anti-heroes that we despise: Shakespeare's scheming Iago in "Othello", Verdi's evil Scarpia in "Tosca", Shakespeare's monstrous Richard III, the unscrupulous Fagin in Dickens'"Oliver Twist", the Joker in Batman comics and movies, the awesome Darth Vader in "Star Wars." The "Dark Side", or what Jung has called "The Shadow", is an enormous source of pleasure, not least in the way that it can help us to experience a joyous fury within a protective frame.

One of the great pleasures of watching professional wrestling to those who are taken in by this bizarre charade, is the frequent scenario in which one wrestler becomes the 'heel' by being grotesquely boastful, or disparaging his opponent, or his opponent's relationship to his mother, or by theatrically cheating, or taking unfair advantage of his opponent, or attacking an official. He then becomes the wrestler who, at least temporarily, one loves to hate. The spectators can become a seething mass of vituperation as they succumb to the joys of anger, and cheer his opponent to victory. While this wrestling experience derives from cynical manipulation, pleasurable anger is also felt more spontaneously by spectators from time to time in other sports, especially, it seems, against referees in football. Booing, jeering, whistling, screaming obscenities, and other public demonstrations of dissatisfaction with referees, can, in my own experience (I have to admit), be a tremendously therapeutic source of release when one engages in it.

Paradoxical anger takes an extreme form in soccer hooligans, whose pleasure comes from confronting, and taunting, and eventually fighting not only supporters of the other side, but also the police, innocent bystanders and as much of the world as they can get their hands on. A wonderful account of the joys of such angry confrontation comes from Bill Buford's book "Among the Thugs." (6) In this journalistic report, he described how he himself became a soccer hooligan in order to experience what was going on 'from the inside.' He followed his team not only nationally, but within Europe and had the full experience when he was badly beaten by the police in Sardinia.

He discovered, to his own immense surprise, just how powerfully pleasurable the hooliganism was, and especially the violence. The book is full of descriptions of gangs of hooligans, usually drunk, assuming the character of an angry crowd – typically during their march to or from the stadium – and how the crowd builds up to, and eventually erupts in the euphoria of violence. Throughout we see the delights of everything from the mild drunken anger of swearing and rowdiness and obscenity to the extreme aggression of knifing and kicking and beating. But here, according to Buford, is the key to understanding why people become hooligans and indulge in such craziness. It is because it is fun to be angry and violent, and to express this, especially when everything is amplified by taking place in a crowd. To call it fun, though, is not strong enough. It becomes a kind of ecstasy. To quote Buford: "I had not expected the violence to be so pleasurable. I would have assumed, if I had thought to think about it, that the violence would be exciting – in the way that a traffic accident is exciting – but the pure elemental pleasure was unlike anything I had foreseen or experienced before. But it was not just any violence. It wasn't just random violence or fights in the pub; it was crowd violence – that was what mattered: the very particular workings of the violence of numbers." (7)

As with all these forms of paradoxical emotion, please be clear: I am not claiming that anger is always rewarding. What I am saying is that it *can* be, and inevitably will be, if one can maintain the anger within a protective frame. In the soccer hooligans case, the protective frame seems to be provided by being drunk in a crowd of like-minded supporters.

Pleasurable Guilt

A friend of mine (with a more practical bent than I have) told me of an incident in which, one evening, in walking past the site of a building being renovated, he saw six wooden tiles piled neatly on the ground. The wood was beautiful and old, with a rich patina, and he had a place in his own home where he reckoned he could use them just nicely. It was unclear to him whether the tiles were being kept until the moment came for the builders to use them, or had been removed and were about to be thrown away. There was no one around to ask so, on the spur of the moment, he just took them. His first momentary feeling, as he described it to me, was one of self-congratulation but then, as he proceeded on his way, this turned to guilt. But the interesting thing is that the guilt was a deliciously pleasant guilt. Instead of trying to justify his action to himself, he found himself accepting that what he had done was wrong and getting a certain *frisson* of pleasure from this.

You might say that, even if you do things that are wrong, like my friend did, you would never get pleasure from it. But consider the following everyday examples, and see if you have never enjoyed doing them, or something like them, precisely because you should not have done them. Have you never enjoyed overeating, not just for the pleasure of the food itself but for the release from an irksome diet? Did you never truant when you were at school, or take a sick day from work when you were not really ill? And was there not a special guilty pleasure about everything you did that day? Admit it: have you never had pleasure from swearing in public, or making jokes that are in bad taste, or being rude to strangers, or catching a glimpse of forbidden flesh? I can personally attest that cigarettes are never as pleasurable again as they were when smoked furtively behind the bicycle shed at school. Have you never bought clothes that you could not really afford, and perhaps hidden them from your spouse until a suitable moment arose to mention them (perhaps when enough time had passed so that you could say, dismissively, "Oh, I bought those ages ago").

There is another whole arena of guilty pleasure, and that is the experience of sex in a form that is believed to be forbidden. (8) Numerous surveys over the years, from Kinsey on, have shown that healthy and normal people enjoy a range of supposedly 'wicked' sexual behaviours. (Do we need a 'thought experiment' at this point?) From religious, or other traditionalist viewpoints, such acts as those involved in oral sex, for example, are sinful. And yet we know that both forms of oral sex, fellatio and cunnilingus, are practiced widely in the adult population.(9) Such acts are therefore only apparently taboo. I have elsewhere (10) called them examples of 'functional fiction' or 'convenient myths.' The 'myth' is that these are rare pathological behaviours, practiced only by perverts, whereas they are in fact boringly widespread. They are 'convenient' because they give people the pleasure of feeling that they are breaking the rules – a feeling of 'being naughty.' Who would deny that such supposed immorality can strongly enhance the intensity of the sexual experience? One writer (11) has pointed out that 75% of American males are technically sexual deviants judging by survey reports.

There is yet another paradox here, which is that the more liberal attitudes towards these practices become general in an enlightened society – the more acceptable these practices become – the less pleasure people will be able to derive from them. In support of this statement is the fact that the use of pornography has declined in countries that have made it legal. The classic and oft-cited case is Denmark, which made pornography legal in 1969. The demand for pornography thereafter fell off steadily. (12) Prohibition, whether of sexual acts, or alcohol, or drugs, seems always to be counter-productive, because it makes what is prohibited even more desirable than it otherwise would have been.

PLEASURABLE PAIN

One of the most remarkable, and to some people shocking, instances of human paradox is the way that some people can relish pain, or at least certain kinds of pain. We are dealing here with masochism and its partner sadism, both of which arise most often in the context of sexuality. How are we to understand the attraction of such sadomasochistic practices? I am talking here about what its devotees refer to as "SM," (or "BDSM" where B and D stand for bondage and discipline). This is a kind of consensual sexual behaviour, usually with props and paraphernalia of various kinds, which allow adherents to act out domination and submission through giving and receiving pain. It may be performed by both males and females, and a given participant may enjoy both being dominant (sadistic) and submissive (masochistic) at different times. (13)

It does not take much thought to see that this is essentially the same as the other examples in this chapter of taking something bad and turning it into something good through a reversal: more specifically of taking something arousing, and reversing into the playful state where the arousal is enjoyed as a kind of excitement. (14)

In the present case, the 'bad' experience involves pain. In fact the pain – more often than not through spanking or whipping – is typically mild, but inevitably produces some level of arousal in the victim which can then be enjoyed by him or her when everything is turned upside down in the playful state. One great advantage that pain has as an instrument of arousal is that it habituates slowly, but continues to maintain itself over time (as anyone with a toothache will know). This is perhaps the reason for its popularity in SM ritual. At the same time, the aggressiveness involved in causing pain may also be arousing to the oppressor, and easily translatable into feelings of sexual arousal. (15) Krafft-Ebing, the great pioneers of sexual research, saw such aggressiveness as an extension of everyday sex involving biting, scratching and rough-and-tumble foreplay. (16)

In the case of sadomasochistic interactions, other sources of arousal can be added in to the arousal from pain and the sexual arousal itself, to make the experience even more enticing. First of all, for the masochist, there can be the arousal that derives from the feeling of vulnerability that comes with being bound. (The term BDSM is used for this version of SM, where B stands for bondage and D for discipline.) Furthermore, if the pain is caused in a humiliating way, as it would be with spanking for example, the arousal from this acute embarrassment can add to the pleasure. Alternatively, for the sadist, there is the arousal that comes from the feeling of power over someone else, which in the playful state becomes the uninhibited joy of being able to do what you want with another human being: to some people a dream come true. SM conjures up images of black masks, blindfolds, handcuffs, whips, chains, nipple clamps, studded belts, and all the other varied instruments of terror and oppression. It is especially ironic that torture devices used to make people conform in previous more dogmatic and brutal ages (think Inquisition) have become the very accessories chosen by those who wish to experience freedom in our own times.

The feeling of doing something forbidden may be another source of arousal, as suggested in the previous section of this chapter, which was on guilty pleasures. The pleasures of SM though, seem to derive more from a sense of release and freedom from normal moral restraints than from guilt. This freedom comes in the masochistic mode primarily from freedom from responsibility (and some masochists even like to be dressed like babies with diapers). In the sadistic mode it comes from not having to justify oneself for one's actions, however outrageous or immoral they seem to be. For someone who is normally bound by the enduring needs of family and work, this may be an enormous, if temporary, release.

To make all this work to produce great feelings, there has to be a strong protective frame, otherwise anxiety will be the outcome rather than sexual excitement. This protective frame is established and assured in a number of ways. First of all, SM sex is set up by consenting adults who usually know and trust each other and may even have a romantic relationship. Not only is participation not forced, but there is also an implicit or explicit contract which establishes what is allowed and not allowed. In this respect, there may be a kind of agreed upon, if improvised, script – for example a mistress and slave script, or a teacher and pupil script. The whole thing is therefore a form of theatrical performance, a charade, in which observers are also participants. Many of the props that are used are exaggerated and preposterous, which also help to induce and maintain the playful state. Although there may be some real pain, the situation is essentially a sex game. Most important of all, there are mutually agreed upon "stop-words" which override anything else, and may be used by the person in the victim role to bring the ritual to an immediate halt at any time, in this way preventing matters going too far. This forms a kind of ultimate protective frame in this situation.

PLEASURABLE CONFUSION

It is generally supposed that people do not like information that contains inconsistencies, dissonances, illogicalities, ambiguities, and what psychologists call incongruities – in other words, situations that are confusing in some way or another. There does not seem to be a good emotion word to describe the negative emotional response that results, but there may be some annoyance and even exasperation. If you have something important to do, and you are therefore in the serious state, you do not want to be frustrated by things that do not make sense and that consequently only add to your difficulties. If you are completing your tax returns, you do not want receipts that are unreadable, ledger entries that say that you both did and did not have a certain expense, and official forms that do not make sense to you. You want everything to be clear and definite. That is a basic requirement of the serious state.

But if we turn to the playful state, we find that things are quite otherwise. Here there are ways available to us of creating dissonances that are, by contrast to the serious state, highly pleasurable. These must not be threatening, otherwise they could not be experienced within a protective frame, so that the playful state could not be maintained. But they must be able to produce at least some arousal. These forms are well known to you, and you might be able to guess what I am coming to. The first major form is humour, and the second art.

In humour, one experiences momentary delightful confusion. A given event (a statement, a situation, an action) seems to have one meaning, but this gives way to a different meaning. Humour therefore always involves two meanings. In one frequent type of humour, a first meaning is established, and then it gives way to a second less immediately obvious meaning, this second meaning always involving some kind of downgrading. Let us take a simple example. One of Groucho Marx's well known quips was: "I had a great evening – unfortunately it was not this evening." The statement has two meanings. In the first, one's assumption is that it is referring to the present evening. In the second part of the statement, this understanding is downgraded, through the implication that the present evening was, after all, not so great. Both meanings are different interpretations of the original "I had a great evening" statement, which therefore turns out to have been unexpectedly ambiguous. And a polite compliment turns into a rude criticism.

"I ate something funny," says one cannibal to another, referring to a clown they had just dragged out of the cooking pot and eaten. In this case the meaning of 'funny' changes from its usual meaning in this phrase – that one has eaten something that might disagree with one's digestion – to the sense of something comic. The subject here is the clown, who is being downgraded through this play on words from a person to a food morsel. But not really – the statement is clearly not intended to be taken as an accurate description of something that really happened, so the protective frame remains in place.

I learned from my daughter Carolyn that she had got into trouble at school for not wearing her school hat while waiting for a bus to get home. "What were you doing at the bus stop without your school hat?" asked her teacher accusingly the next day. She replied "Waiting for the bus." This gave an unexpected, but literally accurate, interpretation of the question. But it was different from the interpretation implied by the teacher. One question, two meanings. A protective frame present while reading the story now allows us to enjoy it, but that was probably not the case for Carolyn at the time: she was given detention.

The psychology of humour is a complicated topic. (17) It is enough here to realise that humour is yet another way of turning the 'bad' into the good. The momentary bewilderment, and the blip of arousal that goes with it, are enjoyed as a special form of excitement, with its own flavour. The downgrading means that there is no threat to the protective frame, which is no doubt part of the reason why the resulting arousal is pleasant rather than unpleasant. If the content of the humour is also arousing or shocking, then the whole effect is enhanced. This is the reason that so much humour is about sex, violence, race, religion or other troubling subjects. Whatever you are most worried about is what you are most likely to find funny – provided only that the protective frame can be maintained.

Turning to art, much contemporary art seems to be designed specifically to cause confusion and surprise, even dismay among those who think of art in a conventional way. To give some celebrated examples:

Exhibit One: Andres Serrano's "Piss Christ", the work of a controversial American photographer, who has produced a series of photographs involving faeces, blood, semen, burn victims, even corpses. But "Piss Christ" (a huge 3 by 5 foot photograph) is his best known work to the public at large, and caused a scandal when it was exhibited in 1989 and won a prize. The photograph is of a plastic crucifix, complete with Christ figure, submerged in a glass of (we are told) the artist's own urine. What is so disconcerting about this, and his other photographs, is that they are very beautiful if one can forget what they are made from and what they are depicting. They therefore produce a confusing mixture of disgust and aesthetic pleasure – and perhaps paradoxical guilt at our enjoying of them, if we do.

Exhibit Two. Damien Hurst's shark preserved in a glass case full of formaldehyde, and entitled "The Physical Impossibility of Death in the Mind of Someone Living" from 1991. This object seems to be very odd, and more zoological than aesthetic. It raises the question "Why?" as in "Why bother?" And yet the image produced does have a kind of power and raises such questions as whether a thing can both be itself and represent itself.

Exhibit Three: Tracey Emin's "My Bed" that was exhibited in 1999 and shortlisted for the prestigious Turner Prize. It consists of her own highly rumpled bed, as if she had just got up. Alongside are strewn an empty vodka bottle, cigarette stubs, worn panties, discarded slippers, condoms, and various other personal items. We have a kind of voyeur's delight in inspecting all this private sluttishness, and with it also some paradoxical guilt.

Since this is art, it is supposed to be 'cut off' from the real world, so that no one should be really threatened or offended. Instead, in the playful state, one is supposed to enjoy the intellectual challenge, the surprise, and the tensions and contradictions. People who object are presumably in the serious state looking for some profound meaning and being angered by its absence. Or perhaps they are naïve enough, in the playful state, to be just looking for something as old-fashioned as beauty.

POSITIVE REVERSALS

The reversals we have looked at in this chapter have been mainly positive. They take something that is producing a bad emotion and, through reversing into the playful state, generate a good emotion instead. Our culture prompts this type of reversal in many ways. We play on the fear of death at Hallowe'en, turning it into a festival of witches and hobgoblins. We convert Bad Friday into Good Friday, and take the day off. We turn major disasters into good television. (Admit it: when the phrase "Breaking News" comes on the screen, do you not feel a little frisson of pleasure?) We take whatever we fear the most, and turn it into a Hollywood movie. So nowadays we have movies about conflict in the Middle East, about terrorism, about global warming and about other natural disasters. A few years ago our movies were frequently about Russian spies and nuclear weapons.

Of course, things can work the other way around. Something that was good can become converted, by means of reversal into the serious state, into something that is really bad. This would be a negative reversal. An earlier example was that of watching TV news about a tornado, and then learning that it is heading your way.

But in our public events, our parades and celebrations and fictions, we tend to do the opposite, by converting bad into good. Our culture tends to *'entertainmentise'* everything it can get hold of, however threatening or despicable (18), transforming it through the mass media into a commodity for consumption. (19) Our society has been called "The Society of the Spectacle" (20) and we can now see how it arises and what psychological mechanisms it draws on.

So a reversal can turn out well or badly. In this chapter we have looked mainly at reversals that have been benevolent, turning the appalling into the appealing. But in the course of the book we shall look at many types of malevolent paradox. The next chapter is about one such: the way that rewards can punish.

CHAPTER 6

PARADOXICAL REWARDS

"Why can rewarding an activity make it less appealing?"

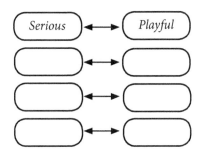

When I was aged 11, my parents gave me a chemistry set for Christmas – the sort that contains a few test tubes, a pipette, a candle to heat things up, some packets and tubes of chemicals, and an instruction booklet with a dozen or so simple experiments laid out like cooking recipes. After the first experiment, I was hooked. I remember that in that experiment I dissolved one chemical in water in a test tube, with the resulting liquid remaining clear and water-like. Then, by pipette, I introduced a single drop of another clear liquid. All of a sudden the whole liquid in the test tube went a deep opaque blue. I was fascinated by this. How could two colourless and transparent liquids together make a beautiful blue liquid? And how could this happen when there was only one tiny drop of one of the liquids? Suffice it to say that this was just the starting point, and that chemistry became one of my main hobbies for the next year or two. I even, with my parents' encouragement, set up the attic in my home as a mini laboratory. When I transferred to the British equivalent of high school at the age of thirteen, chemistry became, for the first time, a subject on the school syllabus. I obviously had a head start over the other pupils in my class. I was praised by teachers, rewarded high marks for homework, passed examinations with flying colours. But then something strange happened: I completely lost interest. The moment I had to strive for marks, and adhere to the laid down syllabus, and swot for exams, all the joy went out of it. My little private laboratory decayed and disintegrated, and soon my passionate interests turned elsewhere (to cricket, if I remember correctly).

My reaction may have been somewhat exaggerated, but this particular phenomenon, if peculiar, is not peculiar to me alone. This is an example of a kind of paradox that has now been well documented. The paradox consists of the fact that rewards, when added to a situation that is already rewarding in itself, can make it *less* rather than more attractive. This really does not seem to make much sense, or at least common sense.

Paradoxical Rewards

This unsettling paradox was first identified and studied by psychologists in the early nineteen seventies. In one of the classic experiments in this field (1), the experimenter asked university students individually to work on a series of spatial-relations puzzles. In this kind of puzzle, they had to use a set of pieces in seven different shapes, in order to construct complicated objects shown in drawings. After a given participant had been working for a certain time, the experimenter would excuse himself saying that he needed to collect another drawing for that person, the chosen drawing supposedly depending on the participant's earlier results which the experimenter would feed into a computer. (This was 1972 and before laptops were around, so this meant that he had to go to a large mainframe in another room!). He made it theatrically clear that he was leaving by noisily opening and closing the door of the laboratory as he went through. In reality he was lying: there was no such drawing.

But now we come to the crux of the matter. An observer watching through a one-way window recorded the amount of time that each student spent continuing to work on the puzzles during this free period, and the extent to which they turned to alternative activities such as reading magazines that were left lying around, or just daydreaming. In fact, this free period, that lasted eight minutes, was really what the experiment was all about. Half the participants had been promised a monetary reward for doing the puzzles, the amount of the payment being determined by task performance, while the other half had been made no such promise. So the question was whether the students who had been promised payment would continue to work on the puzzles during this free period. In fact, the opposite happened: those who had been promised payment, spent *less* time on the puzzles than those who had not. Adding a reward made the participants *less* motivated to do the task.

Not long after, another team of psychologists carried out a similar study, but this time with preschoolers. The children were allowed to draw with Magic Marker pens, but some of these little children were told that if they actually used the pens they would be rewarded with a special certificate decorated with a beautiful bright red ribbon and a big sparkling gold star, which is what in fact happened. Other children were not told this, but were given the same rewards anyway at the end of the activity period. One to two weeks later, they were all observed at free play in the classroom. Those children who had been told that they would be rewarded, and had been rewarded for using the Magic Markers, were now markedly less interested in the pens than those who had not been told this. As in the first experiment, expectation of reward had been counterproductive. It had in fact made something that was attractive and desirable to children, less attractive and desirable – and all this by promising them something extra that was also desirable and attractive! We should note that the children who had not been promised a reward, but were given one anyway, continued to be just as interested in the activity as they had been before. So this means that it is not the reward as such that makes the difference between the two groups of children in this case, but rather the *promise* of a reward. This is consistent with the idea that what is having an effect is not the reward itself but an expectation – a way of seeing the world.

In a related experiment, children were allowed to play with felt-tip pens and pastel crayons. Half the children had to play for a period with the pens before they would be allowed to play with the crayons. With the other half of the children, the opposite was the case: they had to play with the crayons before they could play with the pens. The children were observed two to three weeks later, and they were found to spend less time with the instrument that they were obliged to play with than with the other. Why should any of this have made any difference? And why this kind of difference? (2)

In another study, students were invited to take part in an experiment, for which they would receive credit toward a psychology course. When the subjects arrived, however, they were divided into two halves that were kept separate. Half of them were told that they would not after all receive the credit that they had been promised. The other students were not told this. The behaviour of all students in the experimental task was then measured along a number of dimensions which indicated how motivated they were. All these dimensions showed stronger motivation in those students who were *not* going to be rewarded. In this case, rather than reward having the effect of reducing motivation, taking away reward increased it. (3) So the effect was in the same direction as the earlier experimenter.

Amazingly, just calling something 'work' or 'play' can make all the difference. In one study (4), adults were asked to carry out various kinds of tasks involving Gary Larson "Far Side" cartoons, for example changing the words in each cartoon to alter the meaning. For half the participants, the tasks were referred to by the experimenter as work, and for the other half as play. For the more difficult tasks, participants in the 'play' group reported enjoying the activity more than those in the 'work' group – even though they were doing exactly the same thing. Apparently a rose is not a rose by any other name.

This difference of 'positioning' seems to be particularly important with respect to creative behaviour, which turns out to be more vulnerable to the ravages of reward. In a series of experiments with both children and adults, creativity in various activities (such as making collages, or inventing stories) was found to be less in participants promised a reward. And creativity was greater in participants who were not offered anything beyond the activity itself. (5) Surprisingly, these researchers found that even just thinking about rewards, such as public recognition or money, before starting to write poetry turned out to suppress creativity (as judged for the experimenters by independent professional writers). (6)

Something similar applies to dealing with problems that require the ability to go beyond conventional ways of thinking. There is a classic of this kind, called the 'candle problem' that goes back to the 1930s. The subject is given a candle, a box of tacks and a book of matches. The task is to attach the candle to the wall. You might want to stop for a moment and think how you would do this. Participants naturally try to use each of the tools that they have been given. Otherwise, why were they given to them? They try to tack the candle directly to the wall, or they melt the candle and try to use the candle grease to fix the candle in place. Neither of these approaches work. The solution is to take the box carrying the tacks, tack this to the wall, and then attach the candle, using the candle grease, to the floor of the box. The solution requires the subject to think beyond the conventional uses of each item, so as to see the box as not just a container for the tacks but as a platform for the candle. (7) In an experiment on the effect of rewards, subjects were offered a monetary incentive for completing this task within the speed of the top twenty five per cent of all subjects. In fact, they turned out to be slower than subjects who were offered no reward at all. On average, it took them three and a half minutes longer if they were offered this reward (and this on a task that takes most people between only five and ten minutes). Presumably the emphasis on speed led people to do what seemed the most obvious thing as quickly as possible, without standing back and reconsidering the whole problem from a different and more original standpoint.(8)

The Nature of Play

The existence of this general reward effect is controversial and not all studies replicate it. But the fact is that some, such as those cited here, do. And so this is a phenomenon that does exist and requires explanation. (9) How are we to understand it? (10)

Thinking back to previous chapters, we can get a pretty good idea of what is happening. This is that the addition of a reward redefines the whole situation to the participants as a serious one and brings about a reversal into the serious state. Specifically, the individual starts in the playful state of mind, enjoying what he or she is doing for its own sake. Then the addition of a reward means that there are consequences – and this removes the protective frame. This then redefines the situation as serious rather than playful. The activity is now experienced as being done for the sake of the outcome rather than for its own sake. Because of this the activity becomes less immediately enjoyable in itself and indeed comes to be perceived as being done *only* for the reward (or perhaps to avoid punishment). It is now seen as work, and in a work activity one does the minimum necessary to achieve the end. It's not about adding distractions within a certain mindset (which is what phrases like 'crowding out,' used by some researchers in this field, imply). It's about changing the mindset itself – in other words, the motivational state and with it a whole way of seeing the world. Likewise when the reward is taken away, the playful mindset can return. In these terms, it actually makes sense that in some experiments one sees this effect, but not in others. It is reasonable to suppose that sometimes this redefining 'takes hold' for most subjects, while in other experimental setups the reward is not strong enough to do so.

All this explains why people can throw so much energy into activities from which they gain little or nothing. I am amazed when I listen to call-in sports programs on the radio at the amount of expert knowledge that fans sometimes have, and the time that they must have spent watching their favoured players or teams. When it snowed where I last lived, a neighbour would dig us all out with his snow plough. This was no doubt due in part to his good nature, but there is no mistaking the joy he took in using his plough, especially when things got difficult. A good friend of mine, an artist, and his wife own a farm in Normandy, but they have no intention of farming it. Rather, they are landscaping it, and turning it into a beautiful park, with avenues of trees, a labyrinth, a moat, a small lake, and sculptures that he has created. "What are you going to do with it when it is finished?" I once asked them. From their looks, I could see that that was a thoroughly crass question.

They were not going to "do" anything with it, I realised, apart from cherish it, enjoy it, and share it with friends like me and my wife. In all these examples, the work was gratuitous, over and above what was needed, and done for its own sake.

This is not to say that activity in the playful state cannot have serious consequences, only that these consequences were not what the person had in mind at the time of carrying out the activity. An excellent example of this is the creation of Wikipedia on the internet – the largest encyclopedia in the world – created by thousands of people who have used their own particular areas of expertise to contribute entries for no payment whatsoever. The result consists of something like twenty six million pages. But the point here is that this has been a labour of love, with no financial or other incentives than the work itself (11), even if it has seriously benefited the lives of millions.

In this light it can be seen that when I was "messing around" with chemistry experiments I was indulging in pure play. I was fascinated by what I was observing, and intrigued by the idea of atoms and molecules forming and reforming in some mysterious but beautiful out-of-sight universe that followed its own precise and inviolable rules. But once I returned to school there were consequences for me – even if initially they were good consequences, like high marks – and chemistry now became a form of work. There were goals and deadlines and projects, homework and tests. There were examinations and qualifications to be worked towards, and perhaps a future career. Studying chemistry had become a means to an end. The result of this orientation to results was that the chemistry was no longer interesting in itself. It had become instrumental, and now it provided problems to be coped with rather than challenges to be grappled with joyfully. It had, one might say, gone from romance to prostitution.

When we look at the psychology experiments that I

described earlier in this chapter, we see essentially the same thing. Activities that adults or children enjoy are redefined, by the addition of consequences, as obligations. This is true even if these consequences are in themselves welcome ones. The point is that the activity – solving a puzzle or using Magic Markers – becomes a means to an end *beyond itself* rather than the end *in itself.* (See Appendix Four.)

If we consider creativity, we see that adding rewards to some activity, as well as making the activity seem like a chore, and therefore less enticing, tends to focus the activity on a future goal. This then narrows the possibilities of exploring divergent ideas and approaches. To put it another way, one is more likely to be original if one is allowed to go off on tangents and make new connections, however crazy these may seem at the outset. Experimenting and exploring in ways that are not focused on a particular outcome are, in this respect, more likely to be innovative than those that are not.

This would explain why writers and artists seem so often to need to get away from their normal lives and responsibilities in order to create. One thinks of Montaigne in his tower, Thoreau at Walden Pond, Gauguin in the South Seas, Hemingway in Paris, Dylan Thomas at his boat house, Proust in his cork-lined room. In such detached spaces it is possible to become cut off from the normal chores and deadlines, and escape from the usual round of rewards and punishments. In this way, by setting up a protective frame, it becomes easier to enter the world of creation, and to play imaginatively rather than be caught up in the world of work.

WORK AND PLAY

Earlier I gave a personal example of a switch from seeing things in a playful way to seeing them as work. Let me give another one here. As an undergraduate at Bristol University (in the U.K.) I had a wonderful time studying psychology, largely because I was 'given my head.' I was encouraged to do my own reading and thinking, and to follow my own interests within the subject. The result was that I read widely, with increasing excitement, discussed much with my fellow students in late-night sessions over endless cups of coffee, and thought as deeply as I was able to at the time. After getting my bachelor's degree, and through some fortunate circumstances (12), I was offered a graduate place at Princeton. At Princeton, however, things were disappointingly different. There was course work to be done every day, a timetable of predetermined essays and projects, and little time to think or to do anything outside what had been laid down in one syllabus or another. The result, for me, was not unlike what I described above in relation to chemistry, and the outcome entirely predictable. I lost interest, and towards the end of the first year withdrew from the doctoral program and returned to the UK. It was a few years before I was able to summon up much enthusiasm for psychology again.

My case is no doubt an extreme one, and the other students at Princeton were perfectly satisfied with what they were getting. But for them, studying psychology was a serious means to a serious career, and structure was what they needed and wanted. In contrast, I had a romantic and somewhat impractical view of the subject: for me it was about ideas and insights that could actually help us to understand ourselves and others and provide exciting new ways of seeing the world. The qualification was secondary. I felt that if I stayed on, I would be, to put it rather dramatically, "selling my soul" for a Princeton doctorate. In the light of what I said about the effect of rewards, this now makes sense. By adding the reward of a Princeton degree to the opportunity to learn more psychology, this whole process was turned into a tedious and weighty project with little room for intellectual excitement. To cite an oft repeated phrase that I heard from Professors during that academic year: "If you are going to get ahead in the profession then…" (13) Another phrase reiterated by different professors, and that stuck with me, was: "Good experiments are one percent inspiration and ninety nine percent perspiration." I remember thinking to myself that if this was the case, then I would rather be a lumberjack.

When I took my then six year old grandson Max to a mini-golf range for the first time, he insisted on just hitting the ball over and over, even when it was still moving. My attempts to get him to stop and wait until the ball had come to rest, and then try, carefully, to get it into the hole, were doomed to failure. He was having far too much fun just hitting the ball around (and probably learning a great deal in this way about interacting with moving objects). Eventually, his patience with me snapped. He threw his club down, refused to play anymore, and accused me of "being mean." Clearly I had gone too far, and turned his fun into work. Max's feelings about me, and my feelings about Princeton, were essentially the same, although in neither case were they particularly adaptive or mature.

On another occasion my then seven year old grandson Harry and I went for a walk on a snowy day through a park. He had as a homework assignment to write notes about the park. I insisted that we carry a notebook, and every so often I made us stop so that we could write phrases in it that might be useful to the project. Harry, of course, soon got bored with this and ran ahead. As I watched him, I got drawn into his world, in which everything was magic and new. At one point he stepped lightly on a patch of ice that had formed over a puddle, and we both watched as thousands of little bubbles under the ice shimmered and raced around as he moved the ice gently with his foot. I had never noticed this phenomenon before and I was intrigued. All thoughts of the notebook and the project disappeared, and I wanted my turn at scattering the bubbles. Harry had, for a while, taken me into his childhood state of pure play.

Taking Advantage

A delightful and famous fictional example of the way that a serious chore can be turned into a desirable game, so that work becomes fun, occurs in Mark Twain's novel Tom Sawyer. Tom has been set the unwelcome task, by his Aunt Polly, of whitewashing a fence. In the playful state, this is the last thing that he wants to do. But as his friends come past he pretends to be totally absorbed in a highly satisfying activity. Eventually they ask him if they can have a go too. He is apparently reluctant to relinquish the paint brush, so that his friends have to plead with him and beg. Eventually, out of good nature, or so it seems, he allows them to take turns with each other. He then spends a lazy afternoon watching them do the painting. (14)

The practical implications of all this are obvious. If you want something done with enthusiasm and joy, especially if it is creative, then you must frame it as playful – and this means that adding an awareness of consequences will have to be avoided as far as possible. As I write these words, I do not know if this book will ever be published. I have learned that in order to enjoy – and therefore engage fully – with the writing process, I have to do it at my own speed, without deadlines and also without commitments about exactly what would be covered in each chapter. Therefore, if I can, I avoid signing a contract until after a book is finished. I have found that once a contract is agreed, then much of the fun goes out of the process, and it becomes an obligation and a chore, and often a stressful one.

We should not take from this the notion that there is no place for reward in learning, implying that there is no place for the serious motivational state. There is. There are things that need to be learned that are not particularly interesting in themselves. Practicing scales at the piano, memorising by rote the names for different parts of the body in biology class, learning French vocabulary by memory – in all such cases, the addition of a reward for completing each stage successfully may be needed to take the place of the satisfactions of play.

Indeed, there are situations in which the serious state is more productive than the playful state. In the 'candle' experiment described earlier, if the situation is changed just a little, the advantage reverts to the serious state. If, instead of placing the tacks in a box, they are placed on one side, with the box empty, this implies that the box is a possible tool along with the other objects. In this situation, subjects offered a reward completed the task faster than participants not offered a reward. In other words, when a problem is routine and requires little originality, then a reward can encourage people to work harder and faster. It is important to bear this in mind, as a teacher, or manager, or parent. If a task requires originality then adding rewards may just get in the way; if a task is routine or repetitive, a reward may help productivity. It all depends if the serious or the playful motivational state is needed.

In more general terms, we need both the serious and the playful motivational states to get through life. If all work and no play make Jack a dull boy, all play and no work make him a layabout. If we need to spend time smelling the roses, we may also need to spend time planting the roses and cultivating them.

Behaviourism

This discussion of rewards leads us to one of the most fundamental issues concerning human nature and the way that it can be studied.

There is a very influential school in psychology known as "Behaviourism," that is popularly thought of as all about "rats in mazes." (15) This school is less influential now than it used to be, but during much of the last century it was the dominant approach in psychology.

Behaviourism claims, as the name suggests, that animals, including human beings, are psychologically nothing more than the behaviours that they perform. Psychology is then the elucidation of the relationship between objectively measurable inputs (and the sequence of these inputs over time) and objectively measurable behavioural outputs. If we can predict one from the other, as Behaviourists believe that we can, then psychology becomes truly objective and scientific. It follows, amazingly, that we can for all practical purposes disregard anything that is going on "inside" the organism such as brain activities, or the subjective meanings that go with them. This has been called by skeptics the "empty organism" approach.

One implication is that no reference is needed to motives in order to explain behaviour, and the whole field of motivational psychology is seen as something of an irrelevance – even a hoax! In this view, we can replace reference to motivation with reference to (objectively measurable) rewards and punishments, which are inputs to the organism. From this carrot-and-stick perspective, we should explain an organism's activity by reference to previous rewards it has been given for this activity, and a lack of activity by punishment that has been given for this activity. Reference is also made to the effects of expected rewards and punishers that do *not* occur. (This is a tricky one to explain in Behaviourist terms because expectancy implies that, after all, something is going on inside the animal.) In this view, motivation is not needed as a concept in a truly scientific psychology.

It has to be admitted that there is something intellectually appealing about the stark simplicity of Behaviourism, just as there is in Shaker furniture or minimalist art. Could we really explain all of human nature in such an elegantly uncluttered way? The whole project is breathtaking. Unfortunately, it will not work for a number of reasons, and one of these is the reliance placed on external rewards. The evidence referred to in this chapter to the way in which people will do things without external rewards – that they will do them for fun, for curiosity, for exploration, in a word, *playfully* – makes the behaviourist system difficult to sustain, since for this reason alone something must be happening internally. The paradoxical fact that, as we have seen, such rewards may also inhibit behaviour, is even more problematic. There is no room for paradox in the puritan world of Behaviourism.

But it is possible to extend this argument in a way that is even more damning to Behaviourism. This is to introduce into the debate the reversal theory idea that there are fundamentally different ways of seeing the world – serious, conforming, mastery, and the rest. Each of these are *internal* contexts – what earlier I called 'intexts' – which guide behaviour in critically different, even opposing, ways at different times. There is a tendency in behaviourist studies to assume that whatever is rewarding will always be rewarding, so food pellets can be used throughout an experiment with rats, or tokens throughout experiment with humans, and comparisons can be made unproblematically across such studies. But work cited earlier in this book shows that people can change what they are seeking, and want different things at different times. A man can at one time want excitement, in which case stimulation would be rewarding. But at another time, he might want tranquility, so that quietness would be rewarding, while stimulation would be a punishment. At one time a woman might want to benefit personally from what she is doing, and at another time be more concerned that an ailing relative should benefit: what would count as a reward in the first case would not count as a reward in the second. These different motivational states give different meanings to life. But there is no room for meaning in Behaviourism.

Nor is this merely an academic point, but has real practical implications, for example in education. This is because all eight states can be called on for learning, and not just the playful state. As I noted above, the serious state can be used to support the practice of basic skills. The conforming state encourages learning through imitation, the rebellious helps learning through thinking critically. The mastery state leads to learning through doing tasks and solving problems, the sympathy state to learning through cooperating with others, the self-oriented state to taking responsibility for learning on one's own and the other-oriented state to learning through teaching others. So the educationist has a range of emotional and motivational tools that can be brought to bear, even in teaching a formal subject topic like mathematics. (16)

CHAPTER 7

IDENTIFYING WITH OTHERS

"Why can it discourage giving to be given in return?"

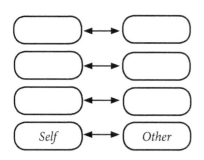

Self ←→ Other

There is a Monty Python sketch in which a merchant banker is asked to donate a pound to help an orphan's home. (1) He is totally confused about why he should do this, since there is no return. Is he buying stock? Is it a loan? "I don't want to seem stupid," he says, "but it looks to me as if I am a pound down on the whole deal."

Economists often seem to be as clueless as this investment banker. They assume much of the time that everything is about personal gain, and consequently they have difficulty understanding why anyone would ever do anything that was not to his or her personal advantage. But people do. Philanthropy is widespread. There is something of John Rockefeller in all of us.

In the Giving Vein

Here is a notable example: blood donation. Why do people willingly undergo this uncomfortable procedure? (2) We can gain some further insight into this by asking a further question: What happens if people are rewarded by being paid to give blood, as happens in many parts of the world? In a classic volume, the British sociologist Richard Titmuss argued that what he called "creative altruism" depended on the expectation of no reward, and that the gift be given to strangers from whom one could not possibly benefit. If giving blood was mainly due to such creative altruism, then paying donors would be detrimental. Titmuss put forward the startling argument that the British healthcare system was free of blood shortages precisely because it was entirely voluntary and altruistic.(3) Other health care systems in other countries would need to take note.

In one study that supports this altruistic view (4), blood donors were recruited either through the offer of a small payment ($10) or without such an inducement. The study took place in community blood centres, one in Kansas City and one in Denver. In each case, a professional recruiter solicited commitments over the phone, and between the two centres over one thousand potential donors were contacted. What was found was that for subjects low in motivation (defined as not having given blood in five years), the offer of payment did increase a little their likelihood of actually turning up. But what was really interesting was that subjects who had *high* motivation (they were on a file saying that they were willing to be contacted in an emergency at any time), were *less likely* to turn up if offered a reward. It is as if they were insulted by the offer, which seemed to question their altruism. The moral is that, if you are a recruiter, you should play to peoples' other-oriented state, in which their need is for others to benefit from their actions. You should not risk the situation becoming redefined by potential donors as in any way selfish, through car stickers, raffle tickets and the like.

Researchers (5) carried out a related study at a blood centre at Gothenburg in Sweden. The subjects were students who had stated that they were interested in becoming donors. As a preliminary, they had to subject themselves to a physical examination to make sure that they were healthy enough to take part in the program. Undergoing this examination effectively committed them to becoming donors. Just before the examination, they were asked if they wished to continue. In fact, the students were divided randomly into three different groups, and in each group the terms were slightly different. In the first group, they were offered no payment for undergoing the examination. In the second group they were offered a small payment (about the equivalent of 7 dollars). In the third, they could choose between taking the payment or giving it to charity (a cancer foundation).

For men there was no significant difference in levels of acceptance between the three groups. But for women there was a marked difference. When payment was introduced, there was a dramatic *decrease* from 52% to 30% in those going ahead with the physical examination. Some of the women just upped and left. But if they were allowed to donate the payment to charity, the acceptance levels returned to no payment levels. So while the effect was not observed in men, the effect of a monetary reward was certainly observable in women. The gender difference is a bit of a mystery, but the point for present purposes is that, at least in some people (i.e. women), we can observe this 'paradoxical giving' effect. It therefore needs to be explained.

Clearly, what was happening was that some of the women donors were in the other-oriented state of mind, in which satisfaction comes from giving. Being given something in return threatened to ruin this way of seeing things. It may even have converted feelings of virtue into feelings of shame. When the possibility arose of giving the payment away (as in the third condition), then feelings of virtue returned since the donors were not gaining from the situation, and were able to maintain the other-orientation. (6)

Why can't you add the enjoyment of being given to the enjoyment of giving? The answer is that these represent opposite ways of seeing the world, and each one takes over the whole of one's mental life at a given time. As we have seen, motivational states are like different lenses. You can only see things through one lens or the other. They cannot be added to each other or mixed.

Not in My Back Yard

Here is another kind of giving – the giving that people do when they are willing to accept something that puts them at a disadvantage, but doing so for the sake of the community as a whole. The local siting of an unwanted facility, like a nuclear power station, a six-lane highway, or a casino, are all good examples.

In a study of this kind of giving in Switzerland (7), people were asked how they would vote about accepting or rejecting a nuclear radioactive waste dump in their home town. The interviews took place a week before an actual referendum that was going to be held on this issue. One might have expected a strong NIMBY response ("Not In My Back Yard"), of the kind that one has seen in many American communities when faced with this kind of choice. But amazingly, this being Switzerland, with its community-oriented culture, a majority said that they would vote in favour. In fact, almost 51% voted in favour of the proposal and only 45% were opposed. This was despite the fact that many felt that there was a risk of serious accidents, and many were also convinced that some local residents would inevitably die in such a case as a result of contamination.

This benevolence is interesting enough, but now we come to the really interesting part. The investigators went on, in the same interview, to ask how their respondents would vote if they were to be given government financial compensation of about 5,000 francs per year per person for the lifetime of the facility. (This would be equivalent to several thousand dollars a year – a tidy sum.) In this case, amazingly, the level of acceptance *dropped*, and dropped to 24.6%. In other words, the offer of compensation resulted in a drop of nearly a half. Everyone who rejected the first offer was then made a better offer. Despite this, only a single respondent who declined the first offer, accepted the second. The pattern remained the same: the offer of compensation turned out to be totally counter-productive. To make sure that this was not a fluke, the investigators repeated the whole procedure with some other communities in another part of Switzerland – and obtained almost identical results.

As with the blood donation studies, what seems to be happening here is that the satisfaction of giving, and being community-oriented, is being spoiled by the intrusion of personal rewards, and therefore the offer as a whole, including these rewards, is rejected. It is not just that the compensation was unwanted, it is that it threatened to *redefine* the respondents' actions as self- rather than other-oriented, taking away the deep satisfaction that would otherwise have been experienced.

Volunteering

We find something of the same pattern when we look at volunteering, i.e. giving time and expertise to worthy causes.

In one survey carried out, again, in Switzerland, the amount of work volunteered related to such payment as was given, in the following way. People worked more for a higher reward than for a smaller reward if a reward was given at all. This makes sense if the reward switched them into, or maintained, the self-oriented state of mind. But here is the interesting thing: people worked more for no reward at all than they did for a small reward, suggesting that the warm glow of giving was more pleasing than the satisfaction of some token compensation.(8)

There is a report on a voluntary poverty relief agency designed to provide emergency assistance to poverty-stricken people in dire need of help. (9) Volunteers did such things as answer phones, deliver food and provide transport to the needy. In order to thank their volunteers, the board of the agency decided to provide a nice "thank you" dinner. But in the event, and to the dismay of the board, less than ten percent of the volunteers turned up. When asked why they had not attended, many of the volunteers said that they joined the organisation in order to combat hunger in others, not to eat a large meal. This is another way of saying that they wanted to give, not to be given.

I am reminded by this of a small incident when I was doing some canvassing for a politician. I was paired to go out door-to-door with another volunteer, and just before we set off she asked at the organisers' desk if there would be free refreshments for volunteers. I felt unreasonably embarrassed by this, however trivial it might have been, and I backed away from the desk. Likewise, the last time that I donated something at a charity shop, I found myself turning down the proferred tax claim form, which seemed to turn the gift into a transaction. These may be small everyday examples, but they illustrate the theme and may remind the reader of similar instances of their own.

This is not to say that thanks are never appreciated. On the contrary, an expression of gratitude can validate that giving has actually been understood to have taken place. For me, a particularly touching example of this came from the residents of a hostel for the homeless in New York, not far from the World Trade Centre. On 9/11 they set up a table on the sidewalk to help people who had escaped to clean up and have something to drink. A couple of days later they received a huge tray of cookies from someone they had helped in this way. They were delighted because although they received gifts all the time, the gifts were usually out of pity. This one was out of gratitude, and gave them the rare pleasure that comes with giving rather than receiving. (10)

The Hedonic Paradox

A number of philosophers have noted that in order to gain pleasure from helping others one must put their good before your own. The paradoxical nature of this situation was first notably pointed out by the British Victorian philosopher Henry Sidgwick who argued that happiness can only come indirectly, as a side-effect of something else. (11)

He illustrated this 'hedonic paradox,' or 'pleasure paradox' as it has also been called, by relating it to various desires. For example, your desire might be for freedom, and when you obtain it you feel pleasure. But the desire you had was not for pleasure – it was for freedom – and only in pursuing this desire would you experience pleasure. He considered in this way a number of other desires that make sense in terms of the polarities that I have been talking about in this book. The 'hedonic paradox' that concerned him most was the one that arises from desiring to help others. When you genuinely want to help other people, he argues, you have a good chance of experiencing pleasure yourself. But this pleasure will only arise when the desire to help others is genuine, and it will be a by-product of this orientation. You may personally benefit, but only by not thinking about yourself. "The self-regarding impulse, if too predominant, defeats its own aim." (12)

GIVING AS A VOCATION

Some people go beyond volunteering and enter into vocations that are largely about being other-oriented and giving. A good example would be people who work in homes for the elderly. Having been the director of just such a home for five years (in South Wales), I have seen at close quarters just how dedicated and selfless nurses and aides can be. It is not that the tasks involved are thankless. On the contrary, the elderly are, on the whole, full of gratitude. But the work was at times heartbreaking, given that residents never recover from ageing, and death is inevitable. But together with the heartbreak, and partly because of it, there were enormous satisfactions that came with caring, especially where close relationships were forged between residents and staff. Among the sorrow there was a great deal of happiness, and a feeling of making a real contribution to the lives of others.

More recently, colleagues carried out research for an organisation operating a chain of geriatric nursing homes. The owners had a problem of high staff turnover, and needed to know what they could do to reduce this. Through thorough one-on-one interviews with members of the nursing home staff, the researchers were able to put their finger on just what was going wrong. It seems that it was company policy for staff to retain their distance from residents, not becoming emotionally involved with them. This policy was put forward with the best of intentions, namely to help staff to retain their emotional equanimity, and avoid being taken advantage of by residents. But the result was that the very thing that made the job deeply worthwhile – the development of close and caring relationships – was the one thing that was being discouraged. Once this was realised it was possible to make the policy changes that were needed, to everyone's benefit, staff and residents alike.

THE GENEROSITY OF ALLOWING OTHERS TO HELP YOU

In order to give people the pleasure of giving, there must be people who need to be given. So here is another kind of paradox, another twist in the argument: it can be a virtue to ask for help. We must allow other people to help us, as we might help them. It has been said that the best way to make a friend is to ask for help. "We need to give. The Dead Sea is dead because it has no outlet. We can't hoard good within us. Where would the sun be if it didn't reflect? You need help, and I need to help you. One half of the world helps the other half; it balances out. We need someone who needs us." (13)

I remember my then wife and I moving into a new house when I was just starting my academic career. Our new next door neighbours were embarrassingly helpful – helping us to put things up, helping us to take things down, doing repairs, bringing us endless cups of tea. But my wife and I felt bad that every time we tried to do something to help them in return, over the ensuing days, we were refused. As we came to see, we were the instruments by means of which these good people were able to get the satisfaction of giving. This sounds like an insincere way of justifying being given. And perhaps it is. But every giving/given relationship has its symmetrical satisfactions. To give is to be given, to be given is to give. Our neighbours did not want anything back, because that would spoil their pleasure in giving. Once we understood this, we took full advantage.

To give another example, I once witnessed my father, who was a very large man, trip, stagger and fall down on the sidewalk of a busy street. In moments, and before I could get to him myself, he was surrounded by an enthusiastic crowd of helpers who fought with each other to haul him back onto his feet, enquire if he was alright, brush him down, and generally fuss over him. As my father confided to me afterwards: "there was not enough of me to go round."

This principle of people liking you when you allow them to do you a favour has been called the Franklin Effect, after Benjamin Franklin, the eighteenth century American statesman and polymath. He confides, in his autobiography (14), how he went about gaining the cooperation of a member of the Pennsylvania State Legislature – apparently a rather taciturn and unfriendly man. What he did was to ask if he could borrow a particular book from him. This was a rare and valuable book, and he knew that it would be an act of great trust by this man to let him take possession of it, even for a short time. Having lent it to him, the man became thereafter considerably more friendly.

The main point that comes out of this is that allowing others to help you can be doing them a good turn. Jesus apparently understood this when he allowed an unnamed sinner to wash his feet, to the annoyance of his followers (Luke's Gospel, 7:36-50). In fact, he was being kind to her by allowing her to be kind to him.

MIXED MOTIVES

While it is reasonable to suppose that the other-oriented state will be the key state in much altruistic behaviour, it may well be that other motivational states will also be directly involved, and either support it in some way or even become the principle focus of the giving.

For example, unselfish behaviour may also stem from the conformist state. Thus one can give for reasons of convention and habit, as in most of the occasions on which one gives tips. In this case the giving may well be of the conformist variety, where not to give would produce feelings of guilt. The same can be true of sending cards, for Christmas and birthdays. In fact, greeting card manufacturers have managed to increase the number of occasions on which we might need to send cards in order not to feel guilty. In recent visits to the Hallmark store I have seen cards for Father's day, Secretary's day, Nurses' day, Doctors' day and even Administrative Professionals' day. No doubt we shall soon have Grandparents' day, not to mention Uncle's day and Estranged Relatives' day and Dog's day. The behaviour apparently involves kindness, but the underlying psychology may be more to do with doing what is expected than it is with generosity.

Altruistic behaviour may also involve the sympathy state. This is suggested in an ingenious experiment involving lost wallets.(15) This utilised 240 wallets, each with the same basic contents – the owner's address, fake membership cards, discount vouchers, and so on. But there was one difference between them. This was that some of the wallets contained a family photograph, specifically a smiling baby, a puppy, a happy family scene, or a happy elderly couple. Other wallets contained a card acknowledging that the owner had recently made a contribution to charity. The remaining wallets contained no additional materials. All the wallets were then randomly and surreptitiously dropped in the street. The question was this: Which wallets would be most likely to be returned?

The answer was clear-cut. The wallets most likely to be returned were, far and away, those containing the photograph of a smiling baby. This was followed by wallets containing other family photographs, while the least likely to be returned were those with no additional personalising items. We may infer that those people who did return the wallet were probably in the other-oriented state when they did so. But it is also reasonable to speculate that the baby photograph put them into the sympathy state – the caring motivational state – and that this combined with the other-oriented state determined the decision to return the wallet in those who actually did so. (One sees something similar with beggars who have pet dogs with them, inducing the sympathy and other-oriented states in passers-by.)

My wife Mitzi and I personally experienced a real-life variation of the wallet experiment. Passing through Charles de Gaulle Airport in Paris, our travel wallets were stolen from our hand luggage. Some months later we were surprised to receive them back in the mail from France, sent anonymously. What was even more surprising was that only our passports had been removed from the wallets. Everything else was still there, including credit cards (which we knew they had not tried to use) and all our cash. My tentative explanation would be either that the thieves were trying to do someone a favour (e.g. a political refugee) in providing them with a passport, and were therefore in the other-oriented state toward this person, and felt good about what they had done, but did not want to harm anyone else. Or perhaps they changed into this state at a certain point after using the passports, felt badly about what they had done, and wanted to minimise their feelings of guilt. What other explanations could there be?

The Abilene Paradox

There is another, rather different, paradox based on the other-oriented state. This has been called "The Abilene Paradox".

According to the psychologist who coined the term, it arose in the following way.(16) On a family weekend, in the desperate heat of a Texas summer, his father suggested a run to Abilene, which was about 53 miles away. His wife and mother-in-law said that this sounded like a good idea. Since everyone was in agreement, he went along with it, albeit reluctantly. They drove two hours there in blazing heat, had a disappointing lunch in a second-rate restaurant, and drove two hours back. When they arrived home, exhausted, his mother-in-law allowed that she would rather have stayed at home. To his amazement his wife and father admitted the same. It turns out that they had all agreed to go because they thought that it was something that everyone else wanted to do. They were all in the other-oriented state, trying to please others they took to be in the self-oriented state. The result was that nobody was pleased.

This paradox has been generalised to situations where organisations "take actions in contradiction to what they really want to do." (17) Among his examples, he cites the Watergate scandal. Everyone involved thought it was a crazy idea, but everyone went along with it, trusting in each others' judgment. It would only have taken one person to disagree strongly, and the whole project might have collapsed, to everyone's benefit. We see this kind of thing in many everyday situations – we all finish up watching the television program that nobody actually wanted to see, or staying up late when everyone really wanted to go to bed, or sending for a pizza that nobody would eat if they were in their right mind, or ordering an expensive bottle of wine that nobody could really afford.

SELF-SACRIFICE: THE REALITY OF ALTRUISM

It is clear from the examples I have given, that people deliberately perform actions that may be detrimental to themselves but that are to the advantage of the group. We can imagine that, in some primitive community, this may consist of devoting energy to communal projects, hunting dangerous animals, exploring new and unknown territory, and testing out new weapons. But where would this human propensity come from? Why, in evolutionary terms, do people ever sacrifice themselves for the sake of others?

In recent years the development of Sociobiology, and its controversial spinoff Evolutionary Psychology, has provided various arguments in favour of the idea that human evolution has a social component, since from the beginnings of recorded history humans are clearly social animals. The basic idea is that the competitive survival of one group against other groups can have evolutionary advantage to members of the successful group as a whole, and that their genetic characteristics can be passed on to the next generation. Also, it is supposed that part of the advantage is likely to derive from the altruism of members of the successful group towards each other. (18) However, for some strange reason, many sociobiologists have been reluctant to allow that people can actually be altruistic, and have tried to 'explain away' unselfishness in various ways. One has been to argue that genes themselves are individualistic, and people help others who are genetically related to them because in this way some of their own genes are helped to survive. This is the 'kin selection theory' which becomes, in a more extreme form, the 'selfish gene' hypothesis. (19) Another is that altruism is 'reciprocal,' so that a person behaves apparently altruistically on the expectation that his or her good turn will be returned, either directly by the recipient or indirectly by other members of the group. (20) From the perspective of the present book, there is no reason why people cannot be seen as genuinely altruistic when they are in the other-oriented state, such genuine altruism being selected because it helps the group, and hence its members, to survive. The group would indeed have an advantage in this respect over other groups with whom it competes and in which altruism may be less developed. The unwillingness for genuine altruism to be recognised by many sociobiologists is puzzling. (21)

Self-sacrifice is not necessarily limited to the other-oriented state and is therefore not necessarily altruistic in origin, but may arise in other ways. Here's one: Taking risks in the playful state, doing so within a protective frame as described in an earlier chapter. This may not pay off for the individual. But taking such risks may have a major payoff to other members of the group, who can learn vicariously from the individual's mistakes, or be warned off certain types of danger, or profit from innovations that work. One thinks here of the actions of explorers, pioneers, hunters, investors, inventors, entrepreneurs, adventurers, and prospectors, all of whom take personal risks that may come to benefit others as well as themselves, or instead of themselves. Another way in which self-sacrifice may arise, occurs when the success of a community (or tribe, political party, religion or cult) gives serious meaning and purpose to an individual's life, such that they are willing to sacrifice themselves to maintain this meaning. We shall return to this in a later chapter.

None of this makes sense if we assume that evolutionary principles apply only to the survival of the individual. But it does make sense if we assume that the survival of the fittest may apply to groups as well as to individuals and that risk-taking may be selected for, through natural selection, because of its advantage to group functioning. (22)

There can, then, be many reasons for giving, and not all giving behaviour is genuinely altruistic. Lobbyists, confidence tricksters, seducers, and jerks of all kinds are self-serving givers, 'giving' in the self-oriented state while feigning other-orientation. After all, as cynics say, there is no such thing as a free lunch. Some may 'give' ostentatiously, in order to show off and be admired. (This would no doubt be particularly satisfying in the mastery state.) Others may 'give' because everyone else is doing so and they want to conform (in the conformist state) by doing the right thing. These are all examples of what we might call 'selfish giving.' But obviously the existence of selfish giving does not mean that people cannot, and do not, also give because they really care for others. We have seen examples in this chapter of such authentic kindness. I can put my hand to my heart and say that I have experienced such kindness in the help I have received from colleagues and others in writing this book.

The psychology of giving is a fertile area for observing human paradox, and we have seen many different kinds of paradox in this chapter: the paradox of giving itself, the paradox of reduced pleasure from being given while giving, the hedonic paradox, the Abilene paradox, and the Franklin paradox. In the next chapter we shall be confronted by some paradoxes of a very different, and more troubling, order.

CHAPTER 8

POSITIVE NEGATIVISM

"Why can doing the right thing be wrong and the wrong thing right?"

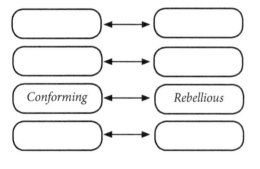

Most people recognise the rebellious state in themselves (1) – the desire to do what one should not do – and they understand how this stands in opposition to the conformist state. Unless there is something radically wrong with us, we know what it feels like to want to 'break free' from time to time. Often we scratch this itch by engaging in such minor acts as being rude, sarcastic, argumentative, hurtful, stubborn, and provocative, known as 'microaggressions.' Some of us take matters even further and indulge in such liberating-seeming activities as drug-taking, sexting, and hooliganism. In the extreme, rebellious behaviour may take the form of some serious form of illegality, immorality, or stupidity.

According to some philosophers, people only do bad

things when they mistakenly think that they are doing good things. (This is a view known as 'internalism.') In the present chapter I will take the view that, on the contrary, people can do bad things in full awareness that they are doing wrong. For them, doing wrong is the whole point.

Often our rebelliousness arises in reaction to some perceived unfairness and is associated with anger and the need for revenge. This would be the sort of reaction one might feel on learning that you have lost your job, or that an erstwhile friend has made fun of you in public. We can call this 'reactive rebelliousness.' It is rebellious in that you want to break the rules by harming someone in some way, and it is reactive in that it is a response to something that has made you 'mad.'

At other times rebelliousness is sought out simply as a desperate antidote to boredom and is associated with a kind of mischievousness, a sort of 'looking for trouble.' In this case we would have what we can call 'proactive rebelliousness,' which starts with the person, who is behaving provocatively, and for seemingly no good reason.(2)

It is surprising that psychology does not pay more attention to rebelliousness, especially since small acts of angry defiance by a single person at a particular moment can escalate into huge and unforeseen changes that echo down the years, for good or ill. In 1823, a schoolboy at Rugby school in England while playing football, picked up the ball in defiance of the rules, and ran with it. His name was William Webb Ellis, and he is usually credited, through this one defiant act, with starting the game of rugby, which has become a major world sport. In 1955, Rosa Park, an African American living in Montgomery, Alabama, stubbornly refused to give up her seat in a segregated bus to a white man. This was the beginning of the Civil Rights movement that changed the face of America. In 1980, a Polish worker named Lech Walesa, on the spur of the moment, climbed over the wall of a shipyard in Gdansk to take part in a strike. He soon became leader of what turned into the Solidarity movement, which played a key role in the fall of Communism. In 1956, taking part in the Castro-led invasion of Cuba, a young doctor named Che Guevara had a choice to make when his group of insurgents came under fire. Should he pick up his medical bag and go help the wounded, or pick up a box of ammunition and go fight. He decided on the ammunition, and thus started a famous career as a revolutionary, playing a major part in the Cuban revolution and beyond.

In the light of this, it is interesting that when, in the course of a self-development workshop, I say that the rebellious state can make an invaluable contribution to an organisation, participants look puzzled. It seems to go against everything that they have been taught. Surely they have to satisfy expectations at work, fit in, do their jobs properly, meet deadlines? If I rephrase rebellion in terms of negative thinking, they become even more puzzled. So I have to explain that by negative thinking I am not referring to pessimistic thinking, I mean critical thinking. I mean questioning, opposing, and being sceptical. But how can such rebelliousness help anything? One answer lies in the following declension: In order for things to improve, there must be change. In order for things to change, someone has to see the weaknesses in the way that things are. In order to see the weaknesses in the way that things are, someone should be thinking critically. In order to be thinking critically, it helps to be in the rebellious state of mind. In this sense, rebellion is a key motivator of change.

Of course, the rebellious state is often far from being helpful. Like all eight of the motivational states it can take both desirable and undesirable forms. On the undesirable side – the 'dark side' – we cannot help thinking of behaviour that is disruptive: damaging argument for argument's sake, unpredictable wildness, unhelpful anger, even criminal aggression. We think of Eliot Spitzer's ill-advised rule-breaking with prostitutes. But having said this, we must recognise that on the desirable side, there are times when rebelliousness is invaluable. In these cases we have a paradox. This is that 'bad' behaviour – behaviour that breaks the rules in some way – can lead to 'good' results. More succinctly: bad is good. Let us look at some areas of life where this is demonstrably the case.

When Doing the Right Thing is Wrong

The point is that following the rules, and doing what you are told to do can be counter-productive. By "rules" here I mean any kind of social pressure, from direct orders by your boss, to vague expectations that one will behave in a conventionally polite manner. Following rules is of course exactly what one delights in doing in the conformist state, but it is uncomfortably constraining in the rebellious state. Obviously, without most people being willing to conform most of the time, social life would become chaotic and unbearable. Civilized interactions require that everyone knows what is expected of them. Efficiency at work requires that people know their roles and the routines that they must follow. Playing sport requires that everyone understands what is permitted and what is not. Taking part in rituals (e.g. weddings) helps people to mark special occasions in well understood ways that support social institutions.

All the same, there are times when change is needed more than continuity, and when the Emperor must be told that he has no clothes. While life would become impossible if the rebellious motivational state held sway most of the time – think what it would be like if every morning everyone in the office argued about what they should be doing, and who was going to be boss that day. All the same, there are moments when rebellion is essential. This is seen at its most dramatic when an absence of rebelliousness leads to disaster.

There are innumerable examples from military history. (3) One example that leaps to mind is the famous charge by the mounted Light Brigade at the Battle of Balaclava (1854) during the Crimean War. This was one of the biggest debacles in the British history of military combat. At a critical moment in the battle against the Russians, Lord Raglan, the British Commander-in-Chief, ordered "the cavalry to advance rapidly to the front… to prevent the enemy carrying away the guns." Unfortunately, to obey the order meant certain destruction and devastation, since the cavalry would have to charge into a valley – later called the "Valley of Death" – with Russian guns mounted not only in front of them but on their flanks. Nevertheless, the cavalry commander, Lord Lucan, while aware of what must inevitably happen, did not challenge the command but, no doubt with a stiff upper lip, ordered the charge to go ahead. "Lord Raglan will have it. We have no choice but to obey." And so they charged, six hundred cavalrymen, resplendent in their blue uniform jackets, sabres glinting, thundering down the valley towards the guns. Witnesses say that it was a glorious sight. But the consequence of this folly was inglorious death: only two hundred of the brigade of six hundred survived the charge. The whole reckless fiasco, is captured in the famous Tennyson poem, known to all British schoolchildren, "The Charge of the Light Brigade." The poem extols the courage and discipline of the men. "Theirs not to reason why, theirs but to do and die." But the more important message for us today is that blind obedience can be disastrous.

In this case, people did something stupid, by doing what they should *not* have done. In the following case, people did something stupid by not doing what they *should* have done.

In 1989 a British Midlands 737 was flying from London to Belfast when the captain and copilot heard an explosion followed by loud vibration. When they shut down the right-hand engine the noise ceased, and so they inferred that the problem was in this engine. The captain, who from his position in the cockpit could not actually see the engines, announced to the passengers that he was going to leave the right-hand engine closed down. This was puzzling to the passengers, because they could see clearly that it was the left-hand engine that was in trouble. Indeed, they could see that it was on fire. One can imagine that there must have been a great deal of muttering among passengers, but not a single person came forward, or tried to contact the flight crew, to point this out, even when the aircraft was losing height. The tragic result was that the plane crashed and 47 passengers were killed. Here we have a dramatic example of everyone conforming and accepting authority. Some negative thinking – and acting – on someone's part, might have saved the day. The terrible irony is that, according to the inquiry that took place later, if the functional right-hand engine had been turned on again its power would have been sufficient for the plane to reach the airport and land safely. (4)

There is experimental evidence that this kind of reaction is not an aberration but that victims do indeed tend to be passive in the face of danger when others are also failing to react to it. In a well-known experiment on what has been called the 'bystander' effect, participants thought that they were going to be interviewed about problems of urban life. While waiting in a side room to be interviewed, and filling in a questionnaire, smoke was fed into the room through a vent. How would the person react to this? When alone in the room, the typical response was to exit smartly and report on what might be a fire. In fact, 75% responded in this way. So far so good. This is what might have been expected. But what if there were two other people present with the subject – supposedly other participants – who failed to show any signs or concern, or to react? (In reality these were of course confederates of the experimenter.) The astonishing thing here is that, in this case, only 10 percent of the experimental subjects did anything about the smoke, apart from coughing, rubbing their eyes, and waving the fumes away. The critical thing is that they did not report it. Clearly they noticed the smoke, but they conformed to the way that the other two were reacting. If there had been a real fire, they would have been toast. In a variant of this procedure, people in groups of three were exposed to the smoke, in this case all three being 'real' subjects, i.e. unaware of the set-up. Here the typical response was, again, to fail to report a possible fire. We seem to have a kind of Abilene paradox here: each person thought that the other two were unconcerned, and therefore did nothing. (5)

It seems that people tend to be obedient to authority, including bureaucracy, and assume that leaders and others know what they are doing. But bureaucracy is fuelled by conformity, and bureaucrats are therefore the least able to deal with the unexpected, and to be flexible, especially in moments of crisis. This was shown in a particularly dramatic form during the response to Hurricane Katrina in New Orleans in late August 2005. Katrina damaged the levee system of the city, which collapsed, causing floods that resulted in nearly two thousand deaths. Here are some by now well-known examples of the way that bureaucracy stood between people and help. A nationwide call went out for firefighters. But the firefighters who arrived were held in Atlanta by FEMA (the Federal Emergency Management Agency) for days of training in community relations and sexual harassment, because it was laid down somewhere that all firefighters in Louisiana must have this training before being allowed to practice. With people dying, this was hardly the moment for worrying about community relations. Indeed, community relations might have been much improved if these emergency workers had been allowed to actually serve the community. Some trucks were sent from Arkansas with food and water, headed to a site near Alexandria which was the staging area for distributing supplies. But they were halted by FEMA about ten miles from the site. FEMA would not let the trucks continue and unload because they did not have a 'tasker number', and waiting for this bit of red tape held the trucks up for a couple of crucial days. Two navy helicopter pilots on their own initiative rescued about 100 survivors. But because they had not received permission they were strongly reprimanded. One was grounded and put in charge of looking after the pets of service members. (6) But the most widely publicised example of bureaucratic stupidity was the 255 yellow school buses that could have been used for evacuating residents of New Orleans before the storm arrived. Unfortunately, nobody gave the command to drive them. The result was that they were left in a parking lot which itself came to be flooded when the hurricane hit, rendering the buses unuseable thereafter. The story of the yellow buses came to symbolise the whole debacle. (7)

OBEDIENCE

This tendency to conform turns out to be extremely strong for most people, as was documented in one of the best known psychological studies of the last century: Stanley Milgram's study of obedience to authority. This was set up to try to understand better how it is that, under a regime like Hitler's, perfectly ordinary people could be turned into mass murderers. (8) What Milgram did was to ask people to take part in an innocuous-seeming experiment on learning. (9) Participants (all of them male) were organised into pairs, and one from each pair was designated as "the teacher" and one as "the learner." This choice was made to seem random, but in fact the real subject of the experiment always finished up as the teacher, and the remaining member of the pair, as the learner. Unbeknown to the real subject, the learner was in fact a confederate of the experimenter who would be play acting. (As so often in social psychology experiments, the experimenter was lying to his subjects.) The teacher was instructed by the experimenter to teach learners to remember word associations, by giving them an electric shock each time that they gave the wrong response to a stimulus word

The teacher was seated in front of a formidable control panel with a button that would administer a shock to the learner when pressed. There was also a dial which allowed him to control the voltage of the shock. The learner was in a separate room, and the teacher and learner communicated by means of an intercom. But the session started with the teacher visiting the learner in his room and seeing the set-up. The teacher was also shown what the shock felt like, by being given a sample shock of 45-volts. After this, the learner was wired up to the electro-shock generator, and the teacher and experimenter returned to their control room.

The experimental procedure required the teacher to read the words to be learned. First would come the stimulus word, and this would be followed by four possible response words read in sequence. The learner had to choose the correct response word and say it back to the teacher. If he made the wrong choice, or no choice at all within a certain time limit, then he was given an electric shock (which of course, unknown to the teacher, was only simulated). The procedure was continued for each stimulus word until the learner gave the correct response. Further, each time he got the response wrong, the teacher was required to step up the intensity of the shock by 15 volts. At a certain voltage level the learner apparently started to display distress that could be heard over the intercom. As the intensity of the shock got greater, he started banging on the wall, screaming to be let out, and in some versions of the experiment, shouting about having a heart condition. (These learner pleas for each shock level were in fact prerecorded.)

The teacher would typically ask for guidance as to whether he should continue, and the experimenter would always tell him to keep going. Eventually, the noise would be replaced by an ominous silence. But the teacher was told to keep going anyway, and to treat a lack of response as a false response to be followed by another, increased, shock. At the intense end of the dial a setting was marked "Danger: severe shock" and two even further increased shock levels were both marked enigmatically with "XXX." The highest of these was shown on the dial to be 450 volts. The question is: At what point would the teacher – the real subject – rebel against the authority of the experimenter and refuse to do what he was being told to do. The results were surprising, indeed dismaying, but they do give us an insight into how it is that people can willingly accept to become part of a totalitarian regime.

Milgram found that no one refused to administer shocks lower than 300 volts – that is, more than six times the intensity of what they had experienced when they themselves sampled a shock. More disturbing: as many as 65% of his subjects gave the final 450 volt shock. They would not necessarily do so without expressing some kind of protest, but they would do what they were told all the same. The experiment has been subsequently repeated many times with many variations, and with different subjects in different countries. By and large, the results always come out the same way, showing people much more prone to obedience to authority figures than had previously been supposed.

The result clearly shows, then, the dangers of people's taste for the conforming state, as played on by fascist regimes, and peoples' willingness to relinquish responsibility and respond to orders. It means that people can be easily induced to carry out acts of cruelty and immorality. This is one of the reasons why the rebellious state is such an important part of human nature: it can provide some kind of a counter-balance against tyranny and, paradoxical as it may seem, against immorality.

Saving the Day

Paradoxically, disobedience can play an essential part in avoiding calamity. In the previous examples, inability to act in a rebellious way led to disaster. In the next example, rebellious action helped to save civilians from disaster.

As everyone knows, the My Lai massacre was a catastrophe, a permanent stain on the US military, and an important factor in turning public opinion against the Vietnam war. But the massacre would have been worse if not for the actions of a helicopter pilot, Hugh Thompson, who was providing helicopter reconnaissance for a ground operation against a hamlet. The hamlet concerned was alleged to be a Viet Cong stronghold, and so he was accompanied by a couple of gunships. At a certain point he started noticing bodies scattered on the ground, all of them women, children and elderly men. Then he noticed people huddled in a ditch. When he landed nearby he found that the ditch was full of the dead, dying, and injured. All of them were unarmed Vietnamese and clearly none of them were soldiers. A group of American soldiers was nearby, so he hurried over to them and asked them to help get the survivors out of the ditch. One of the soldiers grunted that the easiest way would be with a grenade. It was becoming clear to Thompson that a massacre was taking place, and so he went back to the ditch and helped the survivors out himself. Then he called one of the gunships down to pick up the survivors, and kept them around him for their safety. With aid from others on the gunship, he helped all the survivors aboard, where they were flown to safety and medical help.

According to the best estimates, as many as 500 innocent civilians were killed by U.S. forces that day. Amazingly, only one person, Lt. William Calley, was ever convicted of this massacre. The point here is that those who were rescued were saved by a single person taking it on himself to stand up and confront his own side, attempting to reverse the course of what was happening in front of him. It meant defying the strong military pressures to loyalty and conformity that he had previously learned to respect. (10) In my book, this is a kind of heroism (and it is my book).

EINSTEIN, WITTGENSTEIN AND GERTRUDE STEIN

The paradox of bad leading to good also has a special form: This is that destruction can lead to, indeed be an intrinsic part of, construction. Put in another way, there is always a kind of aggressiveness about originality. Strangely, this aggression, when it leads to innovation, represents what is most life-enhancing and affirmative. (The Hindu religion has it right: Siva is both God of destruction and God of Creation. Siva is said to wipe the slate clean before writing anything new on it.)

Originality is by definition rule-breaking. When some action is said to be original this means that it breaks away from the usual and expected ways of doing things. It would be possible to do something original by chance or accident, and even perhaps against one's will. But more usually, the rule-breaking involved is deliberate, and fostered by the innovator. This is another way of saying that innovation stems from the rebellious state of mind, the state of mind in which one wants, roughly speaking, to be 'bad'. Whenever someone talks about the need to 'think outside the box,' I am aware that, because they use a cliche, they themselves may have difficulty in doing so at that moment. In any case, originality is not so much a matter of 'thinking outside the box' as of shattering it, and then putting it together in a new way.

We need here to distinguish between innovation and creativity. It is possible to be creative without being particularly innovative – for example in writing a sonnet, or painting a conventional still life. Innovation on the other hand means being creative in a special way – a way that breaks from and defies previous ways of doing things and displays originality. It is this form of creation that largely depends on the rebellious state. It is not surprising, then, that many highly innovative people turn out to be 'difficult' in their lives in general, since they are presumably often in the rebellious state. This does not mean that they are never conforming, but that the balance in their case is much more towards the negative than it is in most people.

Rebelliousness can enter into innovative behaviour in a number of ways. To explore this, it is instructive to compare three major intellects of the twentieth century (all three, coincidentally, Jewish): Einstein, Wittgenstein and Gertude Stein. All three revolutionised their own fields, as well as defying convention in their personal lives. Of course, it would be perfectly possible, according to reversal theory, for someone to be conventional in their personal everyday behaviour and rebellious only at certain critical moments in their work. But in these three cases we seem to see people for whom the rebellious state occurs frequently. It is then used by them as an essential part of their approach to innovative work.

In the case of Albert Einstein we are confronted with someone whose ideas have revolutionised our very conception of the nature of the universe. What could be more spectacularly rebellious than that? (In celebration, *Time* magazine named him Man of the Century.) To achieve this

POSITIVE NEGATIVISM | 143

he had to overturn certain rules of physics, in other words, certain fundamental assumptions that had gone unchallenged until then. As Einstein himself described the physics of this earlier period: "...dogmatic rigidity prevailed in matters of principle: In the beginning (if there was such a thing), God created Newton's laws of motion together with the necessary masses and forces." (11) Einstein's originality derived from his critical examination of these unexamined 'principles' and the substitution of other, initially shocking, principles. Thus in his Special Theory of Relativity he overturned the idea that the dimensions of time and space are absolute and cannot change, constancy being attributed instead to the speed of light. An implication was that simultaneity is a meaningless concept. In his General Theory of Relativity he showed that gravity and space are not distinct but are intimately related. These are complex concepts. The point for present purposes is that, in a very obvious way, his originality related to rule-breaking. (12) It seems reasonable to assume that this thirst for challenging previous ideas derived from the rebellious motivational state, and when we look at his life, we see that rebelliousness was natural for him.

Einstein showed contempt for authority throughout his life, but especially in his earlier years before he emigrated to America and when he was still living in Switzerland. He is reputed to have said "Long live impudence. It's my guardian angel in the world." (13) He also remarked that "Blind respect for authority is the greatest enemy of truth." This could be taken as his guiding principle in life. (14) As a student, his contempt led him to have bad relations with all his professors at the Zurich Polytechnic, and perhaps this was the reason that he was the only student in his section not to be offered an academic position on graduation. Amazingly, it was not until nine years after he graduated, and four years after the miraculous year (1905) in which he revolutionised science with a set of papers that were to become classics in the history of physics, including his paper on the Special Theory, that he finally managed to obtain a junior professorship. One of the reasons for this delay is probably that his professors felt threatened by his criticism of their work – reminding us of one of the potentially undesirable effects of the rebellious state.

It is still astonishing that such a genius should have been shunned in this way. However, this rejection by him of authority was of the essence of his originality, even if it caused problems for him in his personal life. As a recent biographer has put it: "…Einstein's successes had come in part from his rebelliousness. There was a link between his creativity and his willingness to defy authority… his stubbornness had worked to his advantage." (15) Interestingly, as he aged and became less rebellious, settling comfortably into a bourgeois home in Princeton in his fifties, so he became correspondingly less creative.(16) As he himself put it: "To punish me for my contempt of authority, Fate has made me an authority myself." (17) This is not to imply that rebelliousness was the only motive at work in his theorising. But the rebellious state seems to stand out and to relate to everything that set him apart as a person and as an original thinker.

Looking at the controversial American poet and writer Gertrude Stein (18) we see an altogether different, gleefully playful, delightfully crazy, brand of rebelliousness. Stein was a colourful and larger-than-life personality, something of a self-promoting 'show-off,' who adored attention. She certainly did not hide her light under a bushel, and even proclaimed that she and Einstein were the two greatest thinkers of the twentieth century: "Einstein was the creative philosophic mind of the century and I have been the creative literary mind of the century…" (19)

In her personal life, she was lesbian at a time when this was scandalous. Not that there is anything rebellious about being gay as such. But she lived openly with her partner, Alice B. Toklas, shockingly defying the conventions of polite society in the thirties. She flaunted her homosexuality in her characteristically masculine way of dressing and cutting her hair. She was also rebellious in refusing to learn French, even though she and Toklas lived in France for much of their lives. Potentially much more serious was the way that, during the Second World War, she made no attempt to hide the fact that she and Toklas were Jewish. They were fortunate not to be deported by the Vichy collaborationist government to a concentration camp. Astonishingly, even when they were given inside information that they were about to be arrested, they decided to stand firm rather than trying to escape from France. For reasons still unknown, they escaped the fate that should historically have been theirs. (20)

Generally speaking, Stein's literary rebelliousness seems to have been of a deliciously fun-seeking kind, and her writing is suffused with this playful, even childish, freedom to experiment. Although much of what she wrote is fairly accessible, in some of her works she attempts to communicate even while defying the laws of grammar and logic, and in such cases she twists language almost to the point of breakdown – something that puzzled and even incensed many readers. Her writing frequently alternates repetition and surprise, and sometimes dislocates language and pushes it to the extremes of intelligibility. It is often difficult to tell if it is infantile or profound, as in her famous phrase: "A rose is a rose is a rose is a rose." Perhaps her key innovation was what she called the "continuous present," in which the same words are repeated in different combinations, and with slight variations, so that they seem to go round and round in an endless loop. It could be said that what she is doing here is demonstrating Einstein's idea that time is itself a dimension that can change, by showing how time can be slowed down. On the other hand, it could be said that she was just messing around.

She felt that what she called "aggressive liveliness" was an essential component of artistic revolution, and we can assume that she felt this about her own writing. (21) In describing her method of composition she used the metaphor of a car being taken to pieces before it can be repaired, implying that first must come destruction and only then is creativity possible. (22) Echoing Einstein she said "The creator of the new composition in the arts is an outlaw until he is a classic". (23) In all of this she points to the place of rule-breaking in originality.

The third of our figures, Ludwig Wittgenstein, was a philosopher who, while he spent much of his career at Cambridge, came originally from Austria. He is generally regarded as one of the great figures in philosophy in the twentieth century, and he played a key role in not just one but two revolutions within the field (these revolutions going by the name of Logical Positivism and of Linguistic Philosophy respectively).

Wittgenstein is the perfect example of a 'tormented genius.' As we know from his letters and diaries, and from the reminiscences of a small circle of intimates (24), he was highly self-critical and disciplined, following self-imposed moral principles with an iron determination, and feeling sinful when he fell below his own highest standards. For example, although he came from an extremely rich family in Vienna, he gave away most of his money and as a result was forced to live an austere, even ascetic, life – thus his rooms in Cambridge apparently contained no furniture except a bed and a deck chair.

One of these moral principles was to devote himself to doing something great, and when he was distracted from this mission he felt anxious and depressed. In other words, he was extremely, and perhaps pathologically, serious. A colleague describes how he took Wittgenstein to watch a boat race, but afterwards Wittgenstein was furious saying that "the way we had spent the afternoon was so vile that we ought not to live, or at least he ought not, that nothing is tolerable except producing great works or enjoying those of others". (25) Although there were one or two people with whom, later in life, he developed what we might call a joking relationship (26), and although he was addicted to detective novels, playfulness was distinctly not a dominant state for him. But rebelliousness clearly was. By all accounts, he was often a 'prickly' person to be with, and he opposed much of the world that he found himself in. Among other things, he was anti-science and industry (27), and anti-Cambridge (28), not to mention generally unhappy about living in England.

Given the extent of his seriousness and rebelliousness, we should not be surprised to learn that he was often angry. He was in fact frequently furious with his friends and colleagues (and sometimes behaved violently with his pupils during a time when he was a school teacher). But the way in which his rebelliousness arose illustrates a related paradox. This is that someone who is highly conforming, may be incensed by those who do not follow the same rules, especially moral rules. This induces the rebellious state and feelings of anger, and is what we seem to see in Wittgenstein, who is often disappointed by what he regarded as the lack of moral fibre in others – and also at times in himself. (29)

Whatever the precise ways in which he entered the rebellious state, his grappling with philosophical problems was a struggle against the limits of understanding. He explained on one occasion that what he did involved "running against the walls of our cage". (30) There could not be a better metaphor for the way in which his breakthroughs in philosophy were experienced by him as deriving from defiance and confrontation. His aim was not to *solve* philosophical problems so much as to *dissolve* them – to show that they are pseudoproblems. "What we are destroying is nothing but houses of cards and we are clearing up the ground of language on which they stand." (31) His attack was therefore not so much on problems in philosophy as on philosophy itself, as a viable undertaking, and this is true of both his earlier and later work. What could be more revolutionary than that?

What makes his case especially interesting is that not only did he rebel against much of mainstream philosophy, but later in his career, in developing his second brand of philosophy, he was even rebelled against his own earlier work. This seems "all of a piece" with his self-hatred and feelings of sinfulness.

It is notable that both Wittgenstein and Gertrude Stein take as a central theme in their work the limitations of language. (We can note in passing that for neither of them was English their first language, even though they wrote in English.) For Wittgenstein, language can be misleading in fundamental ways, and this is a source of much agonizing. For Gertrude Stein, in contrast, these limitations are an excuse for delighted experimentation. In both cases, though, we see a defiance towards conventional ways of speaking and communicating. In the case of Einstein, he also has problems in thinking using language, but he by-passes the problem, thinking instead in visual images and carrying out in his imagination what he called "thought experiments" like the famous one in which he tried to imagine what it would be like to ride on a beam of light.

We cannot of course prove from three instances such as these, diverse and significant as they might be, that it is necessary to be frequently rebellious in order to be highly original. But it is interesting how often innovative people, whether they are architects, chefs or football players, appear to have difficult and troubled relationships with other people, and to display defiance and opposition in a variety of ways in their lives. The general point is that frequent rebelliousness can lead to innovation on the one hand, or to anti-social disruption on the other, and in some people to both. Rebelliousness does not guarantee originality, but originality would seem to depend heavily on rebelliousness when it occurs. And the rebelliousness can be expressed in combination with other states such as the playful state in the case of Gertrude Stein and the serious state in the case of Wittgenstein.

But what, you might object, about the technique of 'brainstorming' which has been used so widely since Osborn (32) introduced it in the fifties as a technique for coming up with new ideas? After all, "Don't criticize" is its central tenet for producing quantities of ideas to be sifted through at a later stage. However, its effectiveness appears to be something of a myth. Nemeth (33) gave five-person teams of students at Berkeley a problem: "How can traffic congestion be reduced in the San Fancisco Bay area?" Each team was assigned to one of three conditions: a brainstorming 'no criticism' condition, a condition in which team members were encouraged to criticise each other, and a no-special-instruction condition. All teams were allowed twenty minutes to come up with as many answers as they could. The teams in the 'criticism' condition were the clear winners, generating 20% more ideas than either of the other two teams.

When "No" Means "Yes."

Here is something that is not often recognised. This is that the rebellious state of mind is essential to the development of a sexually intimate relationship. Such intimacy represents something that is very different from everyday relationships, and involves the overturning of strict and well-understood rules of normal social behaviour. For example, in everyday social behaviour we do not normally kiss strangers on the lips, hold them close to us for an extended period, or stroke the genitals of someone we have just been introduced to. All these things are completely taboo… not to mention of course sexual intercourse itself. It is not that there are no rules in intimacy, but they are very different. In particular, in sexual intimacy, that which was denied is now expected. So how does the transition occur from one set of rules to the other? The answer is that one partner or the other has to take a chance and be rebellious, deliberately breaking one of the everyday rules and hope that this impropriety will be accepted by the other. The first kiss on the mouth may lead to prolonged kissing – or to a slap. The first touching by a man of the female breast may lead to further cuddling by the woman, or to shocked withdrawal. The point is that rules must be broken, and that to achieve intimacy something both risky and 'wrong' has to be done. But afterwards, what was prohibited now becomes required and what was objectionable now becomes welcome. Where a prolonged kiss would have been outlandish, now, on the next and subsequent meetings, it becomes expected – and something is felt to be wrong if it is withheld. The paradox is that what is 'bad' becomes 'good' and that, to use the language of anthropology, taboos become fetishes.

Sexuality is therefore necessarily bound up with rebelliousness. This is true in another sense, too. This is that orgasm is typically experienced as a kind of release, a feeling of freedom, a breaking through of some kind of barrier. It becomes a quintessential experience of successful rebelliousness. As one writer has put it, an orgasm is "a sudden feeling that you have escaped from the anxiety, have found your way, are able to see with remarkable clarity, or that you soar, or fall, into freedom… the feeling of constriction followed by release." (34)

This helps to explain a puzzle, which is why sexual words like "fuck" are used in anger, as swear words. One might have thought that any reference to love making would be tender and beautiful. But now we can see that anger and sexuality share a feature in common – rebelliousness – which makes it possible to use one as a metaphor of the other.

A final point: sexual rule-breaking is a risky business, especially, in our culture, for the male. Thus it can lead to embarrassment at the least, arrest for indecent behaviour, or, at the worst, for attempted rape. And such rebelliousness is subject to all kinds of misunderstanding. This is particularly the case where a woman is displaying ambiguous behaviour by ostensibly maintaining the rules of respectability on the one hand, while at the same time allowing the man to make some advances from which she can withdraw at any time with modesty still intact. It is often said by feminists that "no" means "no." And usually this is true – and clearly true. Unfortunately, "no" can also on occasion mean "maybe" or "later" or even "yes," and is not necessarily always designed to lead to a complete halt to further advances.(35) In the words of a character in Little Women: "Girls are so queer you never know what they mean. They say no when they mean yes, and drive a man out of his wits just for the fun of it." (36)

One wonders if the human race would have survived if "no" did in fact always, and unambiguously, mean "no." Such are the complexities of rebelliousness in intimate relationships.

CHAPTER 9

THE POWER OF SYMPATHY

"Why can persuasion be counter-productive?"

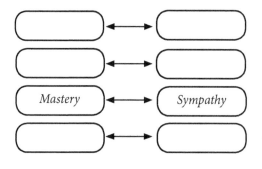

I was staying in New York with friends, and had taken a morning off to do some sight-seeing. I was visiting the tomb of Ulysses S. Grant, the Civil War General whose personality I discussed in chapter 1. I seem to have spent all morning heartlessly warding off the aggressive approaches of beggars and vagrants. But walking through the small park that surrounds the tomb I saw a homeless man lying on a bench with a battered old raincoat draped over him as a makeshift blanket. He took my attention because he was totally unmoving, and I wondered if he was dead. I approached him, and got quite close, still without seeing any movement, and observing that he was an African American, probably in his forties. I was not sure what to do. But in front of the building containing the tomb I could see that there was a uniformed security officer, so I went over to her and told her of my concern. She followed me back to the bench.

"That's just Bill," she said. "He comes here often."

At this point, Bill slowly sat up, a broad grin on his face, and stretched.

"How you doin', Bill?" she asked.

"Jus' fine." He radiated good nature, and flashed white teeth.

"How many times I got to tell you, you can't sleep here?"

"It'll only be for a couple of nights. I shall be able to stay with my cousin then."

"Are you OK? Do you need any help?" I asked him.

"I'm just fine."

"You sure?"

"I'm just fine."

"Well let me help you anyway." I said.

I reached into my wallet and, with a great show of magnanimity, gave him some cash. "Get yourself some breakfast."

Now here is the paradox: why did I resist giving anything to other destitute people, even though they implored me, but did give something to this stranger who was not asking for anything?

The answer of course is that my concern for Bill, and my initial worry that he might be dead, put me into the sympathy and other-oriented states of mind. He did nothing to change that with his cheerfulness and refusal to beg. I felt like a friend. This contrasted with the others who seemed to be challenging me, confronting me with demands, and in this way calling up the mastery and self-oriented states of mind – in which my refusing to give felt to me like remaining in control.

This lesson is one that should be learned by everyone who is engaged in trying to persuade others, whether those doing the persuading are advertisers, lobbyists, spokesmen, salesmen, beggars, or politicians. This lesson is that the more that you confront and cajole people, the less likely you are to succeed – unless you carry a very big stick with which you can force them against their will. Otherwise, by putting pressure on them, you will risk "putting their backs up" so that they refuse to do what they otherwise might have done. In other words, you risk getting them into the mastery and self-oriented states, in which their doing what you demand feels to them like losing. We could call this the paradox of persuasion.(1)

PERSUASION THAT ISN'T

My colleagues and I, at Apter International, have come across this persuasion paradox frequently in our research (2) for social advocacy and other organisations. In this research we use special interview techniques that we have developed to get beyond the kinds of stock answers that people tend to give to questionnaires, or in focus group discussions. Our aim is to find out what is really going on at an emotional and motivational level – what people *really* want rather than what they say that they want, what they *really* think rather than what they admit to. The need for this probing is shown by the fact that people often tell pollsters that they will vote in one way, but then vote in a different way. Or they agree to the pollster that they should behave in a certain socially desirable fashion, but then in actuality behave in an entirely different manner.

In work that we carried out for the South Carolina Highway Commission on seat belt usage (3), we started from the fact that although a vast majority of people report, in response to questionnaires, that they always wear seat belts, observation of traffic by the police shows that considerably fewer do actually wear them than report doing so. So why did those people who did not wear seat belts regularly fail to do so – and why should they say that they did? To answer this question we carried out lengthy in-depth interviews with individual drivers, using the kinds of techniques just referred to, to get beyond the surface level of response.

One of the most interesting things that emerged from this study was that people resented being told what to do in their own cars. Even though most of them said the right things about the need to obey the law, we found by probing beyond their initial statements, that in conforming to the law concerning seat belts, they felt that they were being denied their personal power and independence. In other words the whole issue of seat belts tended to induce the mastery state, and in the mastery state they felt that they were losing out. This was particularly the case with seat belts rather than other laws affecting the driver, because drivers felt that their cars were their own personal space, and that no one had the right to intrude on this space and tell them what they could do in it. Nor did they buy the idea that the state was showing proper concern for their health and wellbeing. As one interviewee argued, if this was the case there should be laws against people being overweight. The upshot of all this is that laws, and advertising campaigns, aimed at increasing seat belt usage, were felt by many drivers as dictatorial. The whole issue of seat belts was experienced as one of confrontation in which, by obeying the law, the driver lost the struggle. This was deeply felt by some people. One driver on being asked how he would decide if the choice was between wearing a seat belt and losing his wife said (without humour) that it would be a tough decision. The paradox is that the greater the pressure on people to wear seat belts, the more that many of them feel the need to push back. One of our respondents even said that he went out of his way to drive past police cars while *not* wearing his belt, in order to feel that he was "winning the game" against them. Nobody wants to feel like a 'loser.'

It can be seen that not only is the mastery state involved here, but also the rebellious state: the enjoyment of doing what one should not do. This is even more apparent in a related study that we carried out for the same agency, but this time on drinking and driving. Here interviewees not only expressed resentment about being controlled, but also made such blunt statements as "We're doing it *because* we are not supposed to," "It's that whole forbidden fruit complex," and "People like to drink and drive *in order to* break the law." Again, this means that, at least for some people, advertising campaigns against drinking and driving simply provide a focus for rebelliousness and are therefore counter-productive. Considerable hostility was also expressed towards friends who tried to prevent them from driving while intoxicated. "If someone takes my keys away, I am *more* likely to drive," one driver insisted. Another said stubbornly "I am going to drive no matter what." (4)

All this presents something of an enigma for those who want to change peoples' behaviour through public campaigns and the like. Pushing people produces a rebound effect, like pushing a spring. But in fact all is not lost. It means, rather, that one must find non-confrontational means of persuasion. One of these would be to emphasise the sympathy motivational state. For instance, in relation to wearing seat belts and to drunken driving, one could draw attention to the pain one would cause to loved ones if one came to harm in a road accident. Or one might emphasize how a person could express rebelliousness and independence through *refusing* to drink when having to drive, despite pressure from friends. Or one could allow the individual to feel moral satisfaction (in this case in the conformist state) by doing the ethically right thing. These are just some examples of what kinds of messages people might find persuasive. The point is that there are many ways one can attempt to change public behaviour through advertising and other forms of messaging, but to use straight coercion of the "Do this or else" variety is asking for trouble.

This was also one of the themes that emerged from qualitative research that we carried out on heterosexual peoples' feelings about same-sex marriage. (5) Rather than influencing peoples' attitudes in what gay activists would see as a helpful way, many people objected to having gay and lesbian views, as they saw it, foisted on them. This was particularly true of Gay Pride marches, and mass marriages, which were seen as "throwing it in your face." One interviewee even went so far as to compare gay marches with demonstrations by the Ku Klux Klan. As with driver behaviour, people do not like to be pressured, and for the same reason. If they succumb to the pressure they feel like losers. In this respect, it is legitimate to wonder whether every gay march might not have lost the movement thousands of votes, with flamboyant public displays of homosexuality losing even more. Instead, our non-gay interviewees reported that they were more likely to respond to sympathy-type messages emphasising the love and loyalty of gay and lesbian couples, and their courage in sticking together despite all the difficulties thrown at them by an unsympathetic society. In this way, non-gays, by being supportive, would be made to feel virtuous, rather than spineless. This was used in subsequent messaging and helped to reframe the whole debate as being about respect for love and caring.

It seems therefore that there are two rather different ways of dealing with the persuasion paradox. One is to help people to see doing what they are being persuaded to do as something that they themselves actually want and would have decided to do for themselves anyway. In other words, they have been given 'ownership,' in which case the new behaviour will feel like winning in the mastery state rather than losing. The other approach would be to help them to reverse into the sympathy state in which being helpful and understanding is experienced as desirable and positive rather than a weakness.

But if we think back to the study by Milgram, described

in the previous chapter, there is something of a puzzle. The Milgram study seemed to show just how easy it is to control people and get them to do what you want. If you remember, subjects were easily persuaded to give harmful electric shocks to fellow-subjects in a psychology laboratory. Unlike people being persuaded to use seat belts, or to support gays and lesbians, it turned out to be easy to persuade people to do things that they would never normally dream of doing, like administering dangerous electric shocks. Why? The difference perhaps is this. In the Milgram study, subjects were placed in a new and ambiguous situation in which there were no clear guidelines to help them. They therefore welcomed orders, because this gave them some structure and told them what was expected of them. In the case of seat belt usage and attitudes to gays, people have already made up their minds and become entrenched in certain behaviours. They do not need to look to others to make up their minds. At this point attempts at persuasion from others are seen as coercive. The moral is that the best moment to persuade someone to do something is when the issues are new. Once people have made up their minds it is difficult to shift them, and attempts to do so are seen as attacks to be rebuffed.

"WE HAVE WAYS OF MAKING YOU TALK."

The most extreme form of persuasion must be that of military interrogation, where a captive is being pressured to provide secret information. Just how effective torture can be in such situations is difficult to determine since, among other things, moral considerations preclude experimental testing in a laboratory. But, from the Spanish Inquisition through the Salem witch trials to the 'enhanced interrogation,' of recent times, it is clear that people will say anything – true or false –

to avoid extreme pain. Therefore their testimony will always necessarily be suspect. In contrast, so-called 'soft interrogation' techniques appear to be highly effective if deployed skillfully, and these are based on sympathy rather than mastery. What is surprising, and not generally known, is that this soft form of interrogation goes back to methods developed by the Luftwaffe, during the Second World War, to elicit information from captured enemy airmen. (6)

How do these 'soft' methods work? The starting point is to develop 'comradeship' between the interrogator and the prisoner. In the Luftwaffe case, this was done by establishing that they were both airmen and could share common experiences. The interrogator also made it clear that he was only doing his job and, like the airman, was not relishing it but was doing no more than his duty required. He would therefore look pained if the prisoner refused to answer a question, and take it as a personal affront to their developing friendship.

A related technique was to impress on the prisoner that he, the interrogator, was actually on his side. This was done by telling the prisoner that he had to establish clearly who he was, so that there could be no suspicion that he was a spy, or a member of the underground, or a saboteur, or some other undesirable. The interrogator would continue that if he could not establish this through the answers to a few simple questions about his identity, then he would have to be turned over to the Gestapo who would probably torture him. This technique was not just about the threat of torture, but about showing the airman that the interrogator was on his side: he did not want him to be under suspicion, and did not want the Gestapo to get their hands on him.

This 'friendly approach' also encouraged general conversation to develop. This could start innocuously enough – by being about sport, the cinema, family matters, mutual problems of all airmen, and so on. The interrogator's interest in the prisoner of war as a person helped the prisoner to feel safe and relaxed, and therefore to lower his guard when more important topics were subtly broached, which would happen once confidence had been fully established.

Another technique was to tell the airman that they already had the requested information, but that it simply had to be confirmed, as a formality, and that he would therefore not be giving anything away. To 'prove' this, the questioner would refer to information that he did indeed already have, so that the prisoner could see that what the interrogator claimed to know was in fact true. It was not difficult to confuse the airman later, since he would be unlikely to remember all the details of what was, and what was not, already known. Also, giving away any information at all, however minor and unimportant, could then be used as a precedent. "Why can't you tell me (this) – you have already told me (that)." Every piece of information was a handle to grab onto and twist.

In these and other ways based on the sympathy state, critical information could often be elicited. It could be argued that such techniques are much more likely to be effective than torture, quite apart from the deep moral issue involved, and the problem of what torture does to the torturer. (7) As a result, this approach has become widespread in modern police interrogation where steps are taken to establish rapport with the suspect: the interrogator might wear similar clothes, discuss common interests and hobbies before getting on to more serious matters, and might touch the suspect reassuringly from time to time. (8) An intriguing extension of this general idea that interrogation is most likely to be successful if the prisoner is in the sympathy state occurred when a terrorist suspect's family was brought in by federal agents to persuade the suspect to talk. Apparently this was successful. (9) It has been reported that, following the scrapping of 'enhanced interrogation techniques' like waterboarding, the FBI, and military interrogators, have been developing more sympathy-based techniques in the "war on terror." For instance, it is reported that one high-value terrorist with connections to Al-Qaeda started talking following the simple expedient of bringing in sugar-free cookies especially for him, since he was diabetic. (10) This is all a kind of chess game and depends on the interrogator using his wits rather than brute force. It is more Sherlock Holmes than Dirty Harry.

GUNS VERSUS PANCAKES

Here's a situation where you might want to be persuasive. This is if a stranger points a gun at you.

Ashley Smith, a young widow living alone in Atlanta, was walking from the car park to her apartment at 2.00 in the morning, when a man approached her and pulled a gun. He forced her into her apartment, where he made her sit in the bathtub. Later he bound her with duct tape and an electric cord.

What she did not know at first was that the man, Brian Nichols, was the same man who had earlier that day escaped from custody in a courthouse where he was about to be tried for rape. He had overpowered a courthouse deputy, taken her gun and shot her with it, then entered the courtroom and shot and killed the judge and court reporter. Later in the escape he had also killed a federal agent. Ashley Smith knew only a smattering of all this from what she had seen on television during the day. What she did realise was that she was confronted with a desperate man who could kill her, without compunction, at any moment.

Our particular interest in this story arises from the fact that instead of fighting, she determined to try to develop a relationship with him. (11) "At this point I was going to agree with everything he said and try to feel his feelings – whatever it took to connect with him and gain his trust. He had to see that he could relate to me". (12) Against every instinct, and holding her fear in control, she tried to move him out of his aggressive mood. So in as casual a way as possible, she started a conversation with him that, in the event, lasted all night. She told him about her own troubled life, her problems with drugs, and about her six-year old daughter who was in the custody of her aunt. She told him about her murdered husband, the circumstances of his death, and the impact of this tragedy on her life. She showed him photographs of both her daughter and husband. In turn she got him to open up about himself, telling her about all the wrongs that had been done to him, and why he had behaved in the way he had in the courtroom. He eventually untied her, but instead of trying to escape she offered him drugs, put a band-aid on his bleeding thumb, and cooked him some pancakes. Without going into all the details of a lengthy night, which included their viewing television coverage of the carnage at the courthouse, and discussing God and the purpose of life, by morning she had established a caring person-to-person relationship with him – so much so that he allowed her to leave the apartment to pick up her daughter. Once outside, she contacted the police, as he must have realised she would. He was arrested without a fight, just as he had promised her if the police ever ran him down. (13)

The point here is that instead of reacting aggressively in the way that most of us would have done – by attacking or making a run for it, either of which could have led to disaster – she did the opposite. She approached him, she opened herself up to him, and she made clear that she wanted to help. In this way their relationship became a sympathy one. In a dramatic fashion, we see illustrated the principle that people may be more open to influence in the sympathy than the mastery state, that persuasion through cooperation can be more effective than struggle, and that vulnerability can be a strength.

We see similar dynamics at work when an intruder, dressed in black from head to foot, pushed his way into the reception office of McNair elementary school. He was armed with a black rifle, an AK-47 and, as quickly became evident, numerous boxes of bullets in a black backpack. He shouted, over and over, "Today we are all going to die."

Antoinette Tuff, who had just arrived and was temporarily in charge of the office – what an example of being in the wrong place at the wrong time – refused to panic. As coolly as she could manage, and as she described it later, fortified by her faith in God, she asked him what he wanted. Over the next hour, she was the only person in direct contact with him, although, unknown to the gunman, she remained on the phone to a dispatcher at the local police who could hear everything that was going on.

Without going into the details of the sequence of events that followed, including a gun battle with the police who arrived to surround the school building, she eventually managed to talk him into giving himself up peacefully. She did this by, bit by bit, befriending him, feeling out why he was so angry, and sharing with him some of her own tribulations (her husband had just left her after 33 years). She also tended to a bullet wound in his hand. In this way she established a sympathy relationship with him and brought everything to an end without a single fatality. Considering that there were over 800 children and teachers in the building, most of them hiding beneath their desks, this was quite an accomplishment. Would this have happened if she had attempted to order the gunman around (mastery), been angry (rebellious), or even been terrified and attempted to escape (self-oriented and serious)? We cannot know, but it seems unlikely. In her own words, "My weapon was compassion". (14) Sympathy triumphed again.

Here's another example of the sympathy state being used to disarm (in both senses of the word) an intruder. It happened at a dinner party in Washington DC. It was a lovely summer evening and they were all eating outside on a patio. Suddenly a hooded man appeared and pointed a gun at the head of one of the guests. He then demanded money. The hostess kept her cool. Instead of panicking, or becoming aggressive, she calmly said that they were just finishing dinner, and asked him if he would like to have a glass of wine with them. The robber accepted and drank the wine that was handed to him (Chateau Malescot St-Exupery, apparently), commenting how good it was. He was then offered the whole bottle. Having had another sip, and also eaten some camembert cheese, he put the gun in his sweatpants. He apologised and excused himself observing, inconsequentially, that he may have come to the wrong house. More surprisingly, he then asked for a hug. Having caught on to what was happening, all the guests gave him a hug, followed by a group hug. They then sent him on his way with a filled crystal wine glass. Police later found the wine glass undamaged on the ground in a nearby alley. (15)

Sympathy Reframing

We are reminded in the last two examples of the effectiveness of food or drink in helping to establish a convivial sympathy state, whether we are talking about pancakes or about Chateau Malescot St-Exupery. Thus the importance of the business lunch in softening people up for negotiation. An excellent example of the deliberate use of food in this way is that of Golda Meir when she was Prime Minister of Israel. Many of her important meetings and negotiations, with both enemies and friends, foreign dignitaries and colleagues, were held in her kitchen. She would make occasional cups of coffee for everyone, and often throw a meal together. This meant that her cabinet meetings were literally the meetings of a "kitchen cabinet". (16) I hardly need to spell out that this would optimise her chances of putting everyone in the sympathy state, domestic colleagues or foreign representatives alike, and therefore reduce mastery confrontation and make people more open to persuasion. (17) As she said: "I am convinced that (such meetings) helped to make the process of government more efficient just because we could talk things out over a cup of coffee or a bit to eat around my kitchen table." (18)

The way in which the sympathy state (like all motivational states) encompasses everything experienced at a given time is illustrated in a study of Christians' feelings about Muslims. (19) Christian students were read a news story about the "Muslimisation of Nazareth," Jesus' home town. A test of imagery showed that the students exposed to this story had more morbid imagery afterwards than a control group of Christian students who had not been exposed in this way. In a second stage of the experiment, half the group who had been read the news story were read another story, this time (unknown to them) made up. It said that 117 devout Muslims on their way to Nazareth had died in a plane crash. In this case the students' thinking became less morbid and derogatory towards Muslims. What surprised the experimenters, however, was that the students became less derogatory not only to Muslims, but also to Hindus, Buddhists and Atheists, even though none of these had, supposedly, died in the crash. Why should there be any change towards these non-Muslims? The answer is that if the fabricated story induces the sympathy state, then there is no reason why the students concerned should not see everyone in sympathy terms for as long as the state continues. From the reversal theory perspective there is nothing odd about this finding. It is about the perspective that one has on the world at that particular moment, and a perspective cannot be divided into parts.

CHAPTER 10

DEAR ENEMY

"Why do people ever willingly help those who oppress or hurt them?"

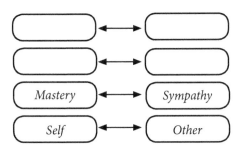

When a person is threatened or harmed, the last thing that one might expect is that he or she would be genuinely concerned with helping their aggressor. But this seemingly inexplicable paradox, in which people do indeed put the needs of their enemies ahead of themselves, is what we shall look at in this chapter. In terms of motivation, this obviously has something to do with the other-oriented state: The meaning of the situation for the individual goes beyond his or her personal needs, as he or she understands them. Instead it involves *identifying* with others and putting their needs first.

One of the most astonishing things about humans is how we can so readily and completely identify with other people, seeing the world temporarily through their eyes and feeling their feelings. We can identify in this way with children, patients, clients, students, team mates, and others. However, this chapter focuses on something stranger – something that goes beyond this. It looks at identification that leads one to be harmed, or at least threatened, but in any case willingly controlled. It is about the paradox of identification with others to one's own disadvantage.(1)

Let us start by noting that there are two versions of identification: a sympathy version and a mastery version. Let's start with sympathy.

THE STOCKHOLM SYNDROME

Here is an amazing example of people being in the other-oriented state of mind when one would have expected them to be in the self-oriented state – and in the sympathy state of mind when one would have thought that they would be in the mastery state.

On August 23, 1973, a 32 year old escapee from prison, armed with a submachine gun, entered one of the largest banks in Stockholm, Sweden, intending to rob it. In doing so he shot and injured a police officer. He then took four bank clerks – three women and one man – as hostages. His first demand was that his prison mate should be released and brought to join him – a demand that was agreed to by the Swedish authorities. The pair now barricaded themselves with their prisoners into the bank's vault, where they all stayed for six days until finally released by a police raid. (2)

The paradox was that the hostages came to bond emotionally with their captors and to feel hostile to the police. This strange phenomenon has become known, after this particular incident, as the "Stockholm syndrome." (3) It has since been observed in other hostage-taking and kidnapping situations, although it is not quite as typical of hostage-taking as one would imagine from the popular press. (4) Nevertheless, it does seem to occur from time to time and therefore requires explanation.

Common sense would tell us that captives would fear, hate and despise their captors, do everything they could to gain release, and welcome their liberators. In many cases of kidnapping, this is in fact what happens. So why did the Stockholm case, and others like it, bring about the opposite effect? Using reversal theory language, the commonsense view would be that hostages would be in the serious state, since their very lives are threatened. They would also be in the rebellious state, since they would want to break free of their captors. They would be in the mastery state since they would desperately like to be in control of the situation. And they would be in the self-oriented state, since they would be primarily concerned with their own safety rather than that of their captors. But with the exception of the serious state, all three of the remaining states were reversed in the Stockholm incident: for much of the time the hostages appeared to be conforming, sympathetic and other-oriented. In particular, they came to care about, and feel affection for, their captors.

Being in the sympathy state does in fact seem to be a good strategy for survival in such situations. If the hostage-takers can be brought to see their hostages as people, with feelings, personal histories, families and life projects, and therefore enter the sympathy state themselves, they are less likely to harm them than if they see their captives as no more than objects to be manipulated for their own ends. In a hostage-taking event in a stalled train in the Netherlands in 1975, by terrorists demanding independence for their country South Molucca, one of the passengers was about to be shot. He asked permission to leave a message for his family, and the terrorists insisted on listening to what he had to say. The message contained very personal material and included reference to his feeling that he "had failed as a human being." Instead of leading him away to be shot, they told him to sit and wait. They then took someone else out to be executed instead. (5)

It may happen to be a good strategy to be in the sympathy state because in expressing the sympathy state one has a chance of bringing about the same state in one's captors and therefore of being treated with some care. We saw this in the case of Ashley Smith, as described in the previous chapter. But how did sympathy get to be experienced in the first place in the Stockholm case? It could be that people deliberately behaved *as if* they were in this state in order to befriend and manipulate their captors, but the evidence seems to be that the caring was far from virtual – the captives became genuinely concerned for their captors. Behaving in a way consistent with a motivational state appears to be a way of actually getting into this state, so perhaps in behaving in a way that simulated caring, the hostages eventually entered the sympathy state themselves. But again, there does not seem to be much evidence for such deliberate play-acting in the Stockholm incident – the sympathy state just seemed to dominate of its own accord after a few hours.

But there is another explanation that seems to me to be the most credible, and it has the advantage of being relatively straightforward. In the Stockholm bank, all six participants were trapped together in the same small, badly ventilated, space for nearly a week. This was unlike those situations where the hostages are guarded by their captors in a separate room, or are blindfolded and kept ignorant of what their captors are up to. In the Stockholm bank, both captors and captives could hardly avoid getting to know one another as people, given the particularly intimate circumstances in which they found themselves. (The vault measured only 11 feet by 47 feet, and 7.5 feet high). As the primary kidnapper said afterwards: "There was nothing to do but to get to know each other." (6)

In contrast, the police were experienced by the captives as a vague and alien force. And later, as time passed, they came to be seen by the hostages as unhelpful and even threateneing. "Why are they still negotiating? Why don't they just agree to what is wanted, and then we can all go home? They obviously do not care about us. What is there to be bargained about when our lives are at stake?" There was also a fear that if the police attacked, they – captors and captives alike – would be equally in danger together. On top of this, little kindnesses by the captors were received with gratitude, and the big kindness of not being harmed by them was received with an enormous sense of indebtedness. Finally, it is possible that the captives saw the kidnappers as doomed, and felt sorry for them.

Put in this way, there does not seem to be so much mystery about the hostages' feelings. While not entirely appropriate, for obvious reasons, their bonding with their captors does become more understandable. It is reported that the women kissed their captors before they were taken away and the man shook hands with them. (7) In the case of one of the female hostages this bonding lasted beyond the ordeal itself, and she remained friendly with one of the hostage-takers, even assisting in his trial defence. (She did not, though, marry him, contrary to popular belief at the time.)

In the Concentration Camp

There is a related process that appears even more puzzling, and this is the way in which prisoners have been known to identify with, admire, and imitate, their captors or abusers. It is an example of what is known as "identification with the aggressor," a term coined by Anna Freud, the psychoanalyst daughter of Sigmund Freud, back in the 1930s. (8) The phenomenon bears some resemblance to the Stockholm syndrome, and indeed has been used in the attempt to explain it. But it is also different in that it is more about copying captors' behaviour than about feeling affectionate towards them, and it seems to occur in the mastery rather than the sympathy state.

The best known, and most dramatic, examples come from the writings of Bruno Bettelheim, an Austrian psychiatrist who was himself, as a Jew, incarcerated in a Nazi concentration camp. While in Dachau, and also in Buchenwald (1938-9), he used his psychiatric skills to study the impact of the camp on other prisoners, helping to preserve his own sanity by this kind of intellectual distancing. After his purchased release and emigration to the United States, he published his observations in an important paper while the war was still in progress, and later in a best-selling book entitled "The Informed Heart." (9)

One of the most intriguing things that he reported is that many prisoners identified with the guards and tried to emulate them. Thus they did things like steal bits of cast-off SS uniforms or mended their prison garb until it resembled the SS uniforms in some fashion. It gave them satisfaction when they could stand well at attention, and give a snappy salute. They adopted the same characteristic habits of speech, and even the same special vocabulary as they heard the SS use in communicating with each other. They even copied the games that the SS guards played during their leisure time, such as a game that involved seeing who could stand being hit the longest without budging. As Bettelheim put it "…as if they were not hit often enough without repeating the experience as a game." (10)

The worst of it was that when some prisoners were put in charge of others, they were often even more aggressive than the guards had been in pushing their fellow prisoners around and threatening them. This was true especially if they had been in the camp a long time. "Old prisoners" prided themselves on being as tough as the SS, and looked down on newer prisoners. Some even came to accept Nazi race ideology and the notion of the superiority of all things German. Bettelheim emphasised that this was not true of all prisoners, and many were courageously defiant throughout their ordeal. But it was definitely true of some.

What Bettelheim claims has been supported by others. Thus a Ukrainian who emigrated to America after the Second World War, described in interview his feelings during the time that he worked in a German forced labour camp, having been captured during the Russian retreat. The most interesting part of this interview came with his description of the way that he hero-worshipped the prison guards. He described how he loved their black leather, the way that they were clean and tall and impeccably turned out. Even when he was hit he admired the strength with which the blow was delivered. But here is the truly significant point: "Loving the arms that hit him, he could think of this power as his own." (11)

In the early seventies, Philip Zimbardo carried out his famous 'Stanford Prison Experiment.' (12) In this study of behaviour in a simulated prison, volunteer students were split arbitrarily into prisoners and guards, and then played out the roles they had been assigned. The whole set-up was very realistic, although obviously everyone knew that it was only a pretence. All the same, people became highly emotionally involved. In fact, the prison guards showed vicious behaviour towards the prisoners, who became genuinely upset. The whole study was designed to last two weeks of continuous imprisonment, but had to be brought to a halt by the end of the first week because of the suffering of the prisoners and the clearly detrimental effect it was having on the psychological wellbeing of many participants. This fascinating, but ethically questionable, study showed just how easy it was to induce cruel and aggressive behaviour, and has been taken by many commentators to throw light on the behaviour of Nazi Concentration camp guards. Zimbardo also used his findings to elucidate the behaviour of American guards at Abu Graib and Gauntanomo.(13) The finding of most interest to our present topic, however, is that when prisoners talked to each other (everything they said in their cells was recorded, unbeknown to them), they referred to each other in the same disparaging way that the guards referred to them, using the very same phrases. Zimbardo cites this as an example of identification with the aggressor. (14)

What seems to be happening in these concentration camps, real or simulated, is that the prisoners concerned reverse from the self-oriented to the other-oriented state. They then identify with their guards and vicariously feel the guards' power. So it is a way of feeling strong rather than weak, even if only by proxy. Unlike the Stockholm Syndrome, the mastery state remains in being in the prisoners. So the feelings are about power, not about kindness. The paradox here is that the weaker you are, the stronger you feel, because the power of your tormentor becomes greater in comparison with yourself. The trick is to experience the power indirectly by identifying with those who have it. This is a key mechanism in understanding so much that is self-damaging and therefore paradoxical in human behaviour.

This identification by some prisoners is not the same as their doing exactly what they were told in order to avoid punishment or even death. Bettelheim cites (15) the example of a group of Jewish bricklayers in Buchenwald who did such excellent work, with such professional pride, that they made themselves nonexpendable, and managed to survive until liberation. But this is a rational tactic that keeps them alive, and is quite different from the emotional identification that I am referring to here, and that seems so paradoxical.

Power is attractive in the mastery state, even if it is threatening, as the Nazis knew so well. One can still understand this appeal in watching films of Hitler speeches and Nazi events, such as we see in Leni Riefentstahl's infamous Nuremberg film "The Will to Power." Who can deny that there is a tremendous seductiveness in the Nazi movement when it is displayed in this way? Who would not like to feel part of this great upsurge of feeling and strength? Nazism was, as much as anything else, an aesthetic: an aesthetic of starkness and contrast, hardness and clarity, direction and purpose. This is not to condone it in any way whatsoever. My point is psychological not political: To identify with the Nazi fascists is to feel power. I defy anyone to watch the Riefenstahl movies without feeling, as they watch, that they want to be part of what they are seeing. In my own case my arm is fairly twitching to be raised in a Nazi salute.

THE TRUTH ABOUT STALINIST SHOW TRIALS

An even more dramatic form of other-oriented motivation is illustrated in the Soviet 'show trials' of the nineteen thirties. In this case, as we shall see, the victims can be understood as trying to achieve something in the mastery state. In this sense their experience was more like that of the concentration camp prisoners than of the Stockholm syndrome captives.

These show trials consisted of three huge public trials of former Communist party leaders, "Old Bolsheviks," whose attachment to the party went back to the Revolution itself in 1917. The trials took place in Moscow between 1936 and 1938. Arising in the context of what historians call the 'great purge,' Stalin used these trials as part of his successful attempt to stamp out any kind of dissidence in the Soviet Union, and enforce his totalitarian rule. All 54 defendants were accused of plotting to assassinate him and restore capitalism.(16) Needless to say, these events were not really trials at all, but exercises in political power.

We now know that the accused were in fact innocent, and that confessions were extracted often through torture, or through threats to their families. (This was admitted by Krushchev during his historical denouncement of Stalin in 1956). But the astonishing thing is that many of the accused, in their public statements, not only admitted their guilt, but, despite their knowledge of the deep unfairness that they were suffering from, extolled the virtues of the Soviet Union and pleaded with people to continue to pursue the aims of the Party. And in their self-criticism they took the part of the Party against themselves, characterising themselves as "the dregs of the land," "fascist murderers," and "traitors who should be shot." One of them even seriously asked Stalin if he could personally execute his fellow "traitors" as an act of contrition. (This request was refused.) (17)

Nikolai Bukharin, who had played a particularly important part in the historical development of Russian communism, in his last plea before the court, captured this identification with the Party:

"For three months I refused to say anything. Then I began to testify. Why? Because while in prison I made a revaluation of my entire past. For when you ask yourself: 'If you must die, what are you dying for?' – an absolute black vacuity suddenly arises before you with startling vividness. There was nothing to die for, if one wanted to die unrepented. And, on the contrary, everything positive that glistens in the Soviet Union acquires new dimensions in a man's mind. This in the end disarmed me completely and led me to bend my knees before the Party and the country… The monstrousness of my crimes is immeasurable, especially in the new stage of the struggle of the USSR… It is in the consciousness of this that I await the verdict. What matters is not our personal feelings of the repentant enemy but the flourishing progress of the USSR and its international importance." (18)

There seems to be something more going on in this self-abasement than submission to torture, understandable though this would be. It is rather that the only thing that gives meaning to the lives of communists like Bukharin is their devotion to communism, and it is this that makes them willing to sacrifice themselves, even to the extent to confessing to crimes that they did not commit. They saw their confessions as being for the sake of the common good and the betterment of the party. The amazing thing is that Bukharin and others were willing not only to sacrifice their lives in this way, but also their honour and reputation before history.

Arthur Koestler the Hungarian-born novelist and essayist has convincingly captured this mindset in his classic novel "Darkness at Noon" (19) which is about an "Old Bolshevik," Rubashov, who has been arrested. Although this is a novel, Koestler knew some of the defendants in Stalin's trials, including Bukharin, and clearly based much of the novel on this knowledge. Indeed, he claims that the novel is "A synthesis of the lives of a number of those who were victims of the Moscow trials." He depicts Rubashov as a firm communist, a patriot, and a loyal follower of the dictator (called "No.1" in the novel). But at an earlier time he had been an opponent of the dictator. He recognises that his conviction is inevitable – that is the way that these things work – but needs to decide on the best way to respond. It becomes clear to him during interrogations that he needs to perform a major service to the party, and that this is to invoke hatred in the masses for any form of opposition to the leader, including his own. He would therefore have to acquiesce to the demands of his interrogator that he admit in open court that he has engaged not just in opposition to the leader, but in counter-revolution, and done so as an agent of a foreign power – which are complete lies.

At one point his interrogator says to him that "…The party must be as if cast from one mould – filled with blind obedience and absolute trust. You… have made a rent in the Party. If your repentance is real, then you must help us to heal this rent. I have told you, it is the last service the Party will ask of you." This Rubashov does, and at the show trial he says "I will describe to you my fall, that it may be a warning to those who in this decisive hour still waver, and have hidden doubts in the leadership of the Party and the rightness of the Party line." Such a confession would have to take enormous self-sacrifice given that it is based on untruth. While many confessed for many different reasons, Koestler is telling us that one reason for doing so is to sacrifice oneself to a historically greater good, and one that gave meaning to the lives of both the victims and their oppressors. "There was a certain nobility, in my opinion, even in their false confessions and their deaths," wrote a Soviet general who fled the Soviet Union. (20) Their behaviour only seems paradoxical if we assume that they are in the self-oriented state.

IDENTIFICATION

This kind of behaviour depends on the ability that people have to identify with others – to be, in the terms I have been using here, in the other-oriented state. This is a state that, if we are normal, we all seem to experience frequently during the course of everyday life. We watch movies on television and identify with the hero or heroine. We listen sympathetically to friends telling us of their concerns. We are 'taken out of ourselves' when music overwhelms us. We feel uplifted by a beautiful landscape. In all these ways, and many others, our own self becomes less important to us than something that transcends our limited personal identities.

It may seem extraordinary that people could identify with others to the extent that we have just seen, in which such identification risks suffering or even death. The examples we looked at seem like a kind of hyper-identification. But consider two things which make them appear more normal. One is the degree to which most parents identify with their children, and would willingly sacrifice themselves for them. This shows that self-sacrifice is built in as part of the loving, sympathy and other-oriented sides of human nature. The second is the widespread nature of identification with teams and groups, this typically being more about mastery than sympathy. A sign of the importance of this, especially in males, is the tendency to join clubs or gangs, and to support sports teams. We can speculate that these two forms of identification, the sympathy and the mastery, have in their origins to do with child-rearing and with hunting respectively. But the point is that, either way, this is an other-oriented phenomenon which can be manipulated to the detriment of the individual, albeit to the possible good of the community. Most people seem to be vulnerable in this respect, and it helps to explain the paradoxical behaviour which we have been looking at in this chapter.

There is another side to this, this one involving the serious state. If having some overall serious meaning in life is an important issue for the individual, then this may override personal safety and advantage. If the community, or some larger investment of purpose, can impose itself on the individual's imagination, then anything is possible. We see it in an extreme form in Islamic suicide-bombing. We see it, at least up until the First World War, in the military concept of 'glory.' We see it in the heroism of firefighters, first responders, bomb disposal experts and swat teams. We see it in the way that great leaders, like Churchill, can call on people to sacrifice themselves for the common good. And we see it in a fully paradoxical form in the false confessions of show trials. These false confessions are paradoxical in a way that is goes beyond other kinds of heroics, in that those concerned sacrifice not just for their friends and families but for their enemies. This only makes sense if we see it as a way to give life meaning and purpose.

DOMESTIC VIOLENCE

We can conclude that people are able to care for those who would, or actually do, cause them harm. There is a final version of this that I want to touch on, and this is to do with wife battering. The paradox here is that the wife, in the face of repeated brutalisation, typically 'sticks things out.' Why? One possible answer is that the abused wife secretly enjoys her husband's power over her, and provokes it on occasion to gain a feeling of vicarious strength through identification: she experiences the husband's power at second hand. An alternative view might be that although the aggression looks serious from the outside, it is really a kind of game, not unlike the sadomasochistic games we looked at in an earlier chapter, and a game which is sexually exciting to both parties. (21)

However, we must always listen to what people themselves have to say about the meaning of their actions. Lenore Walker did just this with women suffering from domestic violence, as documented in her classic book "The Battered Woman". (22) In contrast to the views just presented, she reports that such domestic violence is indeed for most victims a terrifying ordeal and that the injuries are often serious, if hidden as far as possible by the wife from family and friends. It is neither a game nor an indirect way to feel powerful. It is simply, for the victim, subjection to raw violence.

This being the case, why do such abused women not leave their husbands, or report them to the police? Women have even been known to attack the police who turn up to help them. (23) We do seem to have a paradox here. That they do not overtly turn against their husbands, despite the latters' cruelty, is, according to Walker, not at all paradoxical. It is that they are afraid of, and take seriously, threatened reprisals if they leave, not only against themselves but also against their children. Nor is it just a case of reprisals. Pride may enter into it, a loss of face before friends and family, through the admission that the marriage has failed. This would lead to denial of problems and concealment of injuries. There may also be a kind of 'learned helplessness,' a feeling that, in the last resort, they can do little or nothing about what is happening to them. In some cases they even ask themselves whether, in some way, they might not really be to blame for what has happened. "Can I rescue the situation if only I can learn to behave better?" While their decision to stay is in most cases sad, even tragic, and certainly displays poor judgment, it does not amount to irrationality or paradox. But there *is* another aspect of this which is relevant to the theme of reversals.

One of the key characteristics of this kind of unhappy interaction is its repetitiveness. This is captured by Walker in her phrase "The Cycle Theory of Violence." (24) She points out that what so often happens is that the relationship goes round-and-round in a circle consisting of three phases. In the first phase, tension between the couple slowly builds up until something 'snaps' and induces the second phase in which there is an explosion of anger on the part of the husband who physically assaults his wife. The third phase sees the husband devastated by what he has done, shamefully begging forgiveness, and promising that nothing like this will ever happen again. This subsequently becomes a tranquil and loving phase, a respite in which the wife may even come to feel affection for her husband once more and in which trust is, more-or-less, re-established between them.

Then everything begins all over again, like a dance with repeated measures. The husband starts to find fault once more, and to feel dissatisfied with his wife; the unfortunate wife defends herself, there is more tension, building up to another explosion of violence, followed by yet more apologies and yet another reconciliation. We can put this in reversal theory terms, by saying that at its heart this cycle involves the alternation of the mastery and sympathy states. Specifically, the man is in the mastery state in phase 1, trying with increasing difficulty to dominate his wife. He desperately acts out the need for mastery in phase 2 through physical violence. In phase 3 he attempts in the sympathy state to re-establish a loving and intimate relationship. For the woman, phase 1 may well be a loving sympathy phase that turns sooner or later to mastery during phase 2 (but mastery that is not successful in getting into control), with a return to sympathy in phase 3.

Now we come to an observation that is particularly interesting from the point of view of reversal theory, because it supports the idea of reversal due to a process of internal satiation. (It will be remembered from an earlier chapter that reversal theory goes beyond situationism in arguing that people can change because internal contexts change, especially through the satiation of motivational states.) This observation is that for the man, the changes seem to occur not in response to some external event. Rather, they arrive seemingly "out of the blue." According to Walker, "The number of times a battered woman went through the cycle of violence, she still could not predict exactly when an acute battering incident would occur." (25)

In this case, the reversals are not caused by something specific happening, although there may be some minor event which acts as the occasion for a particular reversal. Rather there is a buildup of psychological pressure, a process of satiation of the ongoing state, and this process inevitably, sooner or later, reaches the tipping point represented by a reversal. Whatever has happened to trigger a reversal at that point, may well not have been strong enough to do so at an earlier point in the cycle. It is merely that it happened to do so this time around.

In this way, sympathy leads to mastery and mastery leads to sympathy. Batterers are neither cruel nor kind, but both at different points in the cycle. Their personalities alternate and are self-contradictory. While external situations may play a limited part in determining their behaviour, internal processes are even more important. It would not be too much to claim that the whole phenomenon of repeated domestic violence illustrates the limitations of both trait and situationist theory. This is because neither take into account the way that motivational states can change at the behest of internal rather than external processes.

THE STORY OF MATILDA

I have a final narrative for this chapter. I want you to make up your own minds this time. Will it be possible to make sense of what happened in the terms suggested in this chapter? If so, what might the specific explanation be?

We move to Normandy and Flanders in the eleventh century. Our story concerns Duke William of Normandy, later to be William the Conqueror, and his courting of Princess Matilda, daughter of Count Baldwin V of Flanders. We start with William formally asking Matilda's father for her hand in marriage. This would be a brilliant match in that it would mean that Normandy and Flanders would be joined dynastically and become a powerful European force. Unfortunately, Matilda adamantly refused her father on the grounds that she would never lower herself to marry a bastard (which William in fact was). She said that she would rather become a nun.

When William heard of this stinging rebuff, he was outraged, and rode angrily, with some trusted companions, to

Flanders where he confronted her as she came out of church with her maids. (Accounts differ as to whether this took place in Lille or in Bruges.) There are different versions as to exactly what happened next, but they all involve a physical attack. In one account he cuts open the front of her dress with the tip of his sword. In another he pulls her to the ground by her long braids, splattering her rich dress with mud. Another adds that he stamped on her while she was on the ground. Then he rides off.

Now we come to the paradoxical part. Matilda tells her father that she has changed her mind and that now she wants to marry William after all. In fact no one else will do. The exasperated father, who meanwhile has been making arrangements for a different dynastic marriage, eventually and reluctantly complies. When he asks his daughter what has changed, she is reported to have said "Now I know him better." They do get married, and Matilda gets to be the Queen of England following William's invasion. It would be nice to say that "they lived happily ever after," which would be an exaggeration. But for the times, and with some major ups and downs, it appears overall to have been a good marriage. And Matilda turned out to be a strong and capable queen.

What really happened between them is one of history's little secrets, and one would just love to know what William said to her during his attack. But my question is: Does anything in this chapter give us a possible explanation for Matilda's paradoxical decision? (26)

PART THREE

IMPLICATIONS

CHAPTER 11

ECONOMICS UNBOUND

"Rational or irrational? Neither: Multi-rational."

In the Batman film *"The Dark Knight",* the character called the Joker makes a bonfire of a huge pile of cash, saying that crime is not about economics, it is about fun. In pointing out that money is not always the supreme motivator, the Joker is expressing an idea that has been gaining ground in the social sciences in recent years.

Classical economics assured us that man is rational. (1) This is taken to mean that he is logical, unemotional and self-interested. He is a money-making and spending machine whose calculating nature would be approved by the unemotional Mr. Spock in Star Trek and whose selfishness would be empathised with by Ming the Terrible, Flash Gordon's nemesis. Over fifty years ago, the Nobel prize-winning economist Herbert Simon challenged this idea and suggested that people, as economic agents, are not in fact completely rational. There are limits to rationality, and beyond those limits people may be emotional and illogical. People display therefore what he called "bounded rationality" – they are rational only up to a certain boundary line. This was certainly a step in the right direction, although criticised and ignored by many in the mainstream of economics for many years – which is what usually happens in the academic world with radically new ideas. By 'step in the right direction' I mean a step towards recognising that economic behaviour cannot be fully understood in terms just of rational decisions about money.

A second step in this direction was taken by psychologists Daniel Kahneman and Amos Tversky a quarter of a century later – a step for which Kahneman would also be awarded the Nobel Prize. They showed experimentally that economic decisions are not always objective and straightforward. Rather, they can be strongly influenced by the way that they are 'framed' by people – something that everybody, including advertisers, had known for some time, but seems to have escaped the attention of economists. In putting forward this idea, and evidence for it, they set in motion a whole new field, that of 'Behavioural Economics.' This brings together cognitive psychologists, neurologists and economists to work on human decision-making. One recent result has been a spate of popular best-selling economics books, which is something of a surprise for what has been called 'the dismal science.' (2,3)

ALL EIGHT STATES – AGAIN

Kahneman talked of 'frames' and this is a concept which in one respect is similar to that of 'motivational state' as I have been using it here (the two were originally proposed at roughly the same time). Both concepts imply that there are different ways of experiencing the very same thing. They differ in that Kahneman emphasises the *cognitive* aspect of this – specifically, the different ways that choices can be communicated to people who have to make the choices. A simple cognitive example of framing would be to ask the classic question of whether one would prefer a mug of beer that is half full or half empty. In contrast, I have emphasised the *motivational* aspect – the different motives that different courses of action might be expected to satisfy. Could it be that these eight motivational states form a basic set that would allow us to see peoples' apparent economic irrationality – what happens when they go beyond the bounds of rationality – in a new light? In fact, the ideas being put forward in this book might allow us to put all economic motives – seemingly irrational as well as rational – in a single framework and in this way to systematise some of behavioural economics.

To get a taste of how we might better understand what happens in decision-making by adopting a more motivational point of view, consider the strange psychology of voting behaviour. This is puzzling to economists, and one can see why. One notable economist, Howard Margolis, has even referred to it as the 'paradox of voting.'(4) This is paradoxical because the cost of voting – the time taken, the effort, and the hassle – far outweigh any possible benefits there might be for the voter. Since a single vote is so small in comparison with the total votes cast in an election it is unlikely to make any difference to the outcome. So voting makes little sense in terms of the classical rationalist economic model – as Margolis points out. He goes on to suggest that other processes must be involved, in which choices are made between self and group values, with voting often calling on the latter. It is reasonable to suppose that by 'group values' he is referring to what I have been calling the other-oriented motivational state and explaining voting behaviour in terms of the values of this state. But reversal theory suggests that there are yet other motivational possibilities. In particular, an individual might vote out of a feeling of duty (conformist state), or out of a need to partake in something important (serious state). In other words, taken together, there are other possible psychological benefits of voting beyond those of selfish mastery.

The point is that without a rich enough psychological theory we will not know what questions to ask of people when we are trying to understand the choices that they make in everyday life, including both economic choices and the choice of whether or not to vote. This implies that we need to go beyond behavioural economics into *'experiential economics.'* We need to know the meaning of a given economic behaviour to the person performing it.

A SPECIAL MOMENT: THE ACT OF PURCHASE

What happens when you go shopping? The goods or services that you consider buying offer themselves as so many ways of satisfying particular motivational states, this satisfaction coming later on when you get to benefit from what you have bought. You might buy golf clubs because they will help you to feel more masterful when you get to the golf course. You might, when you buy baby food, expect that this will give you the unselfish satisfactions that go with the sympathy and other-oriented states when you feed your baby. But more interestingly, the act of purchase itself may give rise to different satisfactions related to your ongoing motivational states, quite apart from the hope you might have of later pleasures resulting from your purchase. This *'purchase pleasure'* appears to have been relatively overlooked by economists. So let us examine how this might play out in relation to each of our eight states.

Starting with the serious state, in this state you can congratulate yourself on being prudent and far-sighted in your purchase decisions. In contrast, in the playful state, there is a different pleasure – the excitement of the hunt, as hinted at by the "shop till you drop" catchphrase. In the conformist state you can take satisfaction in knowing that you are doing the right thing, such as buying a birthday present on time, or purchasing a wholegrain product. In the opposite, rebellious, state it is possible to take perverse pleasure in doing the wrong thing, perhaps buying something illegitimate like drugs, pornography or Cuban cigars. In the mastery state you can take satisfaction from having had a good deal, congratulate yourself for having used your expert knowledge to make a clever decision, or enjoyed the cut-and-thrust bargaining. In the sympathy state there can be the joy of luxurious self-indulgence, a joy that can come during the purchase itself and not just afterwards in using the product. Satisfaction in the self-oriented state can come from the knowledge that you have acquired something that you had long coveted for yourself. In the other-oriented state you can congratulate yourself on being caring in buying a gift for someone else that you believe they will enjoy. Clearly, whether in the end you buy or not, and exactly what it is that you buy, is strongly influenced by the motivational states that relate to the shopping experience itself – rather than only to your subsequent experience of the goods and services as a consumer.

Do I need to add that things are more complicated than this? For one thing, a number of different motives can enter into a single act of purchase. In buying a vacuum cleaner I might, during the act of purchase, have simultaneous feelings of seriousness, conformity and mastery, each one vying to be at the centre of attention. One can also move from one motivational state to another in the course of a single shopping expedition. I recall an occasion when my wife Mitzi and I did the round of used car lots. We set out with the idea that we would like a Jaguar. It was a car that we had both wanted all our lives, and I recalled in particular, with great fondness, my father's handsome grey and black 'Jag.' We felt that at last we could afford it, even if only a previously owned one. We set out in a spirit of playfulness, full of excitement and anticipation, but the more we looked, the more problematic things seemed to be. It became apparent that Jags were no longer very reliable, that they cost a lot to repair, and that they were heavy on gasoline. And every Jaguar we found seemed to have something wrong with it: the mileage was too high, the price was too high, the upholstery would need attention, there were significant scratches on the bodywork, there was no warranty beyond the legal minimum, the dealer was particularly shady, and so on. We eventually found that the whole project was giving us precious little pleasure and a great deal of anxiety. We had moved from the playful to the serious state of mind, a state in which buying a Jaguar had come to seem like a worry that we had imposed on ourselves. As it happened we passed a Volvo dealership on our way home that day, and decided to take a quick look. We immediately switched back to the playful state – we no longer felt threatened and everything seemed very easy and 'doable.' An hour or so later, having completed all the paperwork, we had bought a Volvo, and traded in our old… Volvo.

Not only can people find satisfaction in the act of making a purchase decision, but they can willingly and knowingly pay "over the odds." This seems irrational, but when we look at the psychological benefits we see that it can make good psychological sense to the shopper. Take the purchase of designer label clothes – we buy these even though they are more expensive than their non-designer equivalents. Likewise for sports cars, fine wines and watches. The point here, of course, is that one is buying status rather than clothes, and this "conspicuous consumption" (5) gives very real satisfaction in the self-oriented and mastery states. It is not illusory: the purchase *does* provide status. One may also desire to be 'in fashion,' and here we see that what is being purchased is really the conformist pleasure of being 'in' and 'with it' and 'up to date.' Also the sympathy element of self-indulgence might be better satisfied by buying something in which price is secondary. As Oscar Wilde has one of his fictional characters say: "Unnecessary things are our only necessities." (6)

But why would one buy something, other than a necessity, on credit? The answer would seem to be that in the playful state, caught up in the moment, and wanting something 'now,' one may be willing to buy on credit even though this means paying more in the long-term. "Buy now, pay later" has long been a theme in advanced economies. And it makes sense in terms of the playful state, which, as we know, is all about the spontaneity and enjoyment of the moment. (There may also be an element of rebelliousness here, or wanting to feel that one is breaking free of restrictions – in this case financial restrictions.)

In contrast, people in the serious state often make long-term commitments – such as regularly saving money into an account that cannot be opened without penalty before a certain date. This is not only wise in itself but means that people often recognise the central claim of this book, namely that they change, that they move backward and forward over time between opposing psychological needs, and that when they recognise this in themselves they can take appropriate action to avoid unnecessary problems in the future.

The Endowment Effect

There is a general point here. Things that can be bought and sold, are often more than just functional objects. They evoke memories, induce emotions, make promises, console, symbolise values, support self-esteem, provide feelings of personal continuity. In these and other ways, they become an integral part of peoples' lives. Even stocks and shares can have personal values. It is reported that an elderly widow refused her financial adviser's advice to sell stocks in a company that her husband had worked for. It turned out that letting go of the stocks felt like letting go of her husband. The adviser took one of the shares of the stock and framed it, thus allowing the widow to symbolise her loyalty to, and love for, her husband. She could then give herself permission to sell the rest and diversify her portfolio. (7)

In general terms, objects relate to motivational states, and may be tied to more than one at the same time, and over time. In this respect, they can come to have a great richness of meaning, especially emotional meaning. A widespread example of this 'surplus meaning' (8) is the so-called "Endowment Effect". This refers to the fact that people value things more when they own them than before they owned them, and that they are subsequently loath to part with them. This puzzles economists, because it seems that the monetary value of something depends on who owns it, which makes little economic sense. But if we realise that, to some extent, we define ourselves by what we own, then the effect becomes less puzzling. Among other things it explains hoarding.

Here is an experiment that demonstrates this effect in an elegantly simple way. (9) The subjects are a group of students in the same room. Half of them are given mugs and the other half receive nothing. They are then all exposed to a simulated market in which mugs can be bought and sold. Those who now owned the mugs rated their value at three times the value placed on them by those who did not receive mugs. Why? This seems a real puzzle. Reversal theory would suggest that to those who have been given mugs, the value is more than the monetary value. They were *given* the mugs and hence this was experienced by them as a sympathy state satisfaction. Although they know that the gifts were decided randomly, they still remain gifts, and gifts are worth more than the monetary value that they have. They seem to say something about how likeable one is, or about whether luck is on one's side. (Perhaps unconsciously subjects believed that the distribution was not really random at all.)

I collect antiques, and I have a keen sense of ownership that represents a strong case of "endowment." I feel triumphant in having spotted something I want in an antiques shop, in having bought it for a good price, in having researched it on getting home, in having shown off my good taste to others and, hopefully, if I am to be honest, in having created a little envy in them. To me, and I dare to say to all collectors, an antique possession is part of one's very sense of self. This way of seeing things was in sharp contrast with that of my late wife Ivy, who was an established antiques dealer. Dealers cannot afford to have such feelings, otherwise they would never sell anything, and soon go out of business. To them, an antique has to be simply an object to buy and sell, an article of merchandise, a commodity. There can be no sentiment. In short, for them the endowment effect must be absent if life is to be bearable. (As Ivy pointed out to me, fortunately for dealers, people never want to take something back once they have bought it. Antiques dealers already know all about the endowment effect and use it to their advantage.) Our difference of feelings towards antiques led to some (for me) unfortunate occurrences. I would come home from work and notice that there was an empty spot on the wall where a watercolour painting used to hang. Or I would become aware that some prized piece of Staffordshire pottery was no longer on the mantelpiece. It would turn out that Ivy had had a call by a customer for just such an item, and had taken advantage of the fact that we had at home exactly what was being looked for, that could then be sold for a nice profit. This seemed to her to be entirely reasonable, and she was genuinely surprised, each time this happened, that I should be upset. But for me it invalidated the whole purpose of collecting. If I could not be sure, on purchasing something, that it would be mine for ever, and help to define me for eternity, then this part of my life would lose much of its meaning. I have been persuaded that my view of collectible objects was no more rational than hers – but it was certainly different, and it was mine. (10)

THE WORKPLACE AND ITS SATISFACTIONS

Economic decisions include not only purchasing decisions, but also selling decisions. The major selling decisions in most of our lives are the ones that involve selling our own labour. How much are we willing to sell ourselves for? If classic economics has problems with the rationality of purchase, it has at least equal problems with the rationality of salaries and wages, because it is clear that people do not necessarily prepare themselves for, and devote themselves to, the jobs that would pay them the most. This is particularly true of those with a sense of vocation – teachers, priests, nurses, soldiers, among others. The point hardly needs labouring. Accepting relatively low wages might seem irrational from a classical economic point of view, but in terms of psychological rewards, and the motivational states that are implicated, it can make complete sense. Earning money, and therefore competing for the highest wages, might give satisfaction in the self-oriented and mastery states. But helping others by means of one's work (e.g. as a physiotherapist, or an ambulance driver) might, in the other-oriented and sympathy states, provide even greater satisfaction. Doing something that one enjoys in itself (e.g. being a publican, or a scientist, or a kennel owner) might give huge pleasure in the playful state. Doing something that calls on one's spirit of critical innovation (e.g. as a management consultant, or an art teacher) might be a wonderful expression of the rebellious state. What this comes to is that we cannot realistically expect to predict peoples' economic behaviour in real life situations, including their career choices, unless we take into account their different and varying motivations.

We should also remember that, given the amount of time that we spend at work, and the variety of motivational states that sooner or later come into play in the course of the working day, it makes sense for an employer to provide a workplace in which all these needs can be catered for. Ideally the atmosphere should be a motivationally rich one in which people are aware of the consequences of their work (*serious state*), the work is stimulating (*playful state*), there are routines and procedures that provide structure, so that everyone knows what they are supposed to be doing (*conforming state*), innovation is encouraged (*rebellious state*), professionalism is valued (*mastery and self-oriented states*), and there is a friendly collegial atmosphere (*sympathy and other-oriented*). In brief: work is not just about money, but should be about all the things that make life worth living. Nor are any of these things necessarily in conflict with the needs of the organisation itself. They can in fact be harnessed to improve performance to the satisfaction of both employers and employees. (11)

MULTI-RATIONALITY

In recent years, as we have seen, economists have become more open to the idea that man is to some degree irrational, and that some economic decisions may be irrational.(12) Reversal theory takes a different view from either the traditional 'rationalist' or this newer more fashionable 'irrationalist' view. What I am driving at here is that man is neither rational nor irrational, but is rather *multi-rational*. This means that there are different values (represented by different motivational states) and that each state generates its own rationality and makes its own choices and judgments. But each state appears to be irrational to people starting from different values, i.e. in different motivational states. Thus to someone in the serious state, the risk-taking of someone in the playful state seems irrational. Why take any unnecessary risks? The rational thing, it appears, is to be cautious, and to think in the long-term. But to someone in the playful state, this long-term thinking seems irrational – you may not live long enough to enjoy the profits, and the prudent investment process is no fun. Carpe Diem! The fact is that both views are rational – but in their own way. Similarly, being charitable and giving money away seems odd to someone in the self-oriented state, but makes perfect sense to someone in the other-oriented state. To the latter, making more money for oneself when one already has enough might seem odd. Why try to accumulate larger amounts of money than one needs, especially when there are so many poor people around who could make really good use of it?

Each motivational state is rational in its own way then, being based on its own value. A value, such as achievement or love, is not rational or irrational in itself. It is like an axiom, or premise in a mathematical system – something that cannot itself be proved or disproved, but acts as a starting point for rational reasoning. To give a rather abstract example, in comparing Euclid's with Riemann's geometry, one cannot say that one is rational and the other irrational, but only that they are both rational in their own ways, based on different starting assumptions. (One of Euclid's axioms is that two parallel lines will never meet, however far one extends them. This is rejected by Riemann.)

I have been using the terms 'rational' and 'irrational' in a rather intuitive way here, and a more precise definition is available in economics. This derives from the concept of 'utility,' which means the value or benefit that one gets from buying some object or service. This is similar to the term 'satisfaction' that I have been using throughout this book. In making choices between things, we choose the one that has the greatest utility, i.e. the one from which we expect the greatest satisfaction. Given the choice at the greengrocers, does one choose apples or oranges? The way that one chooses should depend on their relative utility. In the supermarket does one choose a bag of apples or a pair of socks? It seems odd that we can compare such different things on a single utility dimension in order to make a choice, but we obviously can because as shoppers we do it all the time. Rationality, in these terms, occurs where people do actually make choices that provide them with the greatest utility. Irrationality, in contrast, occurs when people make less than optimal choices – for example buying apples when, for the same outlay, oranges would have provided them with more utility.

Now I want to suggest here that, generally speaking, people *do* make optimal choices in relation to their ongoing motivational states. In this respect they *do* tend to be rational. But their motivational states change, and hence the utility of different things that they might buy also changes. This is the sense in which people are multi-rational. This multi-rationality derives from the fact that something that might have high utility in one state has low utility in another, and vice-versa. For example, buying a lottery ticket in the playful state, which may have high utility in that state, will have low utility following a subsequent switch to the serious state. It will therefore appear to have low rationality when viewed from the perspective of the serious state. Buying insurance in the serious state may likewise appear to have low utility – to be no fun, and therefore be irrational – in the playful state. In this sense multi-rationality, and movement between different rationalities, leads to a form of what looks from the outside like irrationality. It might seem irrational to someone in San Francisco to go West to reach Chicago, but not to the person starting from New York.

MAKING SENSE OF ODD BEHAVIOURS
_____

In terms of motivational states, and changes between them, we can begin to make sense of many of the irrational-seeming behaviours that have been investigated by behavioural economists. To illustrate this, here are three representative examples of studies that produce puzzling results – but results that begin to be understandable in reversal theory terms.

The first is a study concerning the way that ten day-care centres in Israel attempted to deal with parents who were late in picking up their children (13) What they did was to impose a fine for parents who were more than ten minutes late. The result was surprising: the rate of late pick-ups more than doubled. This has been explained by saying that the day-care centres had substituted an economic incentive for a moral incentive, and the economic incentive was weaker. (14) We can put this more systematically in the terms used in this book, by saying that the fine, seen as a payment for looking after their children a little longer, involved a number of reversals in parents. Firstly, it changed the situation from one in which the sympathy state was focal, with personal relationship to teachers being paramount, to one in which the mastery state was focal, so that there were feelings of choice and control for late pick-up. Secondly there may have been a reversal from the conformist state, with punctuality being a moral obligation (so that parents felt guilty if they were late), to the situation being a rebellious one in which pressure from the school was seen as constraining and annoying – and to be opposed. Thirdly it is possible that there was a reversal from the other-oriented state, in which the needs of the school came first, to the self-oriented state, in which the needs of the parents prevailed. Thus the institution of a penalty turned out to be disastrously counter-productive for the day-care centres.

The next study concerns choices affecting the present

versus choices affecting the future. (15) The experimenters simply asked people to choose three rental movies. In one condition, the subjects were asked to choose a single movie on three occasions. In the other, subjects were required to choose all three at once, for future viewing. In the former case they tended to choose 'low brow' movies, in the latter 'highbrow' movies. This makes sense in reversal theory terms if the three-movies-at-a-time case involved more subjects being in the serious state (which they are likely to have been because they were asked to think about the future). In this state they would be more likely to choose movies that would improve them in some way, and therefore have further future consequences. In the single movie condition, subjects were made to be oriented to 'now,' and were therefore more likely to choose movies with no serious consequences for themselves, but just immediate pleasure.

Thirdly, we have an experiment on Loss Aversion: by loss aversion is meant that people choose safe strategies to minimise loss rather than trying to maximise gain. In other words, they hate to lose more than they love to win. For example, participants are asked whether they would rather take $50, or have a bet in which if they win they gain $100 and if they lose they finish with nothing. Secondly, participants are asked whether they would rather take $100 or have a bet in which if they win they gain $200 and if they lose they gain $100. In both cases the choice is between taking a bet and not taking a bet. And in both cases the difference between winning and losing, if the bet is taken, is the same in absolute terms, i.e. $100. But the interesting thing is that a majority of people choose to take the $50 in the first situation, thus avoiding taking the bet, and to take the bet in the second situation. Why? I would suggest that this is all about having, or not having, a protective frame (remember chapter 4). In the first case there is no such frame, because one can finish up with nothing, which would be experienced as a real loss. In the second case there is such a frame: whatever happens one will finish up with something. In a sense in this case one cannot lose. So the second tends to induce the playful state and with it the pleasure of risk and a certain level of excitement. (16)

Putting all this together, the answer to the question of why people – you and I – make irrational economic decisions is that usually we don't. Looking at things in terms of psychological rewards and punishments, we see that generally people do try to obtain whatever rewards they can. It is just that what they find rewarding will differ depending on which motivational states happen to obtain at that moment. Far from being chaotic, there is an overarching structure of alternative desires, and with them alternative realities and rationalities. While each motivational state may seem irrational from the point of view of other states, it is usually thoroughly rational in its own terms.

Utility or Futility?

There is a final point here, and an important one. It has been said that American culture is based on the pursuit of "Life, liberty and the purchase of happiness." Unfortunately, buying things and owning things does not seem to lead inevitably to happiness.

We can see this clearly in historical terms. No one would dispute that, over the last half century, material conditions in Western countries have improved vastly. More people own their own homes, and homes have become larger and more fully furnished with labour-saving devices of all kinds. The majority of families own a car. Computers have for many of us taken over our hours of work, and television has taken over our hours of recreation. It would be tiresome to list all the ways in which material life has improved, in relation to health, diet, education, communication, transport and entertainment. And yet, as the economist Gregg Easterbrook has documented in his book *The Progress Paradox* (17), our happiness has not improved to a commensurate degree. In fact, there is surprising evidence that levels of happiness have, despite all these material improvements, remained unchanged over a span of fifty years. In one study he cites, sixty per cent of Americans described themselves as happy – but this was no more than in 1950. In the same study, the percentage of Americans who described themselves as "very happy" was in fact slightly less than in 1950. (18)

It is possible to find reasons for this, as Easterbrook does, in terms of historical changes in the nature of society. For instance, he talks about "choice anxiety" which comes from the fact that almost every shopper is faced these days with a superabundance of options. (19) There is also "collapse anxiety," which is the fear that civilisation itself is under threat – from terrorists, climate change, and so on. And there may be guilt over hoarding so much, especially in the face of desperate starvation-level poverty in Africa and elsewhere. Put these, and other historical forces, together and they form a strong counter-balance to the pleasure from increasing material affluence. But another way of interpreting all this is simply to say that the effect of economic forces on happiness is strictly limited.

There are other ways of exploring this lack of relationship between material prosperity and feelings of wellbeing. One is to compare people at different income levels. In one study, millionaires as a group were found to be no happier than people of average income. (20) Another way is to compare across countries. Gallup continually surveys citizens in 160 countries, representing 98% of the world's adult population. Although in this case some relationship has been found between material prosperity and life satisfaction, prosperity is not particularly related to happiness in the sense of day-to-day feelings and emotions. These feelings are more closely associated with having friends, feeling in control of one's life, and so on – forms of happiness that would appear to relate directly to the satisfaction of motivational states.(21) There is also evidence that the more *importance* that people attach to material goods, however rich or poor they actually are, the less wellbeing they will experience.(22)

What *does* seem to be the case is that money can often facilitate the satisfaction of different motivational states. As we have seen, it can buy status to please the mastery state, insurance to please the serious state, valuables to please the sympathy state, and so on. But satisfaction can also be achieved in all the motivational states in ways that have little or nothing to do with money, or even with commodities. (23)

Given the enormous problems that stem from unsustainable economic growth, including climate change, and resource depletion, this importance of non-economic factors in happiness must provide us with some hope that man's psychological needs can be met in ways that do not always require material consumption, and certainly not ever-increasing material consumption. Do we need to move from an economic model to a hedonic model of society and measure improvement not in terms of economic growth but what we might call '*hedonic growth.*' This might seem unrealistic, but it becomes feasible when we learn that the Gallup organisation has already set up a wellbeing telephone poll which tracks US citizens' feelings every day of the year. Known as the Gallup-Healthways Well-being Index, it is based on the daily responses of at least 500 people. Even more extraordinary, and welcome, is that the British government has indicated that it is developing an index of national wellbeing to go alongside such economic indicators as the Gross National Product. In the admirable words of the then Prime Minister we should measure progress "…not just by our standard of living, but by our quality of life". (24) To do this, appropriate questions will be included in the U.K. annual General Household Survey. There are signs that other nations may follow suit in the development of *'hedonomics,'* as the measurement of wellbeing is called.

CONCLUSION ON CRAZINESS

As we have seen, many economists and others think that people are irrational, and certainly non-rational forces play a part in our lives. If people were fully rational, then greater utility would necessarily mean greater happiness. But the point I want to make here is that in a complex and ever-changing environment, continual adaptation and re-adaptation call on different ways of thinking at different times – contrasting kinds of rationality associated with different motivational states. Only crazy people are really crazy. The rest of us have just to put up with being inconsistent and using our rational capacities in different ways at different times to pursue alternative values. And, by the way, if you get emotional in doing this, this does not mean that you are being irrational – it is perfectly rational to experience emotions, since they remind you what you want and what is missing from your life at that moment. They help to guide your behaviour.

At base, of course, we do want to be happy. But what is happiness? In the next chapter we shall finally turn to this fundamental question, and to the problem of why happiness is so difficult to achieve in any lasting form. We shall reach some surprising conclusions.

Chapter 12

GETTING TO HAPPINESS

"Why can we never remain happy for long?"

Over two thousand years ago, Aristotle posed the question of why we can never remain happy for long.(1) Most of us would surely agree with Aristotle that happiness is indeed never more than intermittent. It comes and goes, often unpredictably, sometimes even surprisingly. This relates to what many would think of as the quintessential human condition: a struggle for something that is, by its very nature, never more than ephemeral – like grasping snowflakes. It is this very elusiveness that is at the heart of what has been referred to as "Man's divine discontent."

What I want to do here is to put Aristotle's mournful question in the context of the ideas that I have developed so far in this book. As we have seen, each of the eight motivational states has its own distinctive satisfactions. The serious state is open to the possibility of experiencing the satisfaction of achievement, the sympathy state has the potential of experiencing the satisfaction of love, the conforming state is able to experience virtue, and so on. (If you need reminding about these eight forms of satisfaction, you should glance again at Appendix One.)

It is reasonable to suppose that the satisfactions that are experienced by the different states that are active at a given time come together to produce an overall level of satisfaction. If this is strongly positive then it is what we might think of as happiness or subjective wellbeing. Also, of course, the result could be an overall dissatisfaction which, if large enough, could be called unhappiness. In any case, it should be clear that happiness cannot be equated with satisfaction in any one of these particular motivational states, but is a more general term for an overall level of high satisfaction, whatever its particular source or combination of sources. This is part of the reason why one cannot achieve happiness directly, by aiming at it, but only through the satisfaction of particular motivations. (2)

Whatever happened to the word 'pleasure?' I have been avoiding using 'pleasure' as a synonym for 'happiness,' because 'pleasure' is often used in everyday life to refer to the particular kinds of satisfaction that can be experienced in the playful state – such as sensuous gratification, the exercise of physical skills, and intellectual stimulation. These pleasures are all about immediate forms of stimulation. To avoid misunderstanding, throughout the book, and not just in this chapter, I have therefore used the word 'satisfaction' rather than 'pleasure' to cover agreeable feelings in general, whatever the particular form that they take, and whichever motivational states happen to be involved. (3) Then pleasure is no more than one kind of satisfaction, while satisfactions taken together make up happiness.

THE LIMITATIONS ON ENDURING HAPPINESS

So why is happiness so 'slippery'? Why is it that, as often as not, no sooner do we realise that we have it than it is already gone? We can start with some fairly obvious reasons, and it is surprising just how many of them there are.

Lack of end-point. One basic problem is that psychological motivation, unlike biological motivation, has no end-point. Biological motivation has a natural termination – when one can eat no more, has had an orgasm, or collapsed drunk under the table. Admittedly, the biological need will always resurrect and reassert itself again later on, but it can be fulfilled completely at a particular time. In contrast, psychological needs know no end, either at a particular time or over time. One can never have enough love in the sympathy state, or power in the mastery state, or achievement in the serious state. This means that any source of satisfaction can be judged, at a particular time, to be less than was ideally desired, so that the pursuit has to continue. There is, tantalisingly, no end to desire.

A variation on this is that if one has had an intensely satisfying experience, it may be difficult to rise to the same heights again, and one remains, from then on, aware of just how far one is falling short of that once-experienced golden moment. It is known to explorers as "post expedition blues." A classic example is that of the (assumed) suicide of Meriwether Lewis after returning from the famous Lewis and Clark expedition exploring Louisiana. A more recent example: after Buzz Aldrin had successfully flown to the Moon and back, he became severely depressed. In his words "There was no possible way of setting a goal that would match the goals already achieved."(4) Yet another example: Michael Ventris, the architect and linguist who finally, after many scholars had attempted it, deciphered Linear B – a form of writing dating from about 3,500 years ago. After his success he became depressed and crashed his car in an act which is generally thought to have been suicide. (5)

Such post-achievement depression would appear to be a serious-state paradox known to many successful people. The most famous example of success depression from history must be that of Alexander the Great who, at the height of his military conquests, is reputed to have wept because there were no new worlds to conquer.

Unrealistic expectations. If we set our standards for satisfaction too high, we are inevitably going to be disappointed. If we let our imaginations run riot, we will be dissatisfied in the face of reality. If we want too much, we shall be found wanting. Our anticipations and our fantasies can easily become our enemies, especially when we judge ourselves as having achieved less satisfaction than we could, or should, have done. Eternal quests, such as the medieval alchemists' search for ways of making gold, or for the Elixir of Life, Christian knights' quest for the Holy Grail, and the Spanish conquistadors' search for Eldorado resonate with us because they represent the endless search for an impossible ideal, with inevitable failure.

Reference anxiety. In any case, there will always be other people who have more – this is what economists call "reference anxiety," and involves what psychologists refer to as "social comparison." It is otherwise known to the rest of us as "keeping up with the Joneses." Social comparison means evaluating yourself by comparing yourself with other people and asking whether you are doing better or worse. Reference anxiety is the concern that you are doing worse. Take the case of Stavros Niarchos, the Greek shipping magnate, and, in his time, one of the richest men in the world. He owned the world's largest private yacht (the 385 foot *Atlantis*), a private island, and he collected race horses and rare paintings. It is said that the poor man was endlessly miserable because his arch rival shipping tycoon Aristotle Onassis might just have been even richer – and also happened to be married to Jackie Kennedy. (6) There is therefore always, in principle, reason for a person to be dissatisfied, since someone else is always doing better, or so it seems. We can note in passing that conspicuous consumption is socially harmful because it has the effect of generating reference anxiety. (7) We are getting here into the psychology of envy.(8)

Social comparison can of course work in the other direction, leading us to feel good about ourselves because we are better off than others. A friend of mine told me that his parents emigrated from Russia during the Great Depression in the thirties. On getting off the boat in New York, they spent their first night in a run-down hotel in Harlem – at the time one of the most poverty-stricken areas in the United States. In the evening, while his mother unpacked, his father went out to look for food. On returning he said: "It is true what they say about America. It is rich. The shops are still open and there are things to buy on the shelves." In comparison with Russians they felt rich indeed.

Diminishing returns. One limitation to happiness is already recognised in economics and is called 'diminishing incremental utility.' What this ungainly phrase refers to is that the more you have of something, the less pleasure you get from each additional unit of it. The third ice cream is less rewarding than the first and the tenth ice cream considerably less rewarding, if not actually nauseating. The ninety third Rolls Royce that you acquire is no doubt less fun than the first.(9)

Habituation. In psychology there is a similar concept to diminishing utility, which is that of habituation. This refers to the fact that the psychological effect of something diminishes during exposure or repetition. This is another way of saying that things tend to pall fairly quickly. It is, of course, one of the reasons for drug addiction – the effects of a drug become less each time it is smoked, swallowed of injected, and so more of it is needed in order to be able to cling to the same effect.

This seems to apply to any form of stimulation. Take the

case of movies of different kinds. In a thriller movie, a chase that goes on too long starts to get wearisome. In a 'slasher' movie, the first murder is likely to be horrifying, but each subsequent murder feels less so, even if it is equally bloody. In a romance, the fifth kiss is less enchanting and erotic than the first. Because of such habituation, a good movie usually varies its sources of interest, and introduces as much surprise and plot twists as it can manage, so as not only to maintain attention but to avoid habituation. The fight against habituation presumably lies behind much contemporary art, continual changes in fashion, the latest 'crazes' in pop music, promiscuous sex, and international tourism – in all of which the cry is "make it new."

There is an astonishing study (10) that compares levels of happiness in accident victims and lottery winners. The accident victims in the study had all been seriously injured within the previous year, and were as a result either paraplegic or quadriplegic. The lottery winners had all recently won sums between 50,000 and 1 million dollars. And yet, comparing the two groups, their levels of happiness (in response to questionnaire items read to them over the phone) were not significantly different. When asked about pleasure related to particular mundane events, the lottery winners, in fact, expressed significantly less pleasure than the victims. One possible explanation for all this is that habituation had led the lottery winners to lose pleasure in their winnings over time, and the accident victims to lose displeasure in their misfortunes for the same reason. This is an extreme example of what has been called the 'treadmill phenomenon' (11) which is that material changes in life cause immediate surges or decreases in happiness, but happiness soon returns to a balanced neutral value. All this reinforces the point made in the previous chapter that happiness and wealth are not necessarily directly related.

Exhaustion. Another reason why purchase and possession do not lead inevitably to happiness is that you may have to devote so much time and energy to building up the funds needed to buy something, that you do not have the time and energy left to enjoy it. The man who buys a luxury yacht may not have the time to sail it. The man with the most expensive bag of golf clubs may have the worst handicap. Perhaps this is what Epicurus was getting at when he said, over two thousand years ago, that happiness requires a certain simplicity of lifestyle. (12) Often people are faced with the choice of doing something that they can afford, but do not have the time to do, or doing something for which they have the time, but cannot afford. This, when we come to think of it, is a key difference between the experience of being an adult and the experience of being a child, except that in this case there is no choice in the matter.

Mistaken goals. There is a lot of evidence to show that we do not really know how we will feel about future events before they actually occur. Since our foresight is limited, and even in some of us delusional, we pursue goals in the future that do not necessarily lead us to happiness, so that we are frequently disappointed. And when we do experience happiness, as often as not we 'stumble' on it by mistake or by chance. (13) As examples of irrational optimism, when people daydream about the future, they tend to see themselves succeeding rather than failing. And people think that they are going to live longer, and be married longer than the average. (14) For these reasons they are likely to make choices, and behave in ways, that do not necessarily lead them to happiness.

REVERSALS AND PRECARIOUS HAPPINESS

We can add to these a far-reaching reason for dissatisfaction, a reason that derives directly from reversal theory. This is that any satisfaction is necessarily temporary, since the desire that gave rise to it will not normally endure. Rather, it will eventually switch to its opposite, perhaps through satiation. It is rather as if in playing rugby or football, every so often, and without warning, the referee blew a special whistle and the direction of play was inverted. So if you were close to, and attacking, your opponent's goal line, you would now find yourself to be defending your own.

This means that reversals sometimes bring good experiences to an abrupt end. In the face of this fragility of experience it is difficult to indulge in self-satisfied feelings of confidence in lasting happiness. In one's emotional life, one is never quite sure of what will happen next.

In the following case, the reversal seemed to take place even before the satisfaction that had been aimed for would have been felt. When soccer players win a game, like any winning athletes, they may be expected to experience some degree of triumph (self-oriented and mastery states). In a study comparing the emotions experienced by soccer players in Canada and Japan (15), this was indeed what was found to be the case in Canadian players. But things were surprisingly different with the Japanese players. Here it was found that winners failed to experience triumph at the end of the game, but instead were overcome with feelings of empathic sadness: they felt sorry for their opponents. It seems that at the final whistle, these winners tended to reverse from the self-oriented to the other-oriented state. On the other hand, if they had lost, then, through the same empathy with their opponents, they tended to have pleasant emotions at the final whistle.

Such reversal keeps everything on the move, never allowing us to settle for long in a rut of self-satisfaction. Metaphorically, the hourglass is turned over regularly to keep the sand flowing, with important consequences for subjective wellbeing. Here are some examples of a kind that you might recognise in your own life. Glance through them and see if any of them strike a chord.

- You buy a new car, and are pleased at the attention it is getting from friends, but then you reverse from the self-oriented to the other-oriented state and feel ashamed at having shown off and caused envy in others.
- You organise a party for friends in your house and, in the other-oriented state, enjoy the pleasure you are giving to them as a host; but then, having reversed to the self-oriented state, you feel resentful that you are not having much fun yourself as you run around trying to please them.
- You go bowling with a group of friends and expect to have fun, but find instead that you are restless: Having reversed from the playful to the serious state, you now feel that you are wasting your time. You keep looking at your watch and thinking about what else you could be doing. You leave early.
- You go to a committee meeting in the serious state, wanting to achieve something worthwhile, but then, after a reversal to the playful state, become bored.
- You are enjoying shopping for clothes for yourself, in the self-oriented state, but then you switch to the other-oriented state and feel guilty. You buy clothes for your children.

Life displays what we might call, with a nod to Herbert Simon, *'bounded stability.'* We get into various motivational ruts, each rut representing a kind of stability and, as I argued in the last chapter, a kind of rationality. But, in the normal way of things we bump from parallel rut to rut, never fully settling down in one or another. In this respect, we have a kind of unstable stability.

GETTING IN THE WAY OF EACH OTHER

As we have seen, at any given moment four motivational states will be active, even if only one is at the focus of attention. This multiplicity of motivation means that there may be conflict between different motives. This means that any satisfaction deriving from one state may be at least partially spoiled by the simultaneous dissatisfaction of other states. In a rebellious state, one might want to be rude to one's boss. But one cannot at the same time satisfy the needs of the serious state, since rebellious satisfaction may have serious consequences that are negative – such as being fired. Wanting to be in control in some situation (*mastery state*) may be inconsistent with putting the needs of others first (*other-oriented state*). Telling your story at a dinner party may mean that you cannot listen to, and empathise with, others who also have a story to tell. In general terms, it may be difficult to satisfy all four active states at the same time, e.g. serious *and* conforming *and* mastery *and* other-oriented. It's like riding a team of four wild horses, while being astride only one of them. As a result, as these examples show, one can experience mixed or even conflicting feelings. Here is a striking example: According to Neil Armstrong's wife, he felt terrible guilt that he got all the acclaim for the efforts of tens of thousands of people working for NASA in putting him on the Moon. (16) Here his feeling of achievement (*serious state*) conflicted with his feeling of solidarity with others (*other-oriented state*).

DIVINE DISCONTENT BUT ETERNAL HOPE

But wait! There is another side to all this. If there is a downside for every upside, then there must be an upside for every downside. The situation is symmetrical. This means that it is possible for us to use this symmetry to our advantage. Whatever bad emotion we are feeling, if we switch to the opposite motivational state we will have a chance of replacing it with a good emotion instead. Here are a few possible examples. Glance through them and see if you have ever experienced anything like any of them.

- One is feeling worried in the serious state of mind about having to give a presentation, but if one can reverse to the playful state the arousal will carry over, and one will feel growing excitement at the prospect.
- One is feeling humiliated at having mispronounced a word in public, but on reversing to the other-oriented state is able to laugh at oneself and feel a little rueful.
- One is feeling guilty in the conformist state about not wearing a tie to a gathering that turns out to be formal; but on switching to the rebellious state one feels good that one has been able to express one's individuality, and to hell with all those 'stuffed shirts.'
- One is feeling sorry for oneself in the sympathy state about having to take a particularly bad tasting medicine, but on switching to the mastery state one feels a small sense of triumph at having been able to manage it.

Even if you cannot readily bring about the needed reversal, and no external change has brought it about for you, then innate instability (due to the satiation process that builds up) will eventually carry you out of the state into its opposite. If satisfaction does not last forever, neither does dissatisfaction. The watchword is always: "This too shall pass."

Happiness Happens

The other side of the coin is that happiness can, like unhappiness, arrive unexpectedly, 'out of the blue,' and seemingly for no special reason. Let me give an everyday kind of example from my own recent experience – an example of a kind that could no doubt be easily matched by anyone reading this.

I had to do jury duty in a suburb of Washington that I was not familiar with. It was early morning in mid-winter, with an icy mist swirling around. Luckily I was able to take a local train from my home to a station that was, apparently, only a few blocks from the court house. When I stepped from the train onto the platform, the morning cold hit me like a shock. I set off walking in what I hoped, from a little map I had clutched in my frozen fingers, was the right direction, but I could not be sure. And my uncertainty was increased by the difficulty that I had in reading the names of roads through the mist. Car headlights floated past mysteriously, and sounds were muffled. The shapes of tall buildings loomed above and disappeared into the clouds. I kept peering at my watch to see how much time I had to get to my destination, and worried about what would happen if I was late. Suddenly, and for no obvious reason, I felt suffused with a kind of joy at being fully alive at this moment and in this place. Oddly, despite the mist, everything seemed to have a particular kind of reassuring solidity about it, to be especially 'real.' The feeling did not last long, and had gone by the time, ten minutes later, that I found myself at the entrance to the courthouse. But while it lasted it was happiness. This clearly was an outcome of a spontaneous switch from the serious to the playful state, converting my anxiety about getting lost, and being late, into a species of excitement. But I fancy that it also went deeper than that. I had recently had a serious medical scare and for a while had been very aware of my own mortality. As a result of the spontaneous reversal on the way to the courthouse, I unexpectedly felt safe again, for the first time in many days. It was a very good feeling, even though it did not last long.

Let me use this minor example of being surprised by happiness, to introduce an example on a different level altogether. How could one possibly feel happy in a Nazi concentration camp? If ever a situation has been devised for keeping people continuously and agonisingly and desperately unhappy, this would have to be it. And yet, astonishingly, we find exactly such happiness in the profound accounts by the psychiatrist Viktor Frankl of his experiences as a prisoner in Auschwitz and other concentration camps. He describes how on one occasion he was part of a work team, marching out in darkness to their work site, on a bitterly cold and wet morning, with little clothing to protect them against icy winds. The man marching next to him mumbled "If only our wives could see us now!" This set off a train of thought, and as they stumbled on through icy puddles, he thought intensely about his wife. He felt that she was there, next to him, smiling and talking to him encouragingly. She felt completely real. Then a man in front of him slipped and fell, and others fell on top of him, forcing a break in his train of thought while a guard whipped them onto their feet again. But as soon as they started trudging forwards once more his wife came back to him, and they resumed their imaginary conversation. He felt overcome by an intense love: "I understood how a man who has nothing left in this world still may know bliss." (17)

PEAK EXPERIENCES

The happiest moments in our lives are ones that nowadays are referred to as 'peak experiences.' If what I have been arguing has validity, then peak experiences must derive from strongly positive motivational state satisfactions. In an extreme they become mystical experiences. This means that there must be eight distinctively different flavours of peak experience (besides mixtures of such experiences). Let us see what each of them looks like, and ask whether you have ever experienced anything like any of these:

- Serious peak experience: the whole of life seems to be suffused with meaning and purpose. It all makes sense. There is a plan and a profound goal to life.
- Playful peak experience: everything seems beautiful and joyful, and only this moment of euphoria matters. It's wonderful just to be alive. For some, the experience of orgasm would fall into this category, for others it is particularly associated with the experience of art and especially great music.
- Conforming peak experience: a feeling of fitting into everything, of everything being harmonious and 'just right.' Also the feeling that one is perfect in some important, especially moral, way. For some it means the blissfully certain knowledge that one is doing God's will.
- Rebellious peak experience: a feeling of being free, of escaping from physical, intellectual, and other kinds of limitation, of breaking out of the bonds of mundanity and soaring above the pettiness of everyday life.
- Mastery peak experience: a feeling of enormous power, of being in control of everything, of being able to succeed at whatever one undertakes, and of overcoming any and all opposition. It is a Godlike feeling of superiority.
- Sympathy peak experience: a blissful feeling of universal love, and a knowledge that this love is at the heart of everything. You are loved, and overflowing with love for others.
- Self-oriented peak experience: a feeling of being the centre and hub of the universe. You were right:

It really is all about you. You are the point where everything comes together. You matter, profoundly and permanently.

- Other-oriented peak experience: a feeling of being part of, and taken up in, something vast, transcendent and humbling. It is what is sometimes referred to as the "Oceanic" feeling. This comes close to what was meant by 'the sublime' in the eighteenth century. It also corresponds to some descriptions of mystical experience, in which the self seems to disappear altogether.

FROM POSITIVE TO REALISTIC PSYCHOLOGY

In psychiatry, as in social, clinical and developmental psychology, there has been a huge change of tone over the last thirty years or so. This can be characterised as the result of a movement away from looking at what is wrong with people to looking at what is right with them, from pessimism to optimism. It has meant moving away from the bleakness of psychoanalysis, and the angst of existentialism, towards a more confidently American and less European spirit of hope. (18) If Freud saw everyone as basically neurotic and nasty, the new model insists that man is fundamentally decent and worthy. In this, the new approach is a true child of the "swinging sixties," the era of love and self-esteem. This approach has also meant moving away from a model of man in which such negatives as anxiety and depression are central, to a model in which positives like joy and creativity – not to mention peak experiences – come to the fore. The resulting approach is generally referred to as "Positive Psychology,"(19) and the modern study of happiness is one of its principal offshoots. (20)

While there is a certain wild-eyed and uncritical enthusiasm among some of its supporters, and while it unfortunately connects up at its fringes with the New Age movement, and with occult beliefs, mainstream Positive Psychology has nevertheless played an indispensable part in 're-balancing' psychology. Psychology had, generally speaking, been focused on the dark and troubled sides of Man, placing mental illness at the heart of things. It could be said to have done this to the detriment of all that is courageous, loving and even spiritual in people. But in its own way Positive Psychology has risked going too far, just as 'negative psychology' did before it. Its resolute cheerfulness can sometimes become a little jarring and the anti-scientism of some of its adherents is, at the least, a matter for concern. More to the point: A complete psychology needs to look at both the negative and the positive, and the relations between them. As we have seen, for every positive there is a negative, and for every negative a positive. We need, therefore, what we might call a *'Realistic Psychology,'* that would be balanced and go beyond both negative psychology and positive psychology to provide the possibility of a complete model of man. What is needed is an 'all-round' approach in which nothing psychological is neglected, be it healthy or unhealthy, saintly or sinful, mindless or mindful.

If the nineteen sixties, with its heady feeling that "everything is possible," spawned positive psychology, then the start of the twenty first century, with its very different backdrop – one of global climate change, terrorism and financial meltdown – is prompting an entirely different outlook. This may be the appropriate moment for a realistic psychology to be born.

CHAPTER 13

A PYRAMID OF PARADOXES

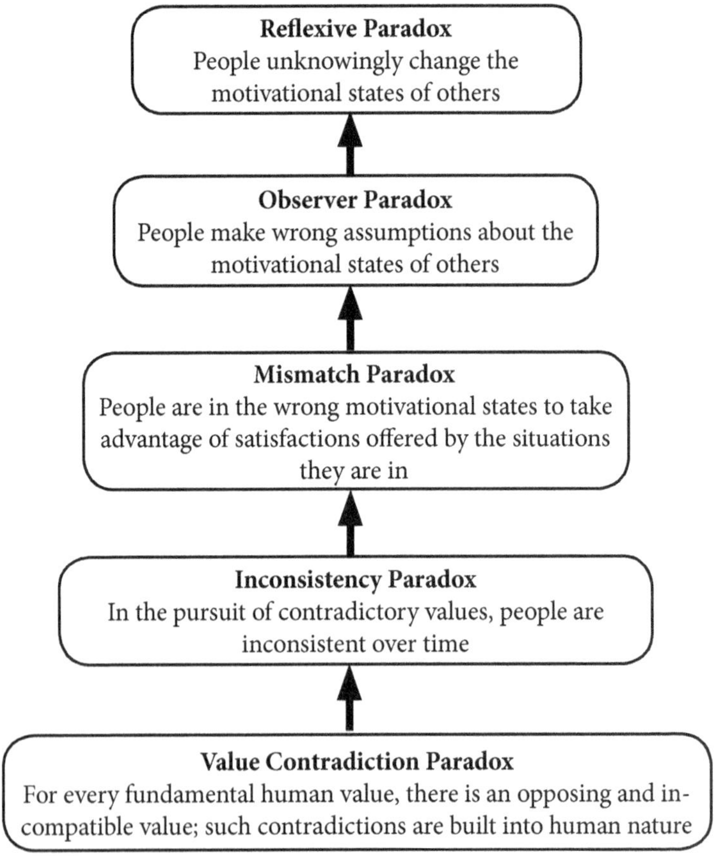

Reflexive Paradox
People unknowingly change the
motivational states of others

Observer Paradox
People make wrong assumptions about the
motivational states of others

Mismatch Paradox
People are in the wrong motivational states to take
advantage of satisfactions offered by the situations
they are in

Inconsistency Paradox
In the pursuit of contradictory values, people are
inconsistent over time

Value Contradiction Paradox
For every fundamental human value, there is an opposing and incompatible value; such contradictions are built into human nature

Figure 3

First a question: What do the following two contrasting human paradoxes – paradoxes that were discussed earlier in the book – have in common? The first is the panic response of people to the radio broadcast of the "War of the Worlds" by Orson Welles. You will recall that many listeners ran out into the streets in terror. The second paradox is the response of many participants in Milgram's obedience study, in which they were required to administer strong and even possibly lethal electric shocks to what they took to be other participants in the experiment.

At first glance these two paradoxes seem very different. In the first, the "War of the Worlds," the problem behaviour occurred because people felt threatened in the serious state. In the second, the Milgram study, the problem occurred in the conformist state because people did what they were told to do without question. The first involved reactions by groups of people as well as individuals, while in the second the focus was on individuals. The first involved a reaction that was, when the truth was found out, merely embarrassing, while the second raised serious moral issues and perhaps strong feelings of guilt in the participants. What they have in common is that they both involved a *mismatch* between peoples' motivational states and the circumstances they found themselves in, producing troubling outcomes. In reacting to the "War of the Worlds," listeners should have realised that they were listening to fiction and enjoyed it in the playful state. In Milgram's experiment, 'collaborators' should have recognised that they were being asked to do something profoundly immoral and reacted with whole-hearted defiance in the rebellious state. In either case, the paradox arose due to a mismatching between motivation and situation.

The paradoxes that I have explored in this book have come in various shapes and sizes. But now an interesting question confronts us: Are there patterns in the paradoxes we have seen? In particular: Can human paradoxes be classified into a set of distinct types, like the mismatching type that I have just identified? Such a typology would categorise the ways in which the paradoxes arise, irrespective of the particular motivational states involved. In fact, it is possible to do just this. Not only can we tease out a number of distinct types of human paradox – five to be exact – but we can also place them in hierarchical order. This provides some additional structure to my account of paradox. (You may find it useful to refer to figure 3 from time to time in reading this chapter.)

Before we discuss this, it might be helpful for me to pause a moment and remind you that by a 'human paradox' I mean some action that is counter-intuitive or perplexing from the perspective of common sense. In other words, a paradox of this kind is something that is difficult to understand in terms of reasonable assumptions, such as the assumption that people would rather be alive than dead, rich than poor, and happy than sad, or the assumption that more of something good makes it even better. This is a very loose definition of paradox, to be sure, because what makes intuitive sense depends on all kinds of different assumptions, including cultural assumptions, and there is no objective way of deciding which are reasonable and which are not. What might seem paradoxical in one culture might seem like common sense in another. Milgram's subjects might be applauded in some cultures, such as Nazi Germany, if not in ours. Voluntarily giving personal money to a political party does not seem odd in the U.S., but would certainly do so in the U.K. Also, what might seem paradoxical to one person might not seem paradoxical to another within the same culture. Having fun completing a tax return or balancing a cheque book, seems paradoxical for me, but not (thank God) for my wife Mitzi who attends to these matters. Shooting deer seems paradoxical to me – why would one want to destroy such beautiful creatures? – but obviously not to hunters. Watching cricket seems paradoxical to my American friends, but not to me, for whom it is as beautiful as ballet and as complex as chess.

Despite this relativity, some universal types of paradox *can* in fact be discerned. But it should be remembered throughout what follows that the analysis is about how people see things rather than how things 'really' are. Human paradox is in the eye of the beholder, and I am trying to make sense of how that eye works.

So let us start with the base of this "pyramid of paradoxes" that we are going to build.

VALUE-CONTRADICTION PARADOX

The basic human paradox, the paradox that supports everything else, is what I am going to call "value-contradiction" paradox. This refers to the awkward fact that for every fundamental human value, there is an opposite value. By a "fundamental value" here, I am referring to the values associated with the eight motivational states that I have referred to throughout this book: achievement, enjoyment, freedom, and the rest. (See Appendix One.) So each value is tied to its symmetrical opposite: achievement is tied to enjoyment, and so on.

If we make the usually unexamined assumption that all values are compatible and if we believe that, in principle, it should be possible to experience every kind of satisfaction at the same time, this idea of value contradiction will seem strange. Life is, unfortunately, more complicated and difficult to navigate than would be the case if there were no such contradictions – certainly more difficult than is supposed in many self-help systems. If we are clever, or lucky, or endowed with wisdom, or have read the right self-help books, we might indeed be able to experience all the kinds of satisfaction that life has to offer – but only over time and in turn. Value-contradiction tells us that there are limits to what is possible, since some values exclude others.

Value-contradiction implies what is known in philosophy as 'value pluralism.' This has it that there are multiple values that cannot be reduced one to another, each existing in its own rights and on its own terms. This is in contrast to what has been called 'value monism,' which argues for a single overriding value such as, to Christians, the value of love, or to Marxists the value of economic power. (1) In more recent times, a notable spokesman for value pluralism was the Oxford political philosopher and historian of ideas, Isaiah Berlin.

My arguments in this book share with Berlin three important points. The first is that value pluralism is *not* a form of relativism. It is *not* the case that "anything goes" and that values are constructed at will, being ever-changing in number and type as we move from culture to culture. Rather, while there may be multiple values, fundamental values are small in number and are fixed by human nature. Each culture may express and maintain values in an endless variety of ways: through clothes, food, religious customs, and so on. But the values themselves are not limitless. Thus one culture may reward military prowess with medals, another with mistresses (as in The Iliad); but the value being celebrated is in both cases that of mastery.

Secondly, these values are not just varied but come in opposites, so that they are unavoidably incompatible. Examples given by Berlin (2) are: justice versus mercy, liberty versus equality, and spontaneity versus planning. As Berlin points out, the members of a pair of such opposites cannot both be meaningfully sought after at the same time. Berlin never developed a theory, or classification system, and was mainly concerned with social values. But we can certainly see the three oppositions just listed as fitting into the reversal theory structure, each being a social/political expression of a personal human value. Thus justice is essentially a mastery state value and mercy a value of the sympathy state. In administering justice, the power of legal principle must hold sway in a detached and objective way, while in mercy the feeling of compassion trumps detached legal principles. Liberty is a rebellious state value, being based on the value of freedom, while equality is clearly a conformist state value – everybody must conform by being the same as everyone else, at least in certain important respects. Spontaneity, as we have discussed it, is a playful state value, and planning is a value of the serious state. (3)

Thirdly, there is no overriding external principle that would allow us to choose between competing values when they occur. Berlin refers to this as '*value incommensurability.*' Likewise in reversal theory, all the ultimate states have equal validity. Of course people often do evaluate values, but they do so typically by trying to reduce one value to another, or as it were, putting it in the service of another. Thus when in the serious state, one might admit that there is a value in being playful from time to time – but only because "this re-charges my batteries so that I have more energy to do important things." In this way the playful state is being made to support the serious state. To take another pair, helping others may be valuable, because later on, and in turn, these other people might help you on the basis that "one good turn deserves another." In this case, the value of serving others has been reduced to the value of making gains for yourself. The point about incommensurability is that there is no ultimate way in which we can justify reducing one motive to another. We cannot claim that one value is inherently more valuable than others: Each value ultimately exists in and for itself and must be judged in its own terms.

Inconsistency Paradox

An effect of value-contradiction is that as people attempt to produce more of one desirable quality, they risk decreasing another. So if a reversal occurs, the behaviour before the reversal may turn out to have been counterproductive. For example, if we attempt, in the mastery state, to dominate someone, and then we experience a reversal to sympathy, the preceding attempt at domination may make it more difficult to get close to that person afterwards: It may damage the chance of developing a more intimate relationship with him or her. Again, if we are critical of some group of people, it may make it difficult subsequently to fit in with them after we reverse from the rebellious to the conformist state.

From the fact of value opposition, emerges the need, if all values are to have a chance of being satisfied sooner or later, to alternate between the values in each pair – which implies inconsistency over time. In other words, the need to pursue different values leads beyond *value*-contradiction to *self*-contradiction. This takes us one step up the paradox hierarchy, from the existence of opposite values to their activation, over time, in real circumstances.

One of the central themes of this book has indeed been about this 'inconsistency paradox' – the puzzles that can arise when people reverse to and fro between motivational states. As we have seen, this means that people are, in effect, different kinds of people at different times pursuing different ends in different ways for different reasons. Their behaviour often does not make sense if we assume that each individual is characterised in all ways and at all times by the same static traits. This was illustrated in the opening chapter through the example of figures like John Rockefeller and Alfred Kinsey who presented dramatically different aspects of themselves on different occasions in their everyday lives. Such people play out their lives on a larger and more public stage than most of us do, with greater consequences for their actions. But I emphasised that such self-contradiction is true of most of us, albeit in less momentous forms. We all show contrasting sides of ourselves to the world under different circumstances. Dare I say that we are all, in a non-clinical sense, multiple personalities (4)?

When people do not understand this, then problems can arise. Here is a striking example. Australian footballers are seen by their fans as hard men: belligerent, tough, looking you in the eye, and looking for a fight. Indeed, on the pitch they do need these kinds of characteristics while they are playing. But fans assume that they must be like this all the time. This means that it is difficult for footballers to go for a quiet drink, because wherever they go they are confronted by fans looking for trouble who assume that the footballer must have the same desire. The footballers are trapped by what are taken by others to be their enduring traits. In the words of one footballer: "Because I am perceived and stereotyped as being aggressive, when I go out at night, people want to challenge you, they want to do what I do on the ground, except they're in a pub." (5)

CONSISTENCY – YET AGAIN

At different points in this book I have contrasted the reversal theory approach with that of trait psychology. I have done this by indicating that although there are no doubt certain kinds of consistency in personality, the trait approach oversimplifies, and risks missing some essential features, especially those that relate to change. It sees people as being like statues rather than dancers. The general point is so central to this book that I will, without apology, revisit it again here.

The basic problem with the trait approach is that it *'chronotypes.'* By this I mean that it overgeneralises across time, by assuming that what is true of a person at one time will also be true of that same person at all other times. It attempts to see states as traits. Unfortunately for trait theory, because a person is observed to be, let us say, agreeable on one occasion, this does not necessarily mean that they will be agreeable when encountered on another occasion. Nor does it imply that they can be categorised once-and-for-all by means of a personality test as "an agreeble person," or pinned at a particular point on an agreeable-to-disagreeable dimension, like an insect on a specimen tray. Such chronotyping is like 'stereotyping,' except that instead of overgeneralising from one piece of information about a person (e.g. that they are female, or Muslim), people overgeneralise from what they observe of a person at one moment to what they expect of that person at another moment. Breaking free from this consistency assumption helps us to understand more complicated and paradoxical behaviour than would otherwise have been possible. It catches in this way something of the spice of life, something of what makes us fully human, alive and restless, and wonderfully difficult to predict. It is exactly what is missed by trait tests.

What is worse, as I noted earlier in the book, is that personality tests, by telling people "this is how you are," tend to discourage change and encourage a kind of helplessness. Such trait-based tests limit rather than liberate. Yet here is the really strange thing: they are used by counsellors, therapists and coaches precisely to help people to change. Imagine that you are depressed and you take a test that tells you that you have a depressive type of personality. Will this encourage you to change? On the contrary it will validate your depression and make your case seem even more hopeless. If you commit a crime and a personality test tells you that you have an antisocial personality disorder, will this help? No, it will provide you with a perfect excuse not to become law-abiding. If you are lonely and have difficulty relating to others, will learning from a personality test that you are unsociable help in any way at all? No, it will rather condemn you. It will allow you to tell yourself that "this is, after all, how I am. I am only being myself."

So why do we want to chronotype ourselves? I am always amazed that in self-development workshops the first question that people have seems to be: "What type am I?" And this is encouraged by personality questionnaires such as the Myers-Briggs Personality Inventory which supplies clients in workshops with just such 'typing' – to their apparent enormous satisfaction. An obvious reason for this satisfaction is that it gives people a kind of handle on things, helping them to make sense of, and seemingly escape from, their own complications. But as noted before, there may be a deeper and more serious reason. This is the belief that we have a permanent soul – and in this sense a permanent personality – that survives death. In this respect, self-chronotyping fits in nicely with the beliefs of Christianity and other world religions. Putting it bluntly, if we did not have permanent personality characteristics, what would it mean to survive? How could there be salvation? How could we even be judged by God? From this perspective there is nothing surprising in people wanting to know who they are. There is, though, at least one major religion that takes a different view, and that is Buddhism, with the view that life is constantly flowing and changing and that there is no real self at all. (6) In this respect, reversal theory comes close to Buddhism.

Mismatch Paradox

Mismatch paradox is the kind of paradox with which I opened this chapter, and it lifts us one further level up the pyramid.

Mismatch paradox comes about when people are in the wrong motivational states to take advantage of the situations in which they find themselves – or indeed to avoid problems in those situations. This means that things go awry, and that their actions are unhelpful and may even be counterproductive. It is like trying to eat a steak with a spoon. Why do people conform to orders that will clearly lead them or others to self-destruction, as happened in the "Charge of the Light Brigade?" Why do people identify with those who put them criminally at risk, as occurred in the Stockholm syndrome? Why does anyone not wear a safety belt, even though it significantly reduces their chances of getting killed or badly maimed should they have a crash? The answer in each case is that people are in the wrong state for the situation that they find themselves in: the commanders of the Light Brigade were in the conforming state at the critical moment of the Battle of Balaclava; the hostages in the bank in Stockholm came to be in the sympathy state; many of those reporting driving without seatbelt protection did so in the playful state, feeling that they could not possibly come to harm: they did not need the safety frame of a safety belt, but experienced instead the fallacious frame of their own beliefs.

These are no doubt extreme examples, but once we become aware of mismatch paradox we start noticing it in our daily lives. In my own case I am aware that when I go to a dinner party with people who I do not know, I am in a serious state of mind. I suppose that I feel threatened. I eventually reverse, but I do not especially enjoy things early in the visit until a reversal into the playful state of mind has occurred. (I am taking the risk that this confession will cut down the invitations I receive.) When I am involved in rituals, like church services, I usually find myself in a horribly rebellious state of mind feeling critical over everything that is being said and done, and uncomfortable that I cannot do anything to oppose its smug certainty, not to mention its self-righteousness. When I am shopping to buy a present I sometimes find myself being distracted by things that I want for myself, and have difficulty in staying other-oriented. I will guess that you can find similar mismatches in your own life. A positive feature of email and other social media is that they give us the opportunity to lay particular messages aside until we are in the right state of mind to respond to them appropriately. For instance, when friends are kind enough to send on to me interesting or amusing things that they have come across, they often arrive on my computer when I happen to be engaged in something that I consider to be serious. Email, unlike the phone, allows me to avoid mismatch and to read what they have sent, and to reply, when I am in a playful mood.

Here's another, this time rather quirky, but personal anecdotal example of mismatch. I arrived at my hotel in Paris the evening before a conference. I was in a serious state of mind because I needed to work on my paper. When I entered my room it was with some dismay: the walls were completely covered with a bright abstract expressionist design consisting of huge jagged swathes of vivid colours. Even the ceiling was covered. It was overwhelming. I was told that no other rooms were available (and that in any case every room had its own artistic style). So I settled down as best as I could to work on my presentation. Eventually it occurred to me to turn off the main lights and work by the light of my laptop screen. As soon as I did so I realised that this would make matters even worse: the painting was phosphorescent! When I got to the conference the next day, rather bleary-eyed, I complained to the organiser who had booked the hotel for me. He looked puzzled. "It's a great hotel," he said "I always take my mistresses there." I have to admit that I could see how this could make sense, but only if you were in his playful state of mind rather than my serious state.

OBSERVER PARADOX

"In supervision you sit down in a boring old chair and talk about how we're getting on and things." (7) This laconic phrase captures beautifully a rather different way in which paradox can arise. This is if one person misjudges the motivational state of the person being interacted with, then the latter's behaviour can seem paradoxical. In the case in question a young delinquent is referring to his regular interviews with a social worker, and clearly he does not find these very captivating. The reason is that the interviewer has not recognised that this youthful offender is in the playful state but simply assumes that he is in the same serious state as himself – and therefore looking for ways to plan his future and stay out of trouble. For the delinquent, the problem is not in planning a future career, or changing his ways, but dealing with all these boring social workers, probation officers, and psychologists who are giving him grief right now. For him, what got him into trouble was doing something that was challenging and fun, such as getting into street fights or drawing graffiti. This did not seem to him to be a problem, or something in need of treatment. Rather, it is what made life interesting and worth living in the first place. Why do these people want an explanation for something that is normal and obvious? The youngster's responses seem paradoxical to the interviewer, who assumes that people want to stay out of trouble, and the interviewer's questions seem paradoxical to the youngsters who assume that people want to have fun. There is a mutual lack of understanding from the observations that each makes of the other.

We all easily make wrong assumptions about the motivational states of others, so that their behaviour seems odd and even irrational. This is why I talked about multi-rationality in the chapter on Economics, and this idea relates widely to observer paradox. The self-sacrifice and false confession of those accused in Stalin's purges make no sense if we assume that the confessions were made in the self-oriented state. But they do make sense if we assume that the accused were in the other-oriented and serious states. No doubt anti-pornography campaigners see pornography as paradoxical. Why do people enjoy what is both sinful and disgusting? But they fail to understand, being in the conformist state, that in the rebellious state, it is exactly this which can be so exciting and liberating for some people. In a similar vein, people engaging in sadomasochism (as we saw in an earlier chapter) are generally consenting and playful. But this is often misunderstood by the law, so that their behaviour is automatically treated in the courtroom as serious assault, in which case it is certainly viewed as both culpable and paradoxical – the deliberate causing and enjoyment of pain and humiliation. (8) In all these cases, behaviour that seems irrational, and paradoxical, makes more sense when we know the real motivational starting point.

Again, we have moved one step up the hierarchy of human paradox. Now we see the motivational state plus environmental context within a further context, which is that of the outside observer. The paradox is only possible because one can never tell with certainty, from their behaviour, what motivational state another person is in. This means that there is always the possibility of error and observer paradox. (9)

There is a sad little story by the French nineteenth century poet Baudelaire that beautifully illustrates the miscomprehension that can arise between people in different motivational states. He is sitting in a Parisian sidewalk café with his lover. They have had a beautiful day together, it is evening, and the café is lit up and sparkling. At the edge of the café, on the sidewalk, he notices a destitute man holding hands with two ragamuffin children. They are staring at the café in wonderment, with large eyes, enchanted by what they are seeing, and knowing that it is a world that they will never enter. He feels pity, and shame that he can afford what they cannot, and at the same time he is enchanted by them. He looks at his beloved and sees her eyes soften as she looks at them too. Then she speaks. "What an irritation!" she says "Can you get the waiter to move them on?" Between the sympathy and the mastery states, there can indeed be a chasm of misunderstanding. (10)

As we saw in an earlier chapter, a widespread type of observer paradox arises from paradoxical emotions. We often do not realise that the emotions that other people experience in the playful state are pleasant, because the emotions typically have names that imply that they are unpleasant – like 'anger' and 'grief.' Since people use these negative words in describing their fun experiences, we fail to notice that the experiences are in fact playful and we are left with the enigma of people apparently setting out to have bad feelings – as when they go to the theatre to see a tragedy or to the cinema to see a horror movie, visit a graveyard as tourists, or drive slowly past a car wreck, eager to see the damage.

In some situations, the content of what is being experienced may remain the same from one time to the next, but the perspective shifts decisively. It is when the latter kind of change occurs in someone being observed, but does so unrecognised by the observer, that we have a frequent kind of observer paradox. The teenager is driving too fast, and assumes, as he observes them, that his friends in the car are enjoying the thrill as much as he is. But his friends are not in control, and having lost their protective frame are terrified. The driver thinks that they are just kidding and drives even faster. When he finally stops he is mystified that his friends are so angry. (Confession time: this is what I did once when I was a teenage driver, speeding, at night through unlit and desolate dockland, dodging cranes and containers. There was no danger from other traffic, but any error could have resulted in the car, with my friends in it, leaping into the black water.)

REFLEXIVE PARADOX

Reflexive paradox is an extension of observer paradox. In this case, in attempting to influence others, we unintentionally, and unknowingly, induce a reversal of motivational state. The effect is that their behaviour is puzzling to us because we did not realise that this is what we had done. As a result, our attempt to influence their subsequent behaviour backfires. It is like resting a writing pad against an open door in order to write a message saying "Do not close this door" – and the pressure of the writing against the door closes it. In such situations our actions reflect back on our intentions. For example, laws that prohibit something, like drugs or pornography, seem often to induce the rebellious state in many people and make such actions doubly attractive.

We are unavoidably reminded here of a basic methodological problem in science, which is that when something is measured, the act of measurement can itself change what is being measured. For instance, the temperature of a thermometer can itself change the temperature of any liquid into which it is placed, either heating it a little or cooling it a little, depending on the comparative temperature of the thermometer and the liquid. As is well known, Quantum mechanics has demonstrated a more profound version of such measurement effects, in which certain quantum properties do not exist until they are actually measured. "Schroedinger's Cat" is a widely used metaphor of the paradox of quantum mechanics: the cat in the box is neither alive nor dead until the box is opened to find out which. (11) Illustrating another kind of reflexivity, George Soros, the multimillionaire financier, has used the concept in his interpretation of what happens in economic systems. A very simple example would be that when you buy shares in a company, by that very act you change the company that you are buying shares in, and change the values of those shares, to however small a degree.(12)

In the reflexive type of human paradox we see something similar, but at the psychological rather than the physical or economic level. What one is doing has an effect beyond what one supposed it would, and an unexpected effect. The police intervening to control soccer hooligans turn the situation into a serious one, with the effect that what was a fun brawl between opposing supporters who are just trying to 'have a good time,' becomes a serious fight with the police. (13) An example, from earlier in the book, is that when we reward children who are enjoying themselves in the classroom, we are surprised when they perform with less enthusiasm than they did before. Their reaction does not make sense to us if we adopt what seems like a reasonable assumption, namely that adding a reward will increase motivation and thereby improve performance. Unfortunately, we have not realised that a reward can also, simultaneously, move people from the playful into the serious state. Thus we have produced a reflexive paradox. Likewise, and for similar reasons, we do not understand that when rewarding others for unselfish behaviour we inadvertently risk bringing about a reversal into the self-oriented state, because they now become focused on the reward for themselves rather than the benefits of their actions for others.

To return to the police and football hooligans, their intervention reframes a playful situation as a serious one, and so makes matters worse for everyone concerned. If we look at the "War of the Worlds" paradox from the point of view of the broadcasters rather than the audience, we see reflexive paradox – in trying to stimulate people they inadvertently brought about a reversal into the serious state. Here is another example from earlier in the book: Discouraging geriatric residential home staff from emotional engagement in the problems of the elderly who are in their special care, removes also the satisfactions that make the job worthwhile. In all such ways, the so-called "Law of Unintended Consequence" comes into effect. In these cases of reflexive paradox we do not just change the situation, we also reframe it for those we are observing, with unexpected results.

We can even reframe things for ourselves. I was recently diagnosed as suffering from sleep apnoea, a condition in which one momentarily stops breathing from time to time during the night. The treatment of choice is a machine that blows air through your mouth and nose all night long, ensuring in this way that your respiration continues and that you therefore get a good night's sleep. To use it, you have to strap on a mask. Unfortunately, this reminds me of the gas mask I had to wear as a child during the bombing blitzes on Bristol, my hometown, during the Second World War. I associate the gas mask with the hum of the bombers getting louder, and with the explosions getting nearer – something that no one who has experienced it will ever forget. What somehow made it worse was that the gas mask, a special one for children, was in the form of a frighteningly bizarre Mickey Mouse mask, painted in vivid colours and with big ears stuck on. When I enter my head into the mask I need for sleeping, this therefore induces the serious state and makes me feel anxious. Being anxious I cannot sleep, and so the very device designed to help me to sleep, no doubt experienced by most users as a protective frame, takes away my own protective frame and actually prevents me from sleeping. This is not a criticism of the machine, which helps many people, but of the way that my particular circumstance causes me to see it in a particular way so that it is difficult for me to take advantage of it.

A Hierarchy of Paradox

As we have seen, these paradoxes are hierarchical: Value opposition, the base paradox, leads to inconsistency paradox, when movement occurs between the pursuit of opposites. Inconsistency paradox leads to mismatch paradox when the movement between opposites is inappropriate. Mismatch paradox leads to observer paradox when the observer is misled about which states are in fact active. And observer paradox leads to reflexive paradox when the observer unwittingly induces unrecognised alternations. Each one depends on the one 'below' it. Each 'supports' the one above it. So each higher paradox simultaneously exemplifies lower order paradoxes as well. This is represented visually in Figure 3 as a pyramid.

As we move up the hierarchy, so the paradoxes become less innate and more avoidable. At the lowest level, value-opposition is built into the very way that people are made – into, as it were, the logic of existence. Together with the self-inconsistency paradox these two levels are intrinsic to human nature. Moving on, we can see that the higher level paradoxes that emerge from them, do so in the course of interactions between people, and between people and the world they find themselves in. They are therefore more conditional and negotiable. If the first two paradoxes are innate, the other three are emergent.

Much of this chapter has been negative in tone, focusing on certain kinds of mistakes that anyone can make. In the next chapter we shall remind ourselves that for every negative there is a positive – if only we can get to it.

CHAPTER 14

THE BENEFITS OF CONTRARY DESIRES

At first sight it appears to make little sense that we have motivational oppositions built into us, and as many as four of them. Would you or I design a human being in this way? Would we put contradiction at the heart of things? And would we do this given that certain kinds of paradoxes can arise as a result? It is possible to fantasise a celestial investigative committee angrily demanding an explanation from the team that designed human beings, pointing out that some deep-seated faults seem to have been revealed, and threatening a species recall.

I have to admit that by taking paradox as a central theme in this book I have tended to emphasise the *problems* that arise from the existence of contrary desires. So let us now look more at the *positive* side of things, and see how reference to these positives might help us to defend ourselves against the committee that has been sent down to investigate.

MOTIVATIONAL MULTIPLICITY

The first positive point is that each individual motivational state makes a necessary contribution to healthy living: all states are needed sooner or later and for different purposes. Let's run quickly through the individual states, reminding ourselves of some of the special advantages that each of them can confer. In seeing these states as distinctive tools for living, we have something like a Swiss Army Knife model of human personality.(1) Let's see when you might want to use each blade.

- If you want a long-term orientation which helps you to keep your eyes on the important goals, avoid distractions, and delay gratification – get into *the serious state.*
- If you want to to have fun, explore, experiment, and be creative – and also to learn survival skills safely by practicing in situations which do not in fact threaten your survival – get into *the playful state.*
- If you want to adapt, and to fit into your group, thus playing a part in developing team work and group cohesiveness, through rules, roles and rituals – get into *the conforming state.*
- If you want to jump start change which will help you, and your group, to recognise and meet new circumstances or to change the circumstances proactively – get into *the rebellious state.*
- If you want to develop new skills, confront danger courageously, and face difficulties and challenges with determination – get into *the mastery state.*
- If you want to develop close and enduring relationships, especially with family members but also with a wider community – get into *the sympathy state.*

- If you want to be self-reliant, and to discover, develop, and make full use of your personal capabilities – get into *the self-oriented state*.
- I you want to help others, especially in practical ways, and contribute to the needs of your community as a whole – get into *the other-oriented state*.

The availability of each of these states is essential if you are to have a chance of living a fulfilled and effective life, both at home and at work. This being so, you might want to cast your eyes over them again and see if you can spot any states that you should cultivate more. What are you missing? What should you make more use of? Which blade remains obstinately stuck in its slot? Note that if you experience each of the states in the positive way described here, then any reversal will involve what I have in an earlier chapter (chapter 2) referred to as a virtuous contradiction: both of the opposites will be beneficial in their own way.

There is a general principle at work here, a principle that operates in all systems, not just biological ones, but also mechanical, sociological, cultural and economic systems. This principle is what we might call the "utility of versatility." In Systems Theory (2) it goes by the more technical term "The Law of Requisite Variety". (3) What this means is that the more varied the responses a system can make towards its environment, and the more different 'ways of being' it can bring to bear, then the stronger its chances of being able to adapt to changes in that environment – and as a result to survive and thrive. In fact, according to this law, in order to be able to survive under all likely conditions, a system (e.g. an organism, an organisation, a piece of equipment) must have at least as much diversity as the environment in which it operates.

To take an obvious example, if an ecological system is to survive a catastrophe, in the sense that at least some species will remain alive after the disastrous changes have occurred, then it must be made up of a sufficient range of different and contrasting species that can react in different ways to the crisis and its aftermath. The greater the diversity of these species, the greater the chance that some will survive, and start rebuilding. This diversity is referred to in biology as *biodiversity*. If the 'system' is a human being, then in order to adapt to a variety of conditions, that person must be able to display what we might call, by analogy with biodiversity, *psychodiversity*. (4) What having eight different motivational states does is to provide plenty of psychodiversity – different ways of engaging psychologically with the environment.

MOTIVATIONAL RICHNESS

We can go beyond thinking of these states in terms of utility and survival. The fact that there is a multiplicity of motivational states, provides people with the chance to lead richer and more fulfilling lives than they otherwise would have done. In a sense people have eights lives instead of one. To live in a worthwhile way, in these terms, means to live fully, experiencing the satisfaction of all the values: achievement, fun, love, power and the rest. To achieve this, one may have to become aware of what one is missing, of the motivational states that appear only rarely in one's life, so that one can direct oneself to experiencing them more often.

From this perspective the tendency in self-help books to concentrate on only one or two values is unfortunate. This is because it oversimplifies both problems and solutions, and may actually open up gaps in peoples' lives and thus diminish them as people, as well as making them less adaptable to change. Thus a huge best-seller like "The Purpose-Driven Life" by Rick Warren (5) is all about the meaning of life, and about life's ultimate purpose for each person, casting all this in terms of Christian evangelism. All well and good, but this book concentrates wholly on the serious state, and looks at life through this single lens. In contrast, self-help books based on Gestalt psychology, emphasise the joys of the moment, and living in the here-and-now. (6) Both of these approaches reduce life to a paltry single value, in one case serious and in the other playful. Likewise, best-selling books by Anthony Robbins emphasise the mastery state, with words like 'power', 'control' and 'mastery' popping up all over the place. (7) But in contrast, other best-sellers focus on sympathy rather than mastery. (8) An extreme example of limitation to a single value is the writing of Ayn Rand (9) who regarded the only worthwhile state as being the self-orientated state. Rand's so-called 'objectivist' view, which extols selfishness, remains popular among many (I wonder why) and led her to become a hugely successful writer.

The point I am getting at here is that there are many worthy and best-selling self-help texts out there, but each tends to be limited by being based on no more than one or two of the full set of eight motivational states and values discussed in this book. Because of this, these books risk doing people a disservice by limiting their possibilities for gaining richness of experience in their lives, and for 'all-round' self-development. A well-lived life is a life of variety. Psychodiversity therefore relates to inner richness as much as to outer effectiveness. The best thing that was ever said to me after a workshop was: "My life is full of possibilities again." (10)

CHANGE ABILITY

But why *opposition*? What is the advantage that comes from motivational states not just floating around randomly like leaves in a pond, but being tied to each other in a firm grid of oppositionality?

One answer is that the availability of opposing states means that there are always completely different approaches to any given problem, so that if one approach does not work out, there is always a contrasting one to try, providing a totally different perspective. An excellent example of this, described earlier in the book, was Ashley Smith's use of the sympathy state, where most of us would have been entrenched in the mastery state, to pacify a murderer on the run. As Hamlet might have said: "There is nothing either good or bad but motivation makes it so. (11)

Another real life example comes from the director of a luxury hotel in the Antilles who was expecting a visit for three days by a group of fifteen South American travel agents looking to do important business with her and with other hoteliers with whom she was working in the same region. (12) She approached their visit with trepidation and planned out all the activities in great detail ahead of time: She did not want anything to go wrong. And indeed everything more or less worked out except that relations seemed rather stiff and formal, and none of the agents got round to mentioning a possible contract. By the final evening of their stay, she felt that things were slipping away. In despair, over dinner she drank more than she should have done, and reversed from serious to playful mode. Indeed, everyone was now in a party mood, and after the meal the agents invited her to a nightclub – which was not on the official program. Suffice it to say that they all had a great time and began to relate to each other at a more personal level. The next morning, a major contract was signed and others promised. Where the serious and mastery approaches had failed, sympathy and playfulness solved the problem.

This use of reversal between opposites is always available

to provide a radically different option when faced with frustrations and difficulties. Suppose that you are on bad terms with someone, try relating to them through the other-oriented rather than the self-oriented state – try to understand the problem as *they* see it. Suppose that you cannot solve a problem using the approach that everyone else uses. Reverse to the rebellious state and critically examine the assumptions that everyone is making and that might be getting in the way of a solution. My daughter Carolyn (aged five at the time) solved the problem of not wanting to wear socks when told that she had to (by me), by tying them around her ankles in a knot

Suppose that you are apprehensive and stressed, working on a big project to a deadline. In this case try to reverse to the playful state so that you will be able to treat the situation as a challenge rather than a threat and so experience excitement rather than anxiety. (Teenagers often seem to understand this better than adults, doing their homework to a background of pop music or television, and in this way maintaining the playful state.) The best athletes also know that, to avoid choking at key moments in a game, they have to concentrate on enjoying the moment. (13) Reversal theory encourages the idea that, whatever the difficulty, there is always something that can be done, including reversing between states or changing the focus among active states. (14)

Relevant to this reversal tactic is the fact that within each motivational state, only emotions related to that state can be experienced, some good and some bad. So if the problem is bound up with a particular emotion, it may be possible to deal with the emotion by changing states. Thus by reversing from the serious to the playful state it may be possible to avoid anxiety, and by switching to the serious state from the playful state it may be possible to avoid boredom. A strong way of putting this is to say that the serious state cannot experience boredom and the playful state cannot experience anxiety. (15)

The implication is obvious. If you want to avoid anxiety, get into the playful state. If you want to avoid boredom, get into the serious state. As a general rule, if you want to avoid being attacked by a shark, get out of the water.

COMPLEMENTARITY

There is another important advantage of opposition between motivational states, and this, strange as it might seem, is the mutual support over time that becomes possible between the conflicting states that make up each pair. What this means is that not only can one increase one's chances of solving a problem by moving between states, but each state can, when active, positively support the needs of the other, and in this way provide a stronger system overall than if there were no paired states. The motivational twins that make up each pair can support as well as undermine each other. Here we perhaps come closest to the answer to the question asked at the start of this chapter: Why do we have contradictory desires in the first place? The answer that I am proposing here is that they can, over time, be complementary and help each other to fulfill their respective functions. This would be a special kind of virtuous contradiction. Let's see how this plays out in each pair. For the sake of simplicity in what follows, I will refer to each state as if it were a person.

Starting with the serious and playful states: Without the serious state to arrange things, the playful state would have little or no time or place to play. It is probably the serious state that organises the vacation, buys the tickets to the theatre, reserves the tennis court, fixes up a babysitter, and makes enough money to support all of this and pay the taxes too. On the other hand, without periods of playful recreation, the serious state would probably not have the energy or concentration to undertake any of these chores, or pursue with sufficient effort any of the important goals of a successful career. In this way each state is positioned, when active, to help its dormant partner.

The conforming and rebellious states help each other primarily with respect to change. Whenever it is necessary to transition to new rules and expectations in life – something the conforming state is keen to avoid – the rebellious state can provide the push from behind that is necessary to make the leap. Moving to a new school, changing careers, relocating, being promoted, or starting a new relationship – all such changes in life provide upset and discomfort to the conformist state, but may be welcomed, celebrated, and felt as a form of release by the rebellious state. On the other hand, the conforming state is needed by the rebellious state to reorder life after change has occurred, and help adaptation to the new situation. After all, we need stability as well as instability. We need brakes as well as accelerators. In this way, again, each state requires the other.

The sympathy and mastery states similarly rely on each other in turn. The sympathy state needs the mastery state to provide the backbone to make things work. In particular, in bringing up children it is necessary to have some degree of discipline, however much one loves one's children and would want them to be happy all the time. Children seem to need structure and to need limits, and will fight until they get them. Another example: competing against friends in the mastery state is an excellent way of developing friendships. Eighteen holes of mastery are followed by sympathy at the "nineteenth hole" (the club bar). In such ways mastery acts in the service of sympathy. Conversely, the mastery state may itself work better if one is on genuinely good personal terms with others. Promotion may be more likely if one is well liked by the boss! Likewise, effective social networking can help a career enormously. In such cases, the sympathy state can be seen to work in the service of mastery.

Finally, the self-oriented state needs the other-oriented state to help to achieve things that are difficult or impossible on one's own. Working with others towards a common cause can eventually lead to satisfaction for oneself as well as everyone else. There is a sense in which, in the end, everything is about self-satisfaction. But sometimes self-satisfaction arrives only through making a detour through the genuine satisfaction of other people, which is what I mean by 'other-oriented.' On the other hand, one can contribute to the success of others (in the other-oriented state) by taking personal responsibility for things (in the self-oriented state). For instance, being an effective leader can be personally fulfilling while also helping to improve the performance of followers. In these ways the self-oriented state can help and support the other-oriented state – and vice-versa. They are unavoidably intertwined.

The point in each of these cases is not just that a person often needs both members of a pair to get some kind of enduring satisfaction, but that the two states in a pair are intrinsically related, and play off each other in a kind of dance in which each in turn supports the other. In this respect it is possible to have what in an earlier chapter, in connection with Florence Nightingale, I called 'virtuous contradiction.' In her case she used both mastery and sympathy states in pursuit of the improvement of hospital conditions. As William Blake the British poet and painter said in a well-known aphorism: "Without contraries is no progression." (16)

HOLDING EACH OTHER IN CHECK

There is also a more subtle connection between motivational states. This is that when a given state is active, the opposite state may have a kind of watching brief, in case the active state goes too far. It may leave the stage, but stand in the wings, sending in prompts and warnings, and holding itself ready to return onstage at a moment's notice. The function of the opposite state here is not so much enablement as limitation. For instance, the serious state may check that the playful state is not going too far with the risks that it takes, and be ready to jump in to rescue the situation if things threaten to get out of hand – if one is gambling more than one can afford to lose, say, or making a drunken fool of oneself in public. The self-oriented state may watch over the other-oriented state to ensure that it is not being taken for a sucker or being walked all over. The sympathy state may make sure that the mastery state is not bullying and humiliating others. (17) The conforming state may make sure that the rebellious state is not throwing valuable things away, or smashing them, through momentary pique.

There may also be precommitment – a kind of 'time binding' in which an ongoing state so sets things up that the opposite state cannot go too far or fast when it climbs into the driver's seat. (18) The word 'binding' in 'time binding' reminds us that in Homer's epic "The Odyssey," Odysseus had himself literally bound to the mast of his ship as it passed the island where the Sirens sang. His aim was to prevent himself being seduced by their voices, jumping overboard to be with them, and drowning. Here, in the serious state, he made arrangements so that he would not do something foolish in the playful state – even ordering his men that they should not respond, when the time came, to his desperate entreaties to be set free.

Victor Hugo, the French author of such classic novels as "the Hunchback of Notre Dame," reported that he would give his clothes to his valet every morning, with the strict instruction not to return them to him, under any circumstances, until he had done his writing for the day. This instruction meant that he was naked and could not go out anywhere and have fun until his serious writing was done. (It seems that Hugo did not have too many clothes.)

In such ways a state may have a limiting influence beyond the time that it is itself in operation. The serious state locks away the alcohol and tobacco for fear that the playful state will overindulge, or drink before driving. (19) The other-oriented state makes public philanthropic commitments that cannot later be renounced when the self-oriented state is in fact being just that: self-oriented. The mastery state engages in long-term challenges and confrontations that cannot easily be avoided in the sympathy state: taking on a leadership role, entering a sporting competition, making boastful claims, starting a feud. In such ways one state may play a part in guiding, to some extent, the behaviour of the other state over time. And this can occur in either direction in any given pair. For instance, not only can the serious state curtail problematic playful state activities, the playful state can ensure that the serious state does not overdo things and become ill through overwork. In this and other ways, the members of a pair are more closely entangled than it might seem at first sight. They hold each other up like two drunks leaning on each other or, to give a more uplifting metaphor, like the opposite halves of a gothic arch holding each other in place.

MOTIVATIONAL INTELLIGENCE

The ability to understand and control your motivational states, and those of others, should provide you with enormous advantages in life. I suggest that, by analogy with 'emotional intelligence,'(20) we call this ability *'motivational intelligence.'* Since motives underlie emotions, we can see motivational intelligence as a more fundamental kind of intelligence.

There are many metaphors that one can use here beyond the Swiss Army Knife analogy I used earlier. One that I find particularly helpful in workshops is the analogy to golf. If we think of life as like a round of golf, then to play well, to display motivational intelligence, you need a number of things. The first is to make use of the complete set of clubs. If you think of a motivational state as being like a golf club, then you can ask: "What is missing from my game – which club or clubs do I only rarely use." Do you tend to live too much in the present, for example, and not make plans for the future? In this case, your serious "club" could be underused or even lost. Do you spend all your time worrying about the future and never stop to smell the roses? You are in danger of "death by projects." In this instance, it will be your playful club that will be missing. Do you spend all your time looking after someone else – children, an aged parent? If so, give yourself permission to spend time for yourself, and with yourself. Whatever club is underused needs to be taken out of the bag, polished up, and put into action as soon as possible. This is a way of saying that the psychologically healthy person displays a certain kind of instability – that he or she is not stuck with a small number of clubs, but can continually change clubs from the complete set.

The second thing that you need to be able to do is to choose the right club for the right situation. Should you tee off on a particular hole with a driver or a long-iron, for example? This is like knowing which state is appropriate for a particular situation: Is this the right moment for commiserating with a friend, asking the boss for a pay rise, driving in heavy traffic? If you are in the self-oriented state when your friend needs sympathy from you, neither of you are likely to be grateful to the other. If you ask for a pay rise in a rebellious state of mind the outcome may not be what you expected. If you drive in the serious state of mind in rush hour, you may feel anxious and frustrated, but get home no sooner than if you were in the playful state of mind enjoying listening to your favourite music on the car radio.

Now we come to the third general level of motivational intelligence. If you have the right club for the right hole, can you actually hit the ball accurately? Do you have the life skills and social competencies to navigate the situation that you find yourself in, and achieve the satisfactions that you are looking for? Are you good at making plans in the serious state, have you developed enthralling interests that can take your attention in the playful state, are you good at negotiating in the mastery state, and so on. Most self-help books seem to operate at this third level alone.

Going beyond the golf analogy, which will not appeal to everyone, you also need to be able to recognise paradoxes when they occur, whether your own or those of others, and to understand what is happening so that you can deal with it. If something you do has the opposite effect on friends to that which you would expect, then look to see if you are giving clear cues so that they know what you are up to. Likewise, see if your understanding of their motivational states is accurate. If someone does something odd, see if you can understand it by looking at it in the light of what you have learned here. In any case, do not assume that they are in the same state that you are in – in other words, at least avoid this kind of elementary observer paradox. Remember, you are never dealing with a person: You are always dealing with a person who is in a certain state of mind.

We can think of playing the 'game of life' well as being successful in all of these ways. In summary, you need to be able to experience all eight states in a reasonably balanced and frequent way, to match each situation that you meet with the appropriate motivational state, and to behave with the skill that allows you to achieve the satisfactions that are available at that time. This may also involve understanding which states other people are inhabiting when you interact with them. These are some of the key skills that go to make up motivational intelligence.

POLAR OPPOSITES IN POLAR EXPLORATION

When someone takes on a large-scale project that requires enormous effort over an extended period of time, and that relies on the ability to remain undaunted in the face of endless challenges, we typically see that every one of the eight motivational states has to be called to action sooner or later for there to be any chance of success.

An admirable example of this is the trek that the British explorer Pen Hadow made from Canada to the North Pole in 2003 and described in his book "Solo." (21) I was fortunate to be able, with a colleague, to interview Pen at his cottage on Dartmoor on his return to England and talk him step by step through the ordeal in order to find out what had sustained him. (22) His trek was one that had never been accomplished before, although many had tried. What he aimed to do was to ski and swim solo, with no aid of any kind, and without resupply by aircraft, 478 miles across the Arctic Ocean to the North Pole. This meant facing, alone, high winds, extremely low temperatures, blinding light, icebergs, glaciers and ridges of banked sea ice. In the event he accomplished it. It took him sixty four days, followed by another nine days when he was trapped at the Pole in such atrocious weather that he could not be rescued by plane. With his supplies dwindling to zero, he was air-lifted out just in time.

The initial motivation for the project could not have been more serious: a solemn vow that he made to his father, when paying his respects to him on his death bed, that he would succeed. (23) This promise became a kind of motivational hub for everything else. It was also a conforming state commitment because of its essentially dutiful nature. The conformist state was also brought into play in a different way through the commitment that Hadow made to all those supporters who were putting faith in him by sponsoring his project.

Not that the project was solely about doing things for others. He was aware of a blazing need to achieve for himself as well. In his interview with us he emphasised that this was not about self-esteem so much as about demonstrating to others in the polar exploration community that he could do what he said he would do. This was still self-oriented: It was just that he did not feel that he had anything to prove to himself, since he was convinced that he would succeed. It was about being seen to achieve by others.

Another particularly important motivation, that came to the fore especially under adverse conditions, was that of power, the need to overcome all frustrations and difficulties at any cost. This mastery state could be expressed as pride in his skill and the desire to perform to the best of his abilities. There were times when he had to relinquish control because of the severity of the weather, confining him to his tent. But apart from this frustration he was able to draw liberally on his need to impose himself on his circumstances.

Two other motivational states also played a part, albeit in a rather different way. These were the playful and rebellious states. In both cases, when these came to the forefront, they filled him with joyful enthusiasm, conferring on him extra strength while they lasted. The rebellious state gave him a feeling of escape from all the mundanities of everyday life: Doing the grocery shopping, answering bills, making the bed. Instead a more heroic world of untouched whiteness and freedom opened itself up in front of him. In the playful state the pure beauty of what he was seeing at times simply overwhelmed him with joy.

This leaves the sympathy state, and at first thought it seems extremely unlikely that this could play a part in such a brute-force endeavour. And yet the sympathy state did, as it turned out, have an important role to play. This arose because he would energise himself by thinking of his wife and children (shades of Frankl here, tramping in the snow). In fact, on one particular day, which was his young son Wilf's birthday, he motivated himself to go further than usual as his special birthday gift to his son.

Sympathy was so important to him that, in fact, he felt the need to conjure up an imaginary relationship with his snow brush, who he named Mavis. He would converse with her regularly, and became very fond of this companion who was sharing his tribulations with him. Alas, the day that Mavis broke, and had to be discarded, was one of the worst days of the whole expedition. He mourned for her.

The reason that I have laid things out in this way is to show that the motivations from all eight states were called on at different points during the ordeal of the trek. If one motivation did not seem to be working then another, or another combination, could be summoned. Between them, one or another always seemed to work and take its turn in pushing the project forward. As Hadow himself volunteered: "Actually, I wasn't really motivated by one single force, it was more like a cocktail of forces to get me to the Pole, that I was constantly drawing on."

SUICIDE BOMBING: THE CURSE OF MOTIVATIONAL RICHNESS

Let's consider another kind of endeavour which, like Hadow's, requires an enormous motivational investment, if somewhat less skill and considerably less endurance: suicide bombing. Here is a paradox if ever there was one. Why should young

Muslim fundamentalists blow themselves and others up for no apparent personal gain, but possible hideous pain for themselves and their victims, and anguish for their families? Well, clearly there are a lot of reasons and this is the point. To make the action acceptable and even attractive, many different reasons must be brought to bear by clerics, friends and others: no single reason may be enough. Many desires must be called on, and promises made by those who would provoke such an action. In fact, it seems that promising the satisfaction of all eight motivational states is the best way forward, so that whichever motivational states a recruit happens to be in at a given moment can be tied to the project, and states can be added to each other for cumulative effect. Seen in this way, the whole dreadful process becomes less paradoxical. One way or another, the recruit is caught in a web of desire and promise from which there is no escape.

To get a better idea of how this works, let us consider what the world looks like to a suicide bomber before the act. Let us see if we can visualise this person, based on accounts that have been given to interviewers by suicide bombers either before the event, or afterwards in the case of failure. (24) What follows is a loose composite from different sources, and I give my identification of the motivational state or states involved at each stage by putting them in parentheses and italics. (25)

Imagine that you are a young Muslim, a true believer, in an Islamic Middle Eastern country. You are middle-class and not particularly poor yourself, but when you look around, you see a world of people who are poverty stricken, hungry, and with little hope of escape from their desperate conditions. You feel angry at the injustice of it all (*rebellious*) and you wonder what you can do to help. You want to make the world a better place (*other-oriented*). Also, you have a beloved uncle who was killed by an American drone and you want vengeance (*mastery, rebelliousness*).

Everyone tells you – your family and friends and Islamist authorities – that the injustice comes from the way that the Christian West, and especially America, is occupying your homeland, exploiting it, corrupting your culture, and intent on destroying your religion. This wicked enemy must be opposed at all costs, and thrown out of the country or killed through the struggle of Jihad (*mastery, other-oriented*). What right do they have to be here in the first place? Why do they hate us and our God? Who do they think they are?

You are recruited by an extremist Islamist group who tell you that there is something you can do about all this. You are told that if you are indeed a true believer, your duty is the destruction of non-believers, and that this is a duty required by the Koran *(conforming)*. You know that duty is the key value in your religion (the word 'Islam' means 'submission') so you are willing to carry through whatever you are ordered to do by your new commanders.

When you are offered the chance of striking God's foes and punishing them, by becoming a suicide bomber, you jump at it. At last you can have an effect: from being a nobody you can become somebody (*mastery, self-oriented*). You can also avenge your uncle (*rebellious).* Best of all, as a reward, you will go to paradise forever. What could conceivably be a stronger incentive than that (*serious, self-oriented*)? Death in such glorious circumstances, as you see it, would not really be death at all, but a way-station on the route to eternal life.

You still have some qualms. One is the pain that you might experience (*self-oriented*). You are told that the moment you press the button, and before your blood even hits the ground, you will find yourself with God in Paradise. There will be no pain. Another concern is the killing of innocent bystanders (*other-oriented*) but you are told that they will forgive you when you all meet in Paradise.

You live in the terrorist group and watch as your friends

and colleagues become martyrs, and you enjoy the feeling of glamour and excitement that surrounds them *(playful)*. You visit your family, who have mixed feelings about what you are going to do, especially your mother; but they are also proud, and this pleases you greatly *(mastery, other-oriented)*. You realise that your younger brothers are looking up to you *(mastery, self-oriented)*. Islamist tradition has it that a martyr can guarantee a place in paradise for 70 people. You feel overwhelming satisfaction at earning salvation for all the members of your family and many of your friends *(sympathy, other-oriented)*.

In case all this is not enough, you are reminded of another reward that you can expect. This is the promise of sexual gratification in Paradise by 70 virgins *(playful, self-oriented)*. (It is not clear what *women* suicide bombers will get, or what will happen to the virgins once they have been deflowered.) You are not aware that there is much dispute among Islamic theologians about what is actually being offered in paradise. But you believe in a Paradise that is delightfully materialist and sensual. You expect that you will lie on a jewelled couch, waited on by immortal youths with everlasting wine.

Now it is your turn: you are to become the next martyr. You feel enormous pride *(mastery, self-oriented)* during the ritual celebration to sanctify your mission, during which you record the video statement that will be your legacy. You feel profound satisfaction that you will be doing something for your country and for your faith through self-sacrifice *(other-oriented)*. There is pleasure in being a centre of attention before the act, and knowing that you will be a hero afterwards, celebrated on Jihadist websites *(mastery, self-oriented)*. In any case, there is no going back, you are openly committed. And you wish to remain loyal to the brotherhood which has become a family to you *(conforming, other-oriented)*.

When the time comes you will strap on your explosive-filled vest and pray. As you approach your target, and search for where you can destroy the most people, you will be smiling. You will concentrate on the fact that you have the passport to Paradise in your hand (*self-oriented*). All you need to do is to press the detonator to be with God. At the end, little else will matter.

There may be disagreement with just how representative this composite portrait is, and how accurately I have attached motivational states to each step in the process. My point, though, does not depend on this. The message is that if all eight motivational states are remorselessly added to each other in the pursuit of a given end, in whatever order, it becomes increasingly difficult for the person subjected to them to resist their cumulative force. This may go some way to explain the paradox of suicide bombing. In such seduction for violence, less is definitely not more.

CHAPTER 15

THE BIOLOGICAL ORIGINS OF OPPOSITION

Getting to grips with how motivational states work as pairs of opposites has helped us to understand human paradox. This has been a focus of this book. Every one of the paradoxes we have looked at has involved one or more of our four pairs of opposites. And every pair of opposites has been implicated in more than one kind of paradox. But there remains a basic and challenging question: Why are motivational states arranged as pairs of opposites in the first place? Where did this polarity come from?

One answer was given in the previous chapter. Oppositeness may offer psychological advantages, some of which may even provide evolutionary advantage by helping fitness and survival. But it is always easy retrospectively to find possible advantages for any identifiable biological characteristic. All the same, if we can assume that psychology in some way emerges from biology, then biology might offer some interesting clues to the origins of psychological opposition.

I am not going to argue here that particular motivational states are related to particular neurological, physiological or hormonal systems. They may well be, but that is a matter for future research. Rather, I want to take a more general and evolutionary perspective, and tentatively suggest that polarity is a fundamental principle in the organisation of biological systems. (1)

If we look to the whole field of life studies, something hits us straight away: This is just how widespread oppositional systems are. We see polarity and reversal wherever we look, so we should not be surprised that this carries over into psychology. Let me touch on three contrasting areas to illustrate the biological proliferation of opposites and reversals: physiological regulation, the movements of simple unicellular organisms, and progammed cell death. (2)

Physiological Oppositions

Did you know that many physiological processes involve systems working in opposition to each other? There are two main ways in which this occurs. The first is like a scrum in rugby or tug-of-war. It is a form of antagonism, in which opposite systems work against each other simultaneously, and hold each other to some degree in check. The second is like taking it in turns to serve in tennis, or to hit the ball in golf. In this case we have alternation, in which the opposing systems take it in turn to be active. This time, jumps occur back and forth from one system to the other. Of the two, the second physiological arrangement – turn taking – is the closer analogy to psychological reversals between motivational states. But let us glance at both kinds since they both involve oppositions.

A good illustration of opposition through antagonism is the way that muscles are arranged in pairs, an agonist and an antagonist. Examples are the extensor and flexor muscles that move the hand, and the biceps and triceps that control movements in the lower arm. As the agonist tenses, to pull the limb in one direction, so the antagonistic muscle relaxes to allow it to do so – and vice versa. Likewise, we see antagonism in the autonomic nervous system, which automatically regulates arousal levels in the body – how 'worked up' you are and how ready for possible action. It is made up of two opposing branches. These two "pull against each other," with one imposing on the other at a given moment to increase bodily arousal and the other, at other moments, to decrease it.

The other kind of physiological opposition, the one involving alternation rather than antagonism, can be seen in systems in which opposites take turns, displaying an internal rhythm. This rhythm may be over-ridden by external events and conditions. Sleeping and waking are a good example, and one that I gave early in the book. We normally experience both over a twenty four hour period, reversing from one to the other. To make things more complex, a further alternation is embedded within just the sleep part of the cycle, namely the alternation between rapid eye-movement (REM) sleep and non rapid-eye movement sleep (the former often being related to dreaming and referred to as paradoxical sleep). This is roughly a 90 minute cycle. So we can have cycles within cycles. (3)

Many biological functions involve alternations. Thus breathing requires the alternation of expiration and inhalation. Walking requires the alternation of leg movements, each one taking the strain in turn to produce what has been called 'controlled falling.' If these two examples of alternation seem a bit obvious, there are others that are not generally known outside the laboratory. For example: the eyes do not remain motionless, even when they stare. Although the looked-at object appears unchanging, and we experience it as smoothly continuous, in fact our two eyes are carrying out, in unison, tiny back-and-forth flickering motions, known as 'saccadic movements,' away from and back to the observed object. But the movements are so fast that, in the normal way of things, we do not notice them.

Another example is the 'nasal cycle,' in which each nostril takes its turn, for an hour or two, to be the main channel for breathing. In other words, at any one time, breathing takes place mainly through one nostril, whether this nostril is the right or the left one. But which nostril is the active one alternates. If you do not believe this, cover each of your nostrils in turn with your hand, while continuing to breathe. You will feel that it is more difficult to breathe through one uncovered nostril than the other. If you try this on subsequent occasions you should find that sooner or later the 'difficult nostril' (if I may put it so inelegantly) will have reversed. (4)

Such biological reversals, from eye movement to nasal alternation, although varying considerably in frequency of change, would seem to be very similar in the way they work to the reversals in motivation that we have been exploring in this book. They involve turn-taking and seem governed by internal rhythms, although rhythms that can be overridden by the environment. This does seem to be a natural way for biological systems to be organised.

YOUR INNER AMOEBA

Reversal goes deeper in biology. If we inspect the very simplest organisms, the tiny single-cell beings known as protozoa, we see reversals of various kinds. Specifically, these microscopic animals display, in their primary behaviour, pairs of states that they reverse between. This primary behaviour is movement devoted to the search for food.

In one study (5), biologists looked at the search behaviour of *amoebae* in an environment that was neutral in the sense that it did not provide any nutrients. You may know that amoebae drag themselves along rather grotesquely by putting out 'feelers,' oozing their 'bodies' into the feelers, and then pushing out new feelers. What the researchers found was that, in searching for food, this movement took place in a sort of slow-motion zig-zag, with a change of direction, a zig or a zag, every couple of minutes. But the interesting thing is that the change of direction was not random but tended to alternate between left and right – and this, believe it or not, in an organism with no nervous system at all. However achieved, this slow left-right wobble meant that the organism could maintain the same general direction over time, while exploring a swath of space on either side of its path. The ability of this tiny creature in this respect inspired the title of the present book.

A further kind of reversal has been found in the protozoon known as *Paramecium*, perhaps the most widely studied of all single-cell organisms (rather like the laboratory rat has been to generations of behaviourist psychologists). It is visible to the naked eye as a speck, but is studied under the microscope where it can be seen to be what is often described as slipper shaped. A paramecium will change direction if food is detectable by it nearby, in order to head towards it. But researchers (6) observing the paramecium's behaviour in the absence of food, found that it would spontaneously change its direction of swimming every five to ten minutes anyway. The researchers emphasise that these two periods, of swimming straight ahead and changing direction, are not related to any change in the environment, which is food-free in this particular experiment. Rather, it is an innate programmed fluctuation. (There is also another kind of reversal that can be observed: when a paramecium bumps into something it cannot get past, it literally reverses at an angle away from it, and then moves forwards again on a new path.)

Biologists studying another kind of protozoan, *Coleps*

hirtus, also found movement reversals occurring, although of a rather different kind. (7) In this case, the microscopic organism that looks something like a hand grenade, searches for food by alternating periods of swimming more or less straight ahead with periods of circular swimming within a small area. It is as if the organism was saying to itself "let's explore this little area a bit by swimming around it" and then after a while, "OK, nothing here, let's move on." These constituted two very definite phases.

Bacteria, which are also minute single-celled organisms (that are so simple that they do not have a nucleus), display a related kind of alternation in their search behaviour. In this case it consists of reversing between swimming and what has been called 'tumbling' which means spinning round and round in a clockwise direction and on the same plane as it was swimming (i.e. not corkscrewing up or down) and then heading off in a new direction. (8) If the bacterium senses that it is moving away from nutrients, it will tumble with little delay. If it senses that it is moving in the right direction it will be less likely to tumble. (I have some fellow feeling with bacteria in this, if not in any other, respect: When I get stuck in my work, and spin round on my swivel chair in exasperation, I conceive of myself as tumbling.)

In the latter two life forms, we see in both cases an opposition between "Steady as she goes" and "Time to try something else," between a kind of stability and a kind of instability. Could these be the progenitors of the serious and playful states? In any case, these examples show us that alternation – reversal – is a very basic dynamic in biological systems.

THE DANCE OF DEATH

As if all this were not enough, in recent years a new development in biology has come to emphasise still further the fundamental part that opposition plays in life processes – and especially in embryology. This is the discovery of a phenomenon to which the awkward name "apoptosis" has been given. (9) By this is meant cellular self-destruction or 'programmed cell death.' This is not the same as cell death through infection or other kinds of externally inflicted injury. Rather it is destruction that comes from within the cell itself – a kind of cell suicide, if you can imagine such a thing. It is typically pre-programmed genetically, and plays a part in the development of the organism. It does this through helping to mold the body in required ways – a carving out through the removal of cells. Thus the shaping of a hand from a developing tissue requires both that growth takes place at some points and is prevented, through cell death, at other points. There has to be an alternation between growth and destruction. Without it, for example, a human hand would be webbed – it is apoptosis that allows individual fingers to develop separately. If it were not for apoptosis I would be walloping rather than typing on my computer keyboard at this very instant. It seems that, as we found in an earlier chapter on rebelliousness: creation and destruction go hand in hand. To make shapes, subtraction is needed as well as addition.

The study of apoptosis has now become a huge field, with over 13,000 papers published annually, two journals, and a scientific society ominously named the Cell Death Society. It turns out that every cell in the body has this capacity to self-destruct and is only prevented from doing so by a continual process of repression of this capacity – a kind of negation of the negation. So the development and maintenance of life – survival and fitness – is dependent on a deep opposition between contrary processes. (10)

BACK TO THE BEGINNING

Suppose that we go right back to the beginning of life and look at the first moments of the newly fertilised egg, the 'little bang' from which every organism develops in biology. What do we find? The very first thing that happens in many plant and animal species is the establishment of polarity. The embryo initially does not know "which side is up," or, for that matter, which side is forwards and which side is sideways. So the very first action in these cases is to set up opposites: up versus down, left versus right, front versus back. The initial site of entry of the sperm may, within minutes, become the first pole, and then the other poles are set up in relation to this. The overall orientation is thought to be established through environmental cues, such as light from above, gravity pulling downwards, water currents or wind pulsing from the side.

Something else interesting now occurs: the very first actions of the organism – all organisms – involve a kind of reversal. What happens is that there is an alternation between two quite different processes. The first is 'mitosis': each cell splits into two. The second is 'DNA synthesis' in which genetic material is built up in each cell in readiness for the next mitosis. This cycle continues in the organism which, starting with a single cell, doubles the number of cells that make it up at each round. In this way it becomes a growing, if initially unformed, mass of cells. These then start to form into the basic shapes of the organism, using the polarities it has set up. The process is more complicated than I have made it sound, and the details differ between organisms. But this is the gist of the story. (11) Further, once a polarity has been established it can then be used to orient parts of the organism in relation to each other so that every cell knows 'where it is' and what it has to do during the course of later development. (12)

PARA-EVOLUTION

The following question can no longer be avoided: Did all such biological forms of opposition emerge through natural selection of the kind supposed by Darwin? Does being characterised by oppositions provide some kind of biological advantage in the struggle for existence? This is difficult to answer because those features that confer survival, and therefore get passed on to later generations, are usually identified in concrete terms – sharper teeth, larger beaks, and the like – rather than in abstract principles like 'opposition'. But it would certainly appear that opposition constitutes a powerful principle of organisation in biological systems, even a foundational one.

There is another speculative possibility that is worth just noting. This is to see opposition as an example of a principle that derives from the very stuff of biological systems, principles that are what we might call *para-evolutionary*. That is, they run in parallel with those deriving from natural selection and interact with them. They are what evolution by natural selection has, as it were, to 'work with.' And they may themselves push towards change and elaboration, prompting their own kind of 'evolution,' independent of survival of the fittest. (See Appendix Five.)

The best example of such a para-evolutionary, rather than evolutionary, principle comes from the last person that one might have expected: Darwin himself and his 'Principle of Antithesis' which he introduces in relation to the instinctive expression of emotions. (13) The idea here is that many emotions go in opposites, but that in each pair of opposites one of the opposing forms of expression has a biological function, and has evolved through natural selection, while the other has no such purpose and merely expresses the fact that the opposite emotion is prevailing. For example, in dogs, hostility is expressed in ways that make the animal seem larger and more dangerous than it otherwise would, and therefore likely to frighten away an enemy. The dog stands erect, its hair bristles, its ears become stiff, its canine teeth are bared, and its tail adopts an upright position. This clearly has a biological function in expressing fierceness, size, and discouraging attack by threatening a potential aggressor. On the other hand, when the dog is placid and friendly, it crouches down, its hair becomes smooth, its ears rest against the head, its canine teeth are covered and its tail is lowered and wagged. According to Darwin, this latter posture functions by expressing the opposite of hostility but in itself, unlike the hostility gestures, has no biological function. This does indeed seem like a para-evolutionary principle and Darwin does not claim that the change is in itself the result of natural selection. A related human example given by Darwin is the way the head is held high in feelings of power and dominance, while it is withdrawn between the shoulders to represent impotence by means of the shrugging gesture. (14)

This antithesis principle of emotional expression seems like a good candidate for a precursor of motivational opposition in human psychology. But what I am suggesting is something broader and more fundamental than this. It is that opposition, polarity, and reversal were not necessarily derived directly through natural selection but might have been derived from biological principles that run in parallel to evolutionary selection. The polarity principle may not be primarily a result of evolution at all, but of something to do with the way that all biochemical systems naturally organise themselves outside of, but interacting with, evolutionary processes. Darwin himself may have been one of the first to recognise this as a possibility.

Taking this all one step further, there is, intriguingly, a whole developing field dealing with 'proto-cells.' This is the study of simple biochemical interactions that produce emergent life-like properties. For instance, oil droplets when placed in different solutions, and injected with certain biochemical substances start to move around spontaneously. They can move towards food, change course, and dance around other similar droplets in a kind of waltz. The point for present purposes is to demonstrate that biochemistry is dynamic, is governed by physical constraints, and naturally generates movement and complexity. (15) It is perhaps here that we need to search for the ultimate origins of opposition.

In any case, whether through evolution or in one of these para-evolutionary ways, opposition seems to be fundamental to living systems. In the words of one notable, if controversial, biologist: *"In the absence of opposition there is no life."* (16) Our bodies are an endless whirl and buzz, pulsating with movement at every level from cell to organ, vibrating with reversals. Nothing is static.

Exactly how biological oppositions might translate into, or influence the development of, psychological oppositions, is a topic that biology tells us little about at present. But the widespread nature of oppositions and reversals at all levels of biological analysis, does seem to suggest that oppositions in psychology have deep roots. They are more than just superficial chance effects, or awkward anomalies. In this wider context, their significance becomes more apparent. In particular, the oppositions that arise within human personality, and the endless changeability that people display, can be seen as inevitable expressions of something organic – something basic to living systems.

Paradox in Paradise

Returning finally to the psychological level, we are forced to recognise that these oppositions, and this restlessness, mean that in principle there can be no permanent state of bliss for us. There can be no grand utopias and no 'end of history.' No perfect arrangement exists that will allow everyone to be happy, or even any one person to be happy all the time. Even in Heaven we would have to relinquish such pleasures as those that come with taking a real risk, arguing, confronting others, displaying courage, being surprised, doing what is prohibited, challenging rules, defeating enemies, overcoming fear, prevailing over frustrations, or achieving in the face of enduring stress and hardship. It is hard to see how we can experience good things, if bad things are no longer possible. In this respect, Paradise seems rather limited, not to say timid. And in any case, who would want to finish up as eternally unchanging? (Perhaps it is in Paradise that trait theory really does work at last.)

But in real life, if we do not expect too much, if we understand the paradoxes that we see around us, and if we have some degree of motivational intelligence, we can at least avoid unnecessary misery and allow ourselves the luxury of hope, together with the ability to relish happiness whenever it does settle itself, however unexpectedly, on our shoulders.

APPENDICES

THE EIGHT
MOTIVATIONAL STATES

It might be useful for you to have, as a reference, a set of descriptions of each of the eight motivational states that make up the four pairs of opposites. Each pair is made up of two ways of experiencing a fundamental aspect of experience, known as a domain. In what follows, each state is characterised in four ways: its style, which gives its name to the state (e.g. serious), its basic value (e.g. achievement), its typical characteristics (e.g. setting goals) and some possible illustrative behaviours (e.g. dieting).

Domain of experience: Means-and-ends

Style: SERIOUS

Basic value: Achievement.

Typical characteristics: Making long-term plans, setting goals, monitoring progress, delaying gratification, tolerating hard work, being aware of consequences, thinking of the future.

Possible illustrative behaviour: Investing, getting insurance, dieting, taking exercise, studying, house-cleaning, visiting the doctor, filling in tax forms, planting seeds, filling up the gas tank, brushing teeth, servicing the car.

Style: **PLAYFUL**

Basic value: Fun.

Typical characteristics: Looking for excitement, sensual, being spontaneous, risk-taking, fantasising, wanting immediate gratification, out for a good time.

Possible illustrative behaviour: Telling jokes, having sex, gambling, playing sport, gossiping, dancing, dining out, watching television, partying, listening to music, looking at pornography, drinking wine, reading a novel, hanging out.

DOMAIN OF EXPERIENCE: RULES

Style: **CONFORMING**

Basic value: Duty.

Typical characteristics: Following orders, obeying the law, joining in rituals, sticking to routines, having faith, respecting customs, being ethical, doing things the traditional way, being superstitious, being honest, being dogmatic.

Possible illustrative behaviour: Buying fashionable clothes, saluting the flag, singing in a choir, praying, following etiquette, being polite, displaying punctuality, telling the truth, dieting, being superstitious.

Style: **REBELLIOUS**

Basic value: Freedom.

Typical characteristics: Breaking taboos, being impolite, being argumentative, departing from convention, being innovative, being eccentric, being obstinate, opposing the status quo, being critical, being sceptical, being disruptive, cheating.

Possible illustrative behaviour: Swearing, drawing graffiti, sexting, wearing unusual clothes, joining a gang, refusing to follow orders, saying original things, flaming, whistle-blowing, smoking, taking drugs, overeating, being sarcastic.

DOMAIN OF EXPERIENCE: TRANSACTIONS

Style: MASTERY

Basic value: Power.

Typical characteristics: Competing, developing skills, undertaking difficult tasks, taking on challenges, admiring strength, being courageous, being confrontational, bargaining.

Possible illustrative behaviour: Getting into fights, playing sport, pursuing politics, riding a motorbike, bullying, playing a musical instrument, teasing, playing cards.

Style: SYMPATHY

Basic value: Love.

Typical characteristic: Being with one's family, reminiscing, discussing personal issues, getting to know someone, showing vulnerability, treating others as people, being sentimental.

Possible illustrative behaviour: Using social media, playing with pets, phoning home, caressing an intimate, cuddling a baby, hanging out with friends, holding hands, sharing memories.

Domain of experience: Relationships

Style: SELF-ORIENTED

Basic value: Self-actualization.

Typical characteristics: Demanding respect, looking for status, wanting to be cared for, attention-seeking, being self-indulgent, being selfish, being vain, being secretive, being personally ambitious, showing off, demanding respect from others.

Possible illustrative behaviour: Having a massage, free-loading, cutting toenails, doing selfies, masturbating, being a jerk, answering personality questionnaires, sunbathing, pushing in front of others, showing off.

Style: OTHER-ORIENTED

Basic value: Transcendence

Typical characteristics: Self-sacrificing, looking after others, parenting, being philanthropic, donating to charity, being unselfish, contributing to a community, volunteering, being a martyr, being loyal.

Possible illustrative behaviour: Writing a reference, giving a friend a recipe, visiting a friend in hospital, teaching, giving a gift, changing a diaper, supporting a political party, playing in a team, supporting a team, leaving a tip, collaborating at work.

There are a number of things to notice about all this. Firstly, motivational states define what people *want*, not what they necessarily get. All kinds of confusions arise if we are not clear about this distinction between desire and satisfaction. For instance, one may fail to achieve anything important, but still be in the serious state. One may fail to be loved but still be in the self-oriented and sympathy states.

Secondly, the illustrative behaviours are indeed illustrative and not definitive, which is why I have called them *possible* illustrative behaviours. The same concrete activity can be used in the service of different states at different times, and so one cannot necessarily tell for sure, from the outside, which value is actually being pursued at a given moment (even if one can make a good guess, or ask the person whose behaviour we are observing). Thus a person may usually play golf in the playful state, but on a particular occasion play it in the serious state, so one cannot infer that golf is playful for him in any permanent sense. It is for this reason that one cannot *define* states in terms of behaviours but only in terms of underlying values. I have given behavioural examples here to give a feeling for what the states-in-action look like in everyday life.

Thirdly, a particular behaviour may be chosen in relation to more than one active state at the same time. Evidence shows, for example, that one may smoke for playful, negativistic and self-oriented reasons all at the same moment (O'Connell & Cook, 2001). Here is another, more general example: usually a self-oriented or other-oriented behaviour is attached to either the sympathy or the mastery state. For instance, if you want to help others (other-oriented), you can do so either through making them feel loved or through making them feel powerful. Indeed, if you think about it, it has to be one way or the other.

A final point is that none of the motivational states are inherently 'good' or 'bad,' although the behaviour expressed in these states may, depending on the situation, be good or bad in the sense of being appropriate or inappropriate, helpful or unhelpful. I have tried here to give examples of both kinds in relation to the illustrative behaviours I have cited.

O'Connell, Kathleen A. & Cook, Mary R. (2001) Smoking and smoking cessation. In Apter, M.J. (ed.) *Motivational Styles in Everyday Life: A Guide to Reversal Theory*. Washington, D.C.: American Psychological Association. Pp. 139-153.

APPENDIX II

EXTRAVERSION AND INTROVERSION

The extraversion-introversion dimension is probably the best known of all the personality dimensions, and the most widely researched over the years. Unfortunately, it has been defined in so many different ways that it has become almost meaningless, even though it is still used frequently in trait studies of personality, especially as one of the so-called "Big Five" personality dimensions that have been particularly fashionable for the last decade or two.

The problems start immediately with Carl Jung's original definition of extraversion (Jung, 1923). He defined it as being oriented to the outside world and introversion to the inner world of mental processes. But what does orientation mean here? It can mean just attention to stimuli from the inside (feelings, images, etc) or the outside (machines, environments, people, etc). This seems to be what Jung meant originally, although even this has its problems. For example, in listening to music is one attending to sensations from the inside or the outside? But Jung goes further and says that the introvert wants everything to depend on his/her own decision, and the extravert wants to conform to what others want (Jung,1928). In this meaning the dimension becomes close to the reversal theory conforming-rebelling dimension. But it also suggests something about what is called in psychology 'locus of control' – in other words, who it is that the person sees as making the decisions that guide behaviour. Elsewhere again it seems to Jung to be about where the reward is searched for – is motivation directed to an outer object or to something subjective. This would make it close to the extrinsic-intrinsic dimension (see Appendix Four) or even to the reversal theory playful-serious dimension. Confusion reigns!

To make matters worse, in the hands of Myers and Briggs in their widely used Type Indicator, extraversion becomes about being sociable and gregarious, while introversion is about being shy and withdrawn. Hans Eysenck's highly influential approach to personality and his Eysenck Personality Inventory (1963) also makes sociability central. But this can easily contradict the Jungian sense of attention to the inside or the outside. According to Jung, repairing one's car at a weekend would presumably be the sort of thing that an extravert would enjoy doing – it is about interacting with the external world, and finding rewards there. But for Eysenck, and for Myers-Briggs, it would be introverted because it is an isolated and even anti-social activity.

Yet a further complication is that Eysenck and Myers-Briggs add impulsiveness into the definition of extraversion, with introversion being characterised by reflectiveness. But this raises all kinds of problems. If someone impulsively played a slot machine, would this be extraversion (because of the impulsiveness) or introversion (because the machine is an objective part of the outside world). And what if someone interacted with a social group in a careful way, manipulating the group according to a plan (as good leaders have to)? Would this be introverted or extraverted? Problems abound.

As if all this were not enough, in the standard inventory measuring the "Big Five" personality traits (Costa & McCrae, 1992), extraversion is associated with the tendency to have positive emotions, a tendency which is supposedly lacking in introverts. Really? I have this image of an introvert having an awful time taking a country walk, or tucked up in bed with a great book. If you reject this extravert negative definition of introversion, then you might enjoy reading Susan Cain (2012) who has advocated for introverts in what she sees as a world made for extraverts.

Note in passing: 'extraversion' is strictly the correct spelling not 'extroversion.' The prefix is 'extra' as in 'extraordinary,' 'extrapolate,' 'extract,' etc., meaning 'outside.'

Cain, Susan (2012) *Quiet: The Power of Introverts in a World that Can't Stop Talking.* New York: Random House.

Costa, P.T. Jr., & McCrae, R.R. (1992*) Revised NEO Personality Inventory (NEO-PI-R) and NEO Five Factor Inventory (NEO-FF) Manual*. Odessa FL: Psychological Assessment Resources.

Eysenck, Hans J. & Eysenck, Sybil B.G. (1963) *Eysenck Personality Inventory.* London: University of London Press.

Jung, Carl. G. (1923) *Psychological Types.* Translated by H.G. Baynes. London: Routledge and Kegan Paul.

Jung, Carl G. (1928) *Contributions to Analytical Psychology.* London: Routledge & Kegan Paul. Extract reproduced in *Personality Assessment* (ed. Boris Semeonoff), 1966, London: Penguin. Pages 79-80.

Myers, I.B., McCaulley, M.H., Quenk, N.L. & Hammer, A.L. (1998) *MBTI Manual, 3rd. edition.* California: Consulting Psychologists Press.

INTERACTIONISM

The brief account I have given of the trait and situationist approaches is necessarily something of an oversimplification of what is now a large literature which also includes so-called "Interactionist" theories about the relationship between situations and traits. In their simplest form, these theories acknowledge that both personal dispositions and environmental contingencies play a part in determining behaviour. In more complex forms it is recognised that different environments may call up different traits, or that different traits may determine which environment people find themselves in or choose to be in. But in all interactionist theories, the individual's traits are seen as essentially constant.

In broad terms it is clear that the spirit of reversal theory is very different, especially in relation to the idea of change within the person. In reversal theory, unlike these other theories, we do not assume that the underlying characteristics of the person remain constant. Even more to the point, reversal theory introduces a third factor into the argument – that of internal change. This makes it a very different kind of theory. In reversal theory there is a kind of 'internal environment,' or 'intext,' made up of changing motivational states following in part their own rules, as well as an external environment.

An interesting development in interactionist theories has been Mischel's "Cognitive-Affective Processing System" in which situations are defined in terms of how the subject sees things, rather than in terms of arbitrary definitions made from the outside by the experimenter. In this way, subjects are more likely to show consistencies across situations, since they will have defined different situations in terms of the things that are important to them in these situations. Such consistency can be described equally well in trait terms (respondents have enduring tendencies to see certain situations in certain ways) or in situational terms (certain situations will be responded to consistently on different occasions). See: Mischel, W. & Shoda, Y. (1995). But again this is different from reversal theory because in reversal theory the same situation, even defined subjectively, can be experienced in different ways at different times depending on which motivational states are active at that time. For example, a given situation might be interpreted subjectively as dangerous, but on some occasions this dangerousness might be welcomed and on other occasions abhorred.

A recent more sophisticated version of situationism, but one which takes a step towards reversal theory by recognising that "character is flexible" (p. 230), is the work of DeSteno and Valdesolo (2011). Their book deals largely with moral judgment. They and their colleagues demonstrate in a series of ingenious experiments that changes in context, sometimes subtle, and involving emotions, can alter people's choices and behaviour, often in surprising ways. But, unlike reversal theory, they see character as varying along a continuum rather than being dichotomous, and regard it as always being controlled by external context.

Another recent advocate of the flexible personality position is Carter (2008). She suggests that, at some level, we are all multiple personalities, extending the clinical term 'multiple personality' (or 'Dissociative Identity Disorder' as it is now called) into a less clinical sense that would include all of us. As she sees it, we all have multiple subpersonalities built around each of the different roles that we perform, with particular memories being more or less accessible in these different roles, and each separate subpersonality representing a profile made up of trait-like characteristics.

One other relevant theory here is Little's interesting "Free Trait Theory" (2005, 2007, 2014). He allows that people will temporarily adopt different 'free traits' at different times in order to achieve their core 'personal projects' in life (e.g. an introvert might be willing to act like an extravert to accomplish some purpose that requires social interaction). In this respect, his theory and reversal theory share the assumption of personality as changing. However, the two theories are fundamentally different in that Little assumes that there are fixed personality characteristics from which free traits are merely deviations.

Carter, Rita (2008) *Multiplicity: The New Science of Personality, Identity and the Self,* New York: Little, Brown and Company.

DeSteno, David & Valdesolo, Piercarlo (2011) *Out of Character: Surprising Truths about the Liar, Cheat, Sinner (and Saint) Lurking in All of Us.* New York: Crown Archetype.

Little, Brian (2005), Personality science and personal projects: Six impossible things before breakfast. *Journal of Research in Personality, 39,* 4-21.

Little, Brian. R., Salmela-Aro, Katarina & Phillips, Susan D.(Eds.) (2007) *Personal Project Pursuit: Goals, Action, and Human Flourishing.* New Jersey: Lawrence Erlbaum.

Little, Brian (2014) *Me, Myself and Us: The Science of Personality and the Art of Wellbeing.* New York: Public Affairs.

Mischel, W. & Shoda, Y. (1995) A cognitive-affective system theory of personality: reconceptualizing situations, dispositions, dynamics, and invariance in personality structure. *Psychological Review, 49:* 229-58.

INTRINSIC AND EXTRINSIC MOTIVATION

The terms 'intrinsic' and 'extrinsic' are typically used to describe what is happening in the studies reported in chapter 6. The idea in these experiments is that extrinsic rewards come to take the place of intrinsic rewards, so that respondents come to undertake the activity for the sake of the rewards that it leads to, rather than enjoying the activity for its own sake.

Unfortunately, this pair of terms has been used in different ways by different researchers. One of these ways is indeed to take intrinsic to mean doing something for its own sake, and extrinsic to mean doing it as instrumental to something else. This would be consistent with the serious/playful distinction that I am using here.

But sometimes a very different definition is given, which is already implied in the name sometimes applied to this field, namely 'Self-Determination Theory.' Specifically, some researchers take intrinsic to mean that one's behaviour is felt to be determined by oneself and extrinsic means that it is experienced as determined by the environment. This is what can be called a 'locus of control' definition (which goes back to de Charms, 1968). It is added to the original definition by Deci and Ryan, the originators of this field of study, who refer to the 'internal perceived locus of control' (Ryan & Deci, 2000, p.54). But this involves a quite different dimension from that described in the first paragraph above. For example, someone could invite me to do something for its own sake (have a drink, play a game of tennis). This would be extrinsic by the locus of control definition, because the person who invites me is part of my environment, but intrinsic by the 'ownsake' definition. Alternatively one could decide for oneself to do something where there were external rewards to work for (for example, to decide in the face of family opposition to become a musician). This would be intrinsic by the locus of control definition – one is making one's own decisions – but extrinsic by the 'instrumental' definition since the hope is that it will eventually provide external rewards like playing in an orchestra and earning money, and one is willing to work towards these. So the two definitions do not necessarily go together. Indeed, they are quite incompatible. You can do fun things that you have been told to do, and serious things that are self-chosen.

As if this were not enough of a problem, various other definitions have also been given. For example, Ormrod (2006) defined intrinsic motivation as the "internal desire to perform a particular task." ("What would an external desire be?" one asks oneself.) Purkey & Schmidt (1987) defined intrinsic motivation as the motivation to engage in activities that are designed to enhance a person's self-concept. In this case we would have to exclude categorisation as intrinsic a whole host of activities that are both self-chosen and pleasurable in themselves, and would therefore fit other 'ownsake' definitions of intrinsic, but do not appear to be about enhancing one's self-concept – like getting drunk, taking drugs, engaging in illicit sex, and so on.

For all these reasons I have decided to stick with the serious/

playful terminology which was, incidentally, introduced at about the same time as the extrinsic/intrinsic pair of terms. In any case, we shall also see, as we continue to go through various kinds of paradox, that the serious/playful distinction on its own does not take us far enough: It helps us to understand certain paradoxes, but we need all four of the reversal theory dimensions to achieve anything like a complete account.

De Charms, R. (1968) *Personal Causation: The Internal Affective Determinants of Behaviour.* New York: AcademicPress.

Ormrod, J.E. (2006) *Educational Psychology: Developing Learners* (5th. Edition) Upper Saddle River, N.J.: Pearson.

Purkey, W.W. & Schmidt, J. (1987) *The Inviting Relationship: An Expanded Perspective for Professional Counseling.* Englewood Cliffs, N.J.: Prentice Hall.

Ryan, Richard M. & Deci, Edward L. (2000) Intrinsic and extrinsic motivations: Classic definitions and new directions. *Contemporary Educational Psychology, 25*, 54-67.

Appendix V

PARA-EVOLUTION

By a para-evolutionary process I mean a process that contributes to the change and elaboration of a species, doing so in a way that goes beyond Darwinian natural selection. Darwin's own Principle of Antithesis (as described in chapter 15) is a good example. It results in a certain development of the behaviour of the organism without this being derived from variation and natural selection alone.

Here is another example of a para-evolutionary principle: It has been suggested that there are basic laws in nature that deal with everything that flows: water, sap, blood, electricity, information – all of which are said to obey a kind of principle of least resistance known as the 'Constructal Law.' The result is the evolution of branching patterns such as we see in rivers, neural networks, trees and lightning. Again, patterns emerge on the basis of something other than natural selection. This particular idea comes out of thermodynamics rather than biology (Bejan & Zane, 2012).

Another kind of para-evolutionary process involves the by-products of evolution. There are two kinds of byproducts. Firstly, there are those which are 'left-overs', that once had a function but, following change, do so no longer. These are known as 'vestigial remains'. A well-known example is that of the tail bone in humans, which is thought, as the name suggests, to be the remains of a tail. There are many other structures in humans which apparently serve no purpose, such as pubic hair, the nails on our fingers, the goose bumps we get when we are cold. They do no harm, so they remain. But they accumulate, so that they become part of an increasingly complicated biological system.

Secondly, there are evolutionary changes that can lead to non-functional byproducts that add something new, but in this case, as in the previous case, the 'something' still does not contribute to survival. The difference from the previous case is that something new has been generated, rather than something old retained. Steven Jay Gould, a foremost evolutionary biologist, likened new byproducts to the architectural features known as spandrels, such as those he noticed on visiting the beautiful San Marcos basilica in Venice (Gould & Lewontin, 1979). When arches come together to make a dome, there are curved triangular walls between them, and these walls are the spandrels. The walls themselves serve no function. But they arise inevitably from something that does have a function, and an essential one, namely the arches that help to hold the building up. Gould suggested that many biological structures that arise during evolution are unavoidable byproducts. A body has myriads of characteristics which serve no evolutionary purpose at all but which have, all the same, arisen through evolution. Bones are white, for example, but this has no evolutionary significance. Everything has to be some colour. He also argued, perhaps surprisingly, that many functions of the brain, such as reading and writing, provide no biological survival advantage. In this respect they are para-evolutionary rather than evolutionary: From an evolutionary perspective, they are no more than offshoots. (Gould, 2002). Psychologists will be reminded here of the behaviourist B.F.Skinner's concept of superstitious behaviour. When an animal like a rat carries out a piece of behaviour that is rewarded, the behaviour will tend to be repeated. But so will other behaviour that the animal happened, by chance, to perform at the same time, such as nose scratching.

A more speculative para-evolutionary idea is that of 'internal selection.' This was suggested by a Scottish financier and industrial engineer who caused controversy some years ago by contrasting "internal selection" with the environmental selection involved in Darwinian evolution, which he called "external selection" (Whyte, 1965). The basic idea here is that the fertilised egg would go through some kind of process of self-testing, and reject any genes that do not meet certain criteria. How it would do this is obscure, but the effect is that genes that have been altered in some way through mutation may be liable to rejection. The criteria would be largely about suitability: Whether the changed gene would fit in and coordinate effectively with other genes and the resulting developing processes. Is the variation one that can be made to work within the developing organism or not? If not, processes within the fertilised egg would kill it off before it had a chance to reach adulthood and reproduce. It is also possible, according to this view, that the gene could be worked on and modified by the organism, either back into the pre-change version of the gene, or into a gene that would be compatible with the embryological development of the organism. In any case, the upshot would be that for a genetic variation to become established it would have to succeed not only by surviving Darwinian external selection through a hostile and competitive environment, but in terms of some kind of internal selection process as well.

Bejan, Adrian & Zane, Peder J. (2012) *Design in Nature: How the Constructal Law Governs Evolution in Biology, Physics,*

Technology and Social Organisations. New York: Random House.

Gould, S.J. (2002) *The Structure of Evolutionary Theory*. Cambridge, M.A.: Harvard University Press.

Gould, S.J. & Lewontin, R.C. (1979) The spandrels of San Marco and the Panglossian paradigm: A critique of the adaptational programme. *Proceedings of the Royal Society of London, Series B* 205, 581-598.

Whyte, Lancelot Law (1965) *Internal Factors in Evolution*. New York: Braziller.

Appendix VI

GLOSSARY OF NEW TERMS

This glossary is made up of new terms that supplement terms already defined within Reversal Theory and documented in other works.

Chronotyping: Characterising someone psychologically on the basis of the observation of only a short temporal segment of their actions. This is a form of over-generalisation, not unlike stereotyping.

Entertainmentisation: The tendency to use unfortunate and tragic real events (such as catastrophes, murder, warfare, and accidents) as the raw material for entertainment of all kinds. This is both a form of trivialisation and of affirmation.

Experiential economics: The study of the subjective meaning that a given piece of economic behaviour has to the person performing it rather than to some third party like an economist or the government.

Humanicide: The destruction of the entire human species.

Inconsistency paradox: The idea that people pursue contradictory values over time.

Intext: The internal context for action, including especially the motivations that give meaning to the action.

Malevolent contradiction: This arises when both members of the same pair of motivational states tend in a given individual to produce behaviour that is inappropriate either in general or in relation to some particular situation. This is a 'loss-loss' situation.

Mismatch paradox: The idea that people sometimes do not adapt what they want to what is, at that moment, readily available to them.

Motivational intelligence: The ability to understand, control, and take full advantage of motivational states in oneself and others. This underlies emotional intelligence.

Motivational richness: The awareness in a given individual of many different psychological desires over time. The pursuit of these multiple desires can give rise to a wide range of different experiences including different kinds of satisfaction.

Multi-rationality: The situation in which different approaches to problems are equally rational but based on different starting assumptions, so that the approaches appear irrational from each other's perspective.

Observer paradox: This occurs when people make the wrong assumptions about what other people want, meaning that the behaviour of these other people is puzzling to them.

Para-evolution: Processes that tend to produce complexity and pattern, but do not use Darwinian natural selection to do so.

Psychodiversity: A psychological system (person, team, etc) is psychodiverse if it has available to it a variety of alternative responses to different problems.

Realistic psychology: An approach to psychology which fully recognises both the positive and the negative in human behaviour and experience, rather than emphasising one or the other.

Reflexive paradox: The puzzlement that arises from the fact that one has changed what someone wants without realising that one has done so.

Success depression: Depression that arises from some kind of intense satisfaction which is unlikely to be repeatable. Often this involves the completion of an important project with no project of concomitant importance to replace it.

Value-contradiction paradox: The idea that for every fundamental human value there is an opposite and incompatible value.

Virtuous contradiction: This arises when both members of a pair of motivational states tend in a given individual to produce behaviour that is appropriate and desirable, either in general or in relation to some particular situation. This is a 'win-win' situation.

CHAPTER NOTES

PREFACE

1. Just a footnote on my footnotes. These take a number of forms. Sometimes they simply document, as they should, the source of information in the text. Sometimes they provide references for further reading. These references are not exhaustive – how could they be? – but consist largely of books that I have myself found particularly helpful. But I must confess that occasionally the footnotes consist of brief personal digressions and provocations – a self-indulgence that I hope you will forgive. There are also six appendices that deal in a little more detail than footnotes with topics that arise in the main text.

INTRODUCTION: THE LOGIC OF DESIRE

1. MacNeice, Louis (1939) *Autumn Journal*, Part XIII, line 36. London: Faber and Faber.
2. Drakulic, Slavenka (2005) *They Would Never Hurt a Fly: War Criminals on Trial in The Hague.* London: Penguin Books

Chapter 6 deals with this particular war criminal.

3. Story published in the Globe and Mail, Saturday December 6th 1997, by Jonathan Silvers and Tom Hagler.

4. This quotation comes from *Man's Search for Meaning* by Viktor Frankl, page 155 of the Washington Square Press, New York, paperback edition, 1984. Frankl, a psychiatrist who in fact worked in the Steinhof before it was taken over by the Nazis, and was later himself in a concentration camp, described the person in question, as he remembered him, as 'satanic.' Disappointingly he does not divulge his name.

5. Reversal Theory is a general theory of motivation, emotion and personality. It was first introduced and explained as a general approach in my 1982 book *The Experience of Motivation: The Theory of Psychological Reversals* (London and New York: Academic Press). Data of various kinds support the theory, including data from experimental, psychometric, psychophysiological and case history studies. An account of this research will be found in my text *Reversal Theory: The Dynamics of Motivation, Emotion and Personality*. (Oxford, Oneworld Publications, 2007.) More detail will be found in Apter, M.J. (Ed.) (2001) *Motivational Styles in Everyday Life: A Guide to Reversal Theory* (Washington, D.C.: American Psychological Association). Chapter 2 of the latter book provides a formal statement of the whole theory, laid out as a set of propositions. Descriptions of applications of the theory will be found, among other places, in Kerr, J.H. (2001) *Counselling Athletes: Applying Reversal Theory,* (London and New York: Routledge), Mallows, D.(2007) *Switch to Better Behaviour Management: Reversal Theory in Practice,* Norfolk: Peter Francis, and in Steve Carter & Jeremy Kourdi (2003) *The Road to Audacity: Being Adventurous in Life and Work*, London: Palgrave Macmillan. Dogor di Nuzzo (2011) *Le Management de*

la Motivation: Améliorer les Services, Cormelles-Le-Royal: EMS. Lunacek, Christophe & Rambaud, Jean (2104) *Le Petit Manuel Anti-Prise de Tête.* Paris: InterEditions, Dunod. Rutledge, D.H. & Tucker, J. (2007) *Reversing Forward: A Practical Guide to Reversal Theory*, Fairfax,VA: Otto Kroeger Associates.

A complete reversal theory bibliography, with reference to more than 500 publications including 20 books, will be found on the Reversal Theory Society website at: www. Reversaltheory.org or Reversaltheory.net. The Society organises an international conference every two years, the eighteenth having taken place in 2017. The society also publishes an open-access journal entitled the *Journal of Motivation, Emotion, and Personality.*

6. These include, in no particular order: stress, risk-taking, addiction, sport, exercise, sexual behaviour, creativity, leadership, teams, aesthetics, humour, depression, anxiety, religion, crime, delinquency, violence, ritual, design, teaching, consumer behaviour, and family relationships. It will be inferred from this that reversal theory is a general theory, with the strengths and weaknesses that go along with this.

7. Intriguingly, one philosopher/mathematician has suggested that self-referential paradoxes are not such a problem if we conceive of them as dynamic rather than static. That is, the contradictory interpretations of the statement are true in turn: First the statement is true, then it is false, then it is true, and so on. Wormell, C.P. (1958) On the paradoxes of self-reference. *Mind, 67,* 266, 267-71. As we shall see, in the present book, paradox and alternation are closely related, if not in quite the way suggested by Wormell. The idea that the universe is in some sense intrinsically paradoxical, and therefore paradox does not need to be avoided in acccounts of it, is developed in: Melhuish, George (1959)

The Paradoxical Universe, Bristol UK: Rankin.

8. A good survey of the seemingly endless definitions of, and ideas about, paradox, from ancient Greeks to the present day, will be found in: Sorensen, Roy (2005) *A Brief History of the Paradox: Philosophy and the Labyrinths of the Mind.* Oxford: Oxford University Press. A readable introduction to the whole field of paradox is: Sainsbury, R.M. (2009) *Paradoxes* (3rd. edition), Cambridge: Cambridge University Press. A useful reference volume is Clark, Michael (2007) *Paradoxes from A to Z.* London: Routledge. This includes 85 named paradoxes. See also: Cuonzo, Margaret (2014) *Paradox,* Cambridge, MA: MIT Press.

9. Alexander Pope, letter to Joseph Addison, 14 December, 1713. In, *Selected English Letters,* Ed. M. Duckitt & H. Wragg, Oxford: Oxford University Press, 1913, page 78.

CHAPTER 1: FOUR LIVES

1. Elkind, Peter (2010) *Rough Justice: The Rise and Fall of Eliot Spitzer.* New York: Portfolio.

2. Ibid.Page 166.

3. Disgraced NY Governor Won't Need New Job, Associated Press, March 12, 2008. Spitzer Fall Began with Bank Reports, New York Times, March 13, 2008. A documentary film by Alex Gibney, entitled "Client 9: The Rise and Fall of Eliot Spitzer", traces both the career and scandal, and contains interview material with Spitzer.

4. Brooke A. Masters (2006) *Spoiling for a Fight: The Rise of Eliot Spitzer.* New York: Holt.

5. Elkind, op.cit., page 291. He also used this term in response to a question in the Gibney film op.cit.

6. Here I am referring to motivation at the psychological rather than the biological level – this is what one wants as a

person, rather than things one wants for oneself as a body. In the psychological case we see pairs of opposites. This does not necessarily occur at the physiological level: The desires to eat, breathe, or urinate, do not have opposite desires.

7. The phrase, much repeated since, was first used by Welsh politician Aneurin Bevan, in attacking a colleague, at the Tribune rally, 29 September, 1954.

8. An excellent detailed account of the story of Rockefeller and Standard Oil will be found in Chernow, Ron (2004) *Titan: The Life of John D. Rockefeller, Sr.* New York: Vintage Books, Random House. A good shorter account is given in: Morris, Charles R. (2005) *The Tycoons,* New York: Holt.

9. Tarbell, Ida (1966) *History of the Standard Oil Company,* Briefer version, ed. D.M. Chalmers, New York: Norton, page 44. Originally published in instalments in McClure's Magazine during 1901-1903.

10. Robert F. Dalzell Jr. & Lee Baldwin Dalzell (2007) *The House the Rockefellers Built.* New York: Holt.

11. Chernow, op.cit, page 190.

12. Chernow, op.cit. page 467.

13. Cited in: Chernow, op.cit., page 412. Interestingly, James himself has been described as "The Man of Two Minds." This is the title of chapter 4 in: Louis Menard (2001) *The Metaphysical Club: A Study of Ideas in America.* New York: Farrer, Straus & Giroux.

14. McFeely, William S. (1981) *Grant: A Biography.* New York: Norton, page 77. This is a scholarly, if acerbic, account of Grant's life.

15. Porter, General Horace (1897) *Campaigning with Grant,* New York: Century Publishing, pages 164-165.

16. Korda, Michael (2004) *Ulysses S. Grant: The Unlikely Hero.* New York: Harper Collins. page 21.

17. McFeely op.cit., page 173.

18. Grant, Ulysses S. (1885-6) *Personal Memoirs of U.S. Grant.* New York: Charles L. Webster, pages 520-21.
19. Simpson, Brooks D. (2000) *Ulysses S. Grant: Triumph Over Adversity: 1822-1865.* Boston: Houghton Mifflin, page 463.
20. Anthony Thwaite (Ed) (2004) Annus Mirabilis, in *Philip Larkin: Collected Poems,* New York: Farrer, Straus & Giroux, page 146.
21. Kinsey, A.C., Pomeroy, W.C., & Martin, C.E. (1948) *Sexual Behaviour in the Human Male.* Philadelphia and London: Saunders.
22. Kinsey, A.C., Pomeroy, W.C., Martin, C.E., & Gebhard, P.H. (1953) *Sexual Behaviour in the Human Female.* Philadelphia and London: Saunders.
23. Kinsey, Alfred C. (1930) *The Gall Wasp Genus Cynips: A Study in the Origin of Species,* Indiana University Studies 16 (84,85,86), pages 1-577.
24. This study of Kinsey, reported in a massive volume of almost one thousand pages, was carried out by James H. Jones, and reported in his book *Alfred Kinsey: A Public/Private Life.* New York: W.W. Norton, 1997. For the shooting script of a movie on Kinsey based on Jones' book, see Condon, Bill (2004): *Kinsey: Public and Private.* New York: Newmarket Press. Further information on Kinsey's perversions will be found in: Jonathan Gathorne-Hardy (1998) *Sex the Measure of All Things: A Life of Alfred C. Kinsey.* London: Chatto & Windus. Republished (2000) by Bloomington, IN: Indiana University Press. This kind of material is summarised in Flynn, Daniel J. (2004) *Intellectual Morons: How Ideology Makes Smart People Fall for Stupid Ideas.* New York: Crown Forum. Chapter 2. This book also contains a critique of Kinsey's research methodology. Judith Reisman has made a career out of attacking Kinsey and, among other things, accusing him of paedophilia. E.g.: Reisman, J. (2010) *Sexual Sabotage: How*

one mad scientist unleashed a plague of corruption and contagion in America, New York: WND Books. The hysterical style of the title gives a good idea of the style of the content.

25. Ibid James H. Jones, page 603.
26. Ibid, page 502.
27. Richard Sale (2003) *Traitors: The Worst Acts of Treason in American History from Benedict Arnold to Robert Hanssen*, New York: Berkeley Books, page 281.
28. All these quotes come from page 142 of: Walter C. Langer (1972) *The Mind of Adolf Hitler: The Secret Wartime Report.* New York: Basic Books.

CHAPTER 2: INVITATION TO THE DANCE

1. Montaigne, M. De (2003) *The Complete Works.* Translated by Donald M. Frame. New York: Everyman's Library, Knopf. Originally published from 1580 onwards. Page 296.
2. Ibid, page 292.
3. Ibid, page 291.
4. Ibid, page 293.
5. Ibid, page 570.
6. Ibid, page 292.
7. There are many ways that we can refer to the nature of such contradictions: For instance as opposing motivations, contrary desires, competing values, incompatible needs, opposing principles, motivational orientations, alternative mindsets or contrasting mentalities. You can take your choice! For consistency in the rest of this book, I will continue, as I did in the previous chapter, to refer to opposing 'motivational states.' This is the term used in the literature about reversal theory.
8. Such terms as 'appropriate' and 'inappropriate' are

obviously very vague and relative, and what may be appropriate to one person may be inappropriate to another. Usually, for practical purposes – e.g. in therapy or coaching – the meaning can be negotiated with the client with respect to particular problems and issues. Typically there will be agreement about what is desirable and what is not. But we can at least distinguish between four general types of inappropriateness. The first is whether the behaviour takes full advantage of what the situation has to offer. The second is whether the behaviour, while being appropriate in the current situation, has negative repercussions later on. The third is whether the behaviour, while being appropriate for oneself, is harmful to others. The fourth is simply whether the behaviour is legal. I have discussed all this in more detail elsewhere, e.g. Chapter 9, Clinical Implications of Reversal Theory, in Apter, M.J. (2007) *Reversal Theory: The Dynamics of Motivation, Emotion and Personality.* Oxford: Oneworld Publications.

9. A famous biographical sketch of Florence Nightingale will be found in Lytton Strachey's classic *"Eminent Victorians."* This was originally published by Chatto and Windus in 1918. Strachey's book ushered in a whole new era of disdainful biography, with contempt for anything Victorian.

10. Robert Jay Lifton (1986) *The Nazi Doctors: Medical Killing and the Psychology* of *Genocide.* New York: Basic Books. See, in particular, pages 185-6. Interestingly, Lifton refers to what he calls 'healing-killing reversals' to refer to Nazi doctors who performed at different times both normal medical functions and mass extermination. This would involve, in my terms, mastery-sympathy reversals.

11. These pairs of states are defined precisely in Reversal Theory, and are given technical names. In case you want to dip into any of the specialist papers that have been

published, you will find the following correspondences useful to know:

The serious state is called the *telic* state.

The playful state is called the *paratelic* state.

The conforming state is called the *conformist* state.

The rebellious state is called the *negativistic* state.

The mastery state is still called the *mastery* state.

The sympathy state is still called the *sympathy* state.

The self-oriented state is called the *autic* state.

The other-oriented state is called the *alloic* state.

12. This interesting perceptual reversal was first noticed by the crystallographer Louis Necker in the late eighteenth century, and it is for this reason that it is called the "Necker Cube." It is an example of what psychologists today call "reversible figures." The term "Neckering" comes from Sawyer, Robert J. (1998) *Factoring Humanity,* New York: Orb.

13. Agassi, Andre (2009) *Open: An Autobiography.* London: HarperCollins.

14. Ibid, page 10.

15. Ibid, page 19.

16. Ibid, page 25.

17. The questionnaire is the "Apter Motivational Style Profile," which is a 40-item personality test, providing for each respondent a profile of the relative importance in their lives of the eight reversal theory states. These norms are based on people with a variety of backgrounds, the largest groups being managers and students in the U.S.A. and the U.K. It is derived from the Motivational Style Profile: Apter, M.J., Mallows, R., & Williams, S. (1998) The development of the Motivational Style Profile, *Personality and Individual Differences, 24,* 7-18.

18. A recent reversal theory state measure, which will probably become the 'go-to' measure for state research, is:

Desselles, M.L., Murphy, S.L. & Theys, E.R. (2014) The development of the reversal theory state measure, *Journal of Motivation, Emotion, and Personality*, Vol.2, 1, 10-21.

19. Walters, J., Apter, M.J. & Svebak, S. (1982) Colour preference, arousal and the theory of psychological reversals. *Motivation and Emotion, 6,* no. 3, 193-215.

20. Lafreniere, K., Cowles, M. & Apter, M.J. (1988) The reversal phenomenon: Reflections on a laboratory study. In, Apter, M.J., Kerr, J.H. & Cowles, M. (Eds.) *Progress in Reversal theory.* Amsterdam: North Holland. Pp. 247-254

21. Rhys, Sylvia (1988) Mastery and sympathy in nursing. In, Apter, M.J., Kerr, J.H., & Cowles, M.P. (eds.) *Progress in Reversal Theory.* Amsterdam: North-Holland. Pp. 329-338.

CHAPTER 3: GOING BEYOND TRAITS

1. Allport, G.W. and Odbert, H.S. (1936) Trait names: A psycho-lexical study. *Psychological Monographs, 47,* 211, 171. See also: Allport, G.W. (1938) *Personality: A Psychological Interpretation*, London: Constable, pp. 311-313.

2. The pattern of eight states has been supported by research, for example the factor analytic studies of Etienne Mullet and his colleagues and students at the University of Toulouse in France. Cottencin, A., Mullet, E., & Sorum, P.C. (2006) Consulting a complementary and alternative medical practitioner: A systematic inventory of motives among French patients. The Journal *of Alternative and Complementary Medicine, 12,* 791-798. Giraudeau, C., Chasseigne, G., Apter, M.J., Mullet, E. (2007) Adults' lay views about intelligence: A reversal theory approach. *Personality and Individual Differences, 42,* 1, 169-179. Makris, I., & Mullet, E. (2009). A systematic inventory of motives for becoming an orchestra conductor: A preliminary study.

Psychology of Music, 37, 443-458. 1-16. Bonin-Scaon, S., Munoz Sastre, M.T., Chasseigne, G., Sorum, P. & Mullet, E. (2009). End-of-life preferences: A theory-driven inventory. *International Journal of Aging and Human Development, 68*(1), 1-26. Lakhdar, M., Vinsonneau, G. Apter, M.J., & Mullet, E. (2007). Conversion in Islam among French adolescents and adults: A systematic inventory of motives. *International Journal of Psychology of Religion,* 17, 1-15. Kpanake, L., Munoz Sastre, M.T., & Mullet, E. (2009) Skin bleaching among Togolese: A preliminary inventory of motives. *Journal of Black Psychology, 38,* 350-268. Kpanake, L., Dassa, K.S., & Mullet, E. (2009) Why most Togolese people do not seek care for malaria in health care facilities: A theory-driven inventory of reasons. *Psychology, Health and Medicine, 14,* 4, 502-10. Neto, F., Mullet E., & Furnham, A. (2009) Sex differences in self-estimation of lay views about intelligence among adolescents. *Personality and Individual Differences, 46*, 4, 541-546. Vera-Cruz, G. Vinsonneau, G. & Mullet, E. (2010) Sexual permissiveness: A Mozambique-France comparison, *Journal of Applied Social Psychology, 40,* 2488-2499. Guedj, M., Munoz Sastre, M.T. & Mullet, E. (2011), Donating organs: a theory-driven inventory of motives, *Psychology, Health and Medicine* 16, 418-429. Neto, F., Pinto, C. & Mullet, E. (in press) Singing Fado: A test of an eight-factor model of motives for performing music, *Psychomusicology: Music, Mind and Brain.* Ballester, S., Chatri, F., Munoz-Sastre, M.T., Riviere, S. & Mullet, E. (2011) Forgiveness and unforgiveness: A systematic inventory of motives, *Social Science Information, 50,* 178-200. Kpanake, L. & Mullet, E. (2011) Motives for skin bleaching among Western Africans*, Household and Personal Care Today.* I cite all of these at length here because it emphasises how the model of eight psychological motives is supported repeatedly in a variety of different contexts and in relation to a wide range of seemingly unrelated research questions. Other papers could have been added to this list. A paper surveying ten such studies is: Mullet, E., Kpanake, L., Zounon, O. Guedj, M., Sastre, M.T.M. (2014) Putting Reversal Theory's model of four domains of experience in the hot seat. *Journal of Motivation, Emotion, and Personality, 2*:1, 1-9.

3. This concept underlies the development and use of all psychometric tests of personality. An entertaining, clear and critical introduction to this area is: Paul, Annie Murphy (2004) *The Cult of Personality.* New York: The Free Press.

4. See for example: Mischel, W. (2004) Toward an integrative science of the person. *Annual Review of Psychology 2004*, 55:1-22.

5. A classic example of this viewpoint is: Goffman, Erving (1959) *The Presentation of Self In Everyday Life.* New York: Anchor.

6. The main proponent of this view has been Mischel, who started the whole trait/situation debate. The classic statement is: Mischel, Walter (1968) *Personality and Assessment.* New York: Wiley. Just in case you are a sociologist rather than a psychologist, I should point out that 'Situationist' here does not refer to one of the groups that took part in the riots in Paris in 1968 who are also, curiously, referred to as 'Situationists,' together with the philosophers and intellectuals who inspired them such as the French intellectual Guy Debord.

7. An entertaining book about what the spaces that you create tell about your personality is: Gosling, Sam (2008) *Snoop: What Your Stuff Says About You.* New York: Basic Books.

8. For example: Bandura, A. (1978) The self system in reciprocal determinism. *American Psychologist, 33,* 344-358. Reciprocal determinism may also be discerned in Evolution: not only are biological characteristics selected by the environment, but environments are selected and

created by species to suit their biological characteristics. It has been argued that this undermines Darwin's theory of evolution: Taylor, Timothy (2010) *The Artificial Ape: How Technology Changed the Course of Human Evolution.* London: Palgrave Macmillan.

9. Interestingly, this inconsistency is recognised by the law in the 'anti-propensity rule' of evidence. This says that how someone usually is, should have little or no bearing on how that person was at the moment that they were alleged to commit the crime. A person should be tried for his bad act not for his bad character. For this reason previous convictions cannot normally be brought in as evidence. Likewise, a defence that says that a crime is inconsistent with someone's good character – the inconsistency personality defence, is not encouraged and is rarely successful. See: Roll, Samuel & Foote, William E. (1984) The inconsistent personality defence. In Dave J. Miller, Derek E. Blackman, & Antony J. Chapman (Eds.) *Psychology and Law,* New York: Wiley, pages 125-150.

10. A classic example of such a list is given in: William McDougall (1923) *Outline of Psychology*, London: Methuen. It includes the instincts of: escape, combat, disgust, parenting, distress, mating, curiosity, submission, self-assertion, seeking company, food-seeking, hoarding, creativeness, laughter. There were also various 'minor' instincts such as sneezing and urination.

11. A powerful recent defence of innate human nature will be found in: Pinker, Steven (2002) *The Blank Slate: The Modern Denial of Human Nature.* London and New York: Penguin Books. In defending the concept of human nature, Pinker is taking on a whole movement in the social sciences which is currently influential and goes by various names including post-structuralism, cultural psychology and discursive psychology.

12. Colin Talbot (2005) *The Paradoxical Primate*. Exeter, U.K.: Imprint Academic. Interestingly, Talbot has also called for a field of study that he would name 'paradoxical systems theory.' Obviously the present book would fit well into this category.

13. Here are a handful of examples, in no special order. "There is probably no reconciling his greatness and his malignancy. He had both." Review by Roger Lowenstein of *"I invented the modern age,"* a biography of Henry Ford, by Vincent Curcio New York: Scribner. Wall Street Journal, May 11, 2013, page C6.

"(He is) full of paradoxes." Biography of *"Young Prince Philip,"* London: Harper, 2011. Review by Frances Wilson, Times Literary Supplement, July 15, 2011, page 34.

"The Prince appears a mass of contradictions," *Heart of a King,* by Catherine Mayer/Aberdeenshire, *Time,* Nov.4, 2013, p.28.

"Steinberg finds a great many contradictory things to say about his subject. Review by anon of *"Bismark: A Life,"* Oxford University Press, 2011, reviewed in The Economist, April 2, 2011, page 80.

"The contradictions were fascinating." About Marlon Brando. In, *Rebel Males: Clift, Brando and Dean,* 1991, London: Hamish Hamilton, page 79.

"Sa vie et son art se sent construits autour de contradictions." House, John, page 13, in *"Renoir,"* Paris: Editions de la Reunion des Musees Nationaux.

"A man whose life and work were characterised by violent contradiction." *Rebel Rebel,* a biography of Arthur Rimbaud. In The New Yorker, August 29, 2011, page 74.

"There were also two Jane Russells." *Obituary* in The Economist, March 12, 2011.

"For my new biography of President Eisenhower, I asked his son John about the apparent even balance between the sunny, genial Ike and the cold blooded Ike. 'Make that 75% cold blooded,' John said with a slight smile." Article on "The upside of mystery" by Evan Thomas, *Time,* October 1, 2012, page 18.

"Baudrillard is a contradictory character." Page 4, Chris Horrocks and Zoran Jertic, *Buadrillard for Beginners,* Icon Books, Cambridge, UK.

"A rolling paradox of contradictions." Review by Jonathan Yardley of *Master of the Mountain: Thomas Jefferson and his Slaves,* by Henry Wiencek, London: Farrar Straus Giroux, 2012, published in the Guardian Weekly, 012.11.12, page 39.

"The list of his contradictions is endless." Paul Johnson on Leo Tolstoy, *Intellectuals,* New York: Harper Perennial, 1988, p.128.

14. If you take the dynamic view that I am presenting here, it opens up whole new areas for future individual difference and personality research. Here are some examples of questions that can be asked now, that would not have arisen before. Do people differ in terms of how frequently they reverse between motivational states – their reversibility or instability? Do people have 'favourite' trajectories, i.e. sequences of states that they tend to cycle around? What different things induce reversals in different people? Do people have characteristic combinations of states that tend to work together? How do people influence the states that others are in? Do people who get on well together, such as the partners in a happy marriage, have similar or complementary motivational state characteristics? Why do some people experience and express certain states in particularly intense ways? Why do individuals tend to focus on some pairs of states rather than others, so that they become central in their lives? These, among others, are topics for future research.

CHAPTER 4: THE PROTECTIVE FRAME

1. "Mount Everest 'death zone' set for spring clean-up as team risk their lives to tidy the world's highest garbage dump." *Mail Online,* 19 April, 2010. "Maxed out on Everest, Mark Jenkins, *National Geographic,* June 2013, pp.84-95.

2. "Storm chasers create chaos." Joe Barrett, *The Wall Street Journal,* April 20, 2012, page A4.

3. "Antarctic concerns grow as tourism numbers rise." USA Today, March 16, 2013.

4. Apter, M.J. (1982) *The Experience of Motivation: The Theory of Psychological Reversals.* London and New York: Academic Press. This was the first book on Reversal Theory, and indicated that the understanding of behavioural paradoxes would be one of the principle aims of the theory. See especially page 10.

5. Many forms of risky physical activity involve playing with gravity. A good discussion will be found in: Soden, Garrett (2003) *Falling: How Our Greatest Fear Became Our Greatest Thrill.* New York: Norton. This book traces the history of all the major games that man has devised that involve gravity.

6. I have used this 'tiger in the cage' metaphor elsewhere, and repeat it here because people seem to find it helpful. I have dealt with the subject of this chapter, excitement-seeking, in a book entirely devoted to this topic: Apter, M.J. (2007) *Danger: Our Quest for Excitement.* Oxford: Oneworld Publications.

7. Those familiar with 'Optimal Arousal Theory' will see that the reversal theory approach is quite different. In place of the homeostasis of optimal arousal theory (in which a single intermediate level of arousal is preferred), reversal theory puts bistability (which has two alternative levels of desired arousal, one high – excitement – and

one low – relaxation). Unfortunately, the single preferred level idea still runs through most present-day research on motivation, but is increasingly difficult to justify. It dates back to: Hebb, D.O. (1956) Drives and the C.N.S. (Conceptual Nervous System) *Psychological Review, 62,* 243-254. A more accurate view comes from research using the "International Affective Picture System" (devised by Lang, P.J., Bradley, M.M. & Cuthbert, B.M., 1999 at the University of Florida) which shows, across many experiments, that the greater the arousal the more a picture is pleasant or unpleasant to look at. See: Margaret M. Bradley (2000) in Caccioppo, J.T., Tassinary, Louis G. & Berntson, Gary G. (Eds) *Handbook of Psychophysiology, 2nd. Edn.,* Cambridge: University Press. A formal analysis of different types of stability will be found in: Apter, M.J. (1981) On the concept of bistability. *International Journal of General Systems, 6,* 225-232.

8. Valentine, C.W. (1956) *The Normal Child and Some of His Abnormalities.* Harmondsworth, U.K.: Penguin Books. Pages 132-3.

9. Ibid. Pages 127-8.

10. From the perspective being developed here – the reversal theory perspective – it is possible to see at least one fundamental way in which Freud went wrong in his theorising. Essentially, he got into a terrible tangle over arousal. On the one hand he saw high arousal as the same as anxiety, and argued that, for this reason, people always want low arousal. Further, they will use various psychological tools, including defence mechanisms (such as sublimation or rationalisation), to achieve this. On the other hand he argued that sex was the master motive: It was what people really wanted more than anything else, and libido and eros suffused their lives. But how could this be, since sexual behaviour is all about achieving *high* arousal in the form

of sexual excitement and intense orgasm? The only way of getting around this theoretical self-contradiction was for him to claim that sex is not really enjoyed at all and makes us feel anxious and guilty – something which seems to fly in the face of everyday experience, not to mention the future of the human race. He could be seen as having spent all his considerable creativity over a long career trying to make sense of this self-created conundrum, elaborating a view of sex which is impossible to reconcile with the reality of healthy sexual experience.

11. Interview in television program "102 Minutes that Changed America," produced by Siskel/Jacobs, and that was shown on the History Channel on 9th September 2013.

12. Apter, M.J. & Batler, R, (1997) Gratuitous risk: A study of parachuting. S.Svebak & M.J. Apter (eds), *Stress and Health: A Reversal Theory Perspective.* Washington, D.C.: Taylor & Francis. Pages 119-129.

13. A similar effect was found in an experiment involving emotions before, during and after, a fast cable ride in a French ski resort: Legrand, F. D. & Apter, M.J. (2004) Why do people perform thrilling activities? A study based on reversal theory. *Psychological Reports, 94,* 307-313.

14. Kerr, J.H., Kawaguchi,C., Oiwa, M., Terayama,Y., & Zukawa, A. (2000) Stress, anxiety and other emotions in Japanese modern dance performance. *Pacific Journal of Psychology, 11,* 1, 16-33.

15. Dutton, D.G. & Aron, A.P. (1974) Some evidence for heightened sexual attraction under conditions of high anxiety. *Journal of Personality and Social Psychology, 30,* 510-517. This can be seen as an example of 'excitation transfer.' For more on this, see: Zillmann, Dolf (1998) *Connections between Sex and Aggression.* Hillsdale, New Jersey: Lawrence Erlbaum.

16. Reversal theory and adult recreation has been explored in detail in: Kerr, J.H. & Apter, M.J. (eds.) (1991) *Adult Play: A Reversal Theory Perspective.* Amsterdam: Swets & Zeitlinger.

17. Nick Spandler, Diary of disaster, in: Chris Bull & Sam Erman (Eds) (2002) *At Ground Zero: 25 Stories from Young Reporters Who Were There.* New York: Avalon, pp.48-51.

18. Bivona, J. & Critelli, J. (2009) The nature of women's rape fantasies: An analysis of prevalence, frequency, and contents. *Journal of Sex Research,* 46:33.

19. Willie Sutton with Edward Linn (1976) *Where the Money Was.* New York: Viking. Page 120.

20. Matsen, Brad (2008) *Titanic's Lost Secrets: The Further Adventures of Shadow Divers,* by John Chatterton and Richie Kohler. New York: Grand Central Publishing. This behaviour is also cited in the definitive book by Walter Lord (1955) *A Night to Remember,* New York: Holt

21. Maxtone-Graham, John (2012) *Titanic Tragedy: A New Look at the Lost Liner.* New York: Norton.

22. Everett, Marshall (2011*) The Story of the Wreck of the Titanic: Eyewitness Accounts from 1912.* Mineola, New York: Dover. Page 88.

23. Douthwaite, Richard & Fallon, Gillian (eds) (2010) *Fleeing Vesuvius,* Ireland: Feasta.

24. Weick, Karl E. (2007) Drop your tools: On reconfiguring management education. *Journal of Management Education, 31*, 1, 5-16. Cited in Hirschorn, Larry & Horowitz, Sharon (2013) Extreme work environment: Beyond anxiety and social defence. ISPSO symposium, Oxford, July 2013.

25. Might we be in a similar situation now with respect to the major global threats that face us stemming from climate change, resource depletion and overpopulation? This is an apocalyptic theme to be reduced to a footnote. But could it be that the possible prospect of what we might want to call 'humanicide' (the killing of the human race) is not

being taken as seriously as it should be, especially by many politicians, because the issues are surrounded by fallacious frames of various kinds? The idea of the 'rapture' certainly provides a protective frame for those who consider themselves to be 'the chosen.' The characterisation of scientists as crazy and out of touch provides another kind of illusory protective frame. So does the opposite idea: the idea that scientists will come up with something to save us, as they always have in the past. This kind of fallacious frame seems to be a fallacious safety-zone frame: The dangers seem to be too far in the future to be a real threat. The possibility of humanicide has led to an astounding new kind of super-Nihilism in some quarters, in which the emergence of humankind is seen as an evolutionary aberration, and it is argued that it would be better if our species disappeared altogether. In some versions the argument extends to life on earth in general. See: Ligotti, Thomas (2010) *The Conspiracy Against the Human Race.* New York: Hippocampus. Also: Gray, John (2002) *Straw Dogs: Thoughts on Human and Other Animals.* New York: Granta Books.

26. This was first published in 1898, and has never been out of print since.

27. Cantril, Hadley (1940) *Invasion from Mars.* Princeton, New Jersey: Princeton University Press. The original novel, the entire text of the play, and various essays, will be found in: *The War of the Worlds: Mars' Invasion of Earth.* Published 2005 by Naperville, Illinois: Sourcebooks (no editor cited). See also: Gallop, Alan (2011) *The Martians are Coming! The True Story of Orson Welles' 1938 Panic Broadcast,* New York: Amberley.

28. BBC World News, Monday 5 April, 2010.

29. The Independent, UK, Monday 15th March, 2010, page 21.

30. Kagan, Jerome (2006) *An Argument for Mind.* New Haven: Yale University Press.

31. Bonierbale, M., Clement, A., Loundou, A., Simeoni, M.C., Barrau, K., Hamidi, K., Apter, M.J., Lancon, C. & Auquier, P., (2006) A new evaluation concept and its measurement: "Male sexual anticipating cognitions." *Journal of Sexual Medicine, 3,* 96-103.

32. Associated Bodywork and Massage Professionals Magazine for the Visually Impaired. March/April 2013 issue. I must confess that this is not a journal that I have often cited.

33. Kerr, John H. (2007) Sudden withdrawal from skydiving: A case study informed by Reversal Theory's concept of protective frames. *Journal of Applied Sport Psychology, 19,* 337-351.

34. Viktor E. Frankl (1986) *The Doctor and the Soul: From Psychotherapy to Logotherapy.* 3rd edition, New York: Vintage Books. Also: Viktor E. Frankl (1973) *Psychotherapy and Existentialism: Selected Papers on Logotherapy.* Harmondsworth, U.K.: Pelican Books. Incidentally, Frankl is the psychiatrist mentioned in the Introduction to this book, in connection with his experience in a concentration camp.

35. Hans O. Gerz, The treatment of the phobic and the obsessive-compulsive using paradoxical intention, see Viktor E. Frankl, in: Frankl op.cit (1973), pp. 194-6.

36. Frankl op.cit (1986) pp. 235-6.

CHAPTER 5: PARADOXICAL EMOTIONS

1. In order to overcome this kind of ambiguity in talking about emotions, reversal theory uses the term 'parapathic' (meaning 'alongside emotions') to refer to nominally unpleasant emotions when they are actually being enjoyed. I will, however, continue to use the term 'paradoxical

emotion' here in the spirit of attempting to avoid technical terms in this text and emphasising the human paradox theme.

2. Many psychological studies of emotions use movies to induce unpleasant emotions, like anxiety, to study in the laboratory. Results from such studies can be misleading because, in any particular case, a supposedly unpleasant emotion may really be a pleasant paradoxical one.

3. Andrade, Eduardo B. & Cohen, Joel B. (2007) On the consumption of negative feelings. *Journal of Consumer Research, 34*, published electronically at http://www.ssrn.com/abstract=892028

4. All these studies on stress that follow are reported in: Martin, R.A., Kuiper, N.A., Olinger, L.J. & Dobbin, J. (1987) Is stress always bad? Telic versus paratelic dominance as a stress moderating variable. *Journal of Personality and Social Psychology, 53,* 970-82. The reversal theory account of stress is developed through a series of papers in: Svebak, S. & Apter, M.J. (eds.) (1997) *Stress and Health: A Reversal Theory Perspective.* London: Taylor & Francis.

5. Actually, at a high level of stress frequency, the playful group also started to show the same relation to stress as the serious group, but this is presumably because at this level of stress they were also starting to experience the serious state more frequently.

6. Buford, Bill (1993) *Among the Thugs.* New York: Vintage.

7. Ibid page 217.

8. Of the many books on sexual fantasy, the best known is probably Nancy Friday's *"My Secret Garden: Women's Sexual Fantasies."* New York: Pocket Books. This bestseller showed that fantasy in women is often about acts that are illicit or immoral. In another study 65% of women reported having fantasies, even during sexual intercourse with their husbands. About half their fantasies were about

doing something forbidden including coercion, group sex and voyeurism. Hariton, E.B. & Singer, J.L. (1974) Women's fantasies during sexual intercourse: Normative and theoretical implications. *Journal of Consulting and Clinical Psychology, 42,* 323-322.

9. Kinsey, for example, found that fellatio and cunnilingus were both practiced, generally, by about half of married couples, and this frequency increased for married couples in later surveys, such as: Hunt, M. (1974) *Sexual Behaviour in the 1970s,* Chicago: Playboy Press. By the nineteen nineties we see oral sex as increasing in non-married couples: Laumann, E., Gagnon, J.H., Michael R.T. & Michaels, S. (1994) *The Social Organisation of Sexuality: Sexual Practice in the United States,* Chicago:University of Chicago Press.

10. Apter, M.J. (1982) *The Experience of Motivation: The Theory of Psychological Reversals.* London and New York: Academic Press, page 219. See also M.J. Apter (2007) *Danger: Our Quest for Excitement.* Oxford: Oneworld Publications, page 120. I want to make clear that the point I am making here is psychological not moral. Whether certain sexual acts are or are not sinful is not the issue here. The issue is about how people experience and use them.

11. Bering, Jesse (2013) *Perv –The Sexual Deviant in All of Us.* New York: *Scientific American*/Farrar, Straus & Giroux.Cited by Mirsky, Steve, p.80, Scientific American, Jan. 2014.

12. Kutchinsky, B. (1973) The effect of easy availability of pornography on the incidence of sex crimes: The Danish experience. *Journal of Social Issues, 29,* 169-181.

13. This does not mean that real sadists do not also exist, for whom the cruelty is what is central to their needs. Fortunately they are rare. Clearly in these pathological cases it is only the sadist and not the victim who enjoys what is happening. And what is happening is obviously not

at all playful for the victim, in that it can have significant consequences, including, in the extremes, even torture and death.

14. The playful nature of sadomasochism is documented in: Thompson, Bill (1994) *Sadomasochism*. London: Cassell. A similar view is taken by Gerald and Caroline Greene in their book *S-M: The Last Taboo,* New York: Blue Moon Books, 1995. In fact, they refer to SM as "a sort of supreme sexual art form" (page 4). See also: Thomas S. Weinberg & G.W. Kamel (1995) *S & M: Studies in Dominance and Submission*, New York: Prometheus Books. The popularity of the novel *Fifty Shades of Grey* (2012) by E.L. James (New York: Random House) attests to peoples' understanding of sexual submission as fun. However, it has been argued that pornography is becoming increasingly sadomasochistic and that, while viewers may take it as fun, what the viewer sees may not be fun at all to the women who are pushed into taking part and who risk damage and real humiliation as a result: Hedges, Chris (2009) *Empire of Illusion: The End of Literacy and the Triumph of Spectacle*, New York: Nation Books.

15. Evidence for the way that aggressive arousal can become experienced as sexual arousal will be found in the research of Dolf Zillmann, as reviewed in his 1984 book cited earlier: *Connections Between Sex and Aggression*. Hillsdale, New Jersey: Lawrence Erlbaum.

16. Krafft-Ebing, Richard von (1965) *Psychopathia Sexualis,* New York: Bell. English translation. Originally published in German in 1886.

17. I am giving here a brief and simplified version of the reversal theory account of humour. In particular, I have avoided the explanatory term 'cognitive synergy' which is used in reversal theory to refer to the way in which two incompatible meanings are made to apply to the same

identity, thus apparently breaking the logician's Law of the Excluded Middle, but 'working together' to produce special psychological effects. More details will be found in my book *The Experience of Motivation: The Theory of Psychological Reversals,* London and New York: Academic Press, 1982, Chapter 8, and also my book *Reversal Theory: The Dynamics of Motivation, Emotion and Personality.* Oxford: Oneworld Press, 2007, Chapter 8. See also: Apter, M.J. & Desselles, M.L. (2012) Disclosure humour and distortion humour: A reversal theory analysis. *Humour, 25* (4) 417-435.

18. This obsession with disaster in Hollywood movies, especially blockbusters, has been referred to by sociologists as 'disaster porn.' The use of this term has been documented by Recuber, Timothy (2013) Disaster Porn, *Contexts,* 12: 2, 28-33.

19. Terrorism in particular can be seen as a form of entertainment, as is well understood by terrorists themselves. To be effective, terrorism must get popular attention, which means that it must be spectacular. Without this theatricality, it would not survive. The best antidote to terrorism would be the refusal of news channels to report on it at all, or to do so in no more than a perfunctory manner.

20. Guy Debord (1967) *La Société du Spectacle.* Paris: Buchet Chastel. See also Hedges, Chris (2009) *Empire of Illusion: The End of Literacy and the Triumph of the Spectacle,* New York: Nation Books.

CHAPTER 6: PARADOXICAL REWARDS

1. In fact, the researcher, Edward L. Deci, asked some other questions in this study, but this was the central question. The reference is: Deci, E.L. (1972) Intrinsic motivation, extrinsic reinforcement, and inequity. *Journal of Personality*

and Social Psychology, 22, 113-120. Other papers in this early research were published with his Rochester University colleague Richard M. Ryan, as well as a founding text: Deci, Edward L. & Ryan, Richard M. (1985) *Intrinsic Motivation and Self-Determination in Human Behaviour.* New York: Plenum.

2. The first experiment described here was by a team from Stanford University: Lepper, M.R., Greene, D. & Nisbett, R.E. (1973) Undermining children's intrinsic interest with extrinsic rewards. *Journal of Personality and Social Psychology, 28,* 129-137. The second was: Lepper, M.R., Sagotsky, G, Dafoe, J.L. & Greene, D. (1982) Consequences of superfluous social constraints: Effects on young children's social inferences and subsequent intrinsic interest. *Journal of Personality and Social Psychology, 42,* 51-65.

3. Weick, K.E. (1964) Reduction of cognitive dissonance through task enhancement and effort expenditure. *Journal of Abnormal and Social Psychology, 68,* 533-539.

4. Reported in Langer, Ellen J. (1997) *The Power of Mindful Learning.* Cambridge, MA: Da Capo Books. Pp. 58-59.

5. Amabile, Teresa M., Hennessy, Beth Ann, & Grossman Barbara S. (1986) Social influences on creativity: The effects of contracted-for reward. *Journal of Personality and Social Psychology, 50,* 14-23.

6. Amabile, Teresa M., (1985) Motivation and creativity: Effects of motivational orientation on creative writers. *Journal of Personality and Social Psychology, 48,* 393-99.

7. This problem was originally devised by Karl Duncker, who referred to it as a problem of 'functional fixedness.' Duncker, K. (1945) On problem solving. *Psychological Monographs, 58,* 5, 1-111.

8. Glucksberg, Sam (1962) The influence of strength of drive on functional fixedness and perceptual recognition. *Journal of Experimental Psychology, 63,* 36-41.

9. More than 100 papers have now been published on this phenomenon, and surveys of the results show that sometimes the effect occurs and sometimes it does not. A good survey paper is: Cameron, J., Banko, K.M. & Pierce, W.D. (2001) Pervasive negative effects of rewards on intrinsic motivation: The myth continues. *The Behaviour Analyst, 24,* 1-44.

10. An excellent review of the whole field will be found in Kohn, Alfie (1993) *Punished by Rewards,* Boston: Houghton-Mifflin. This book also brings out some of the practical implications, especially in the classroom.

11. This point is made by: Pink, Daniel H. (2009) *Drive: The Surprising Truth About What Motivates Us.* New York: Riverhead Books. This book is, in fact, an excellent introduction to the subject-matter of the present chapter. It goes into detail on the experimental foundations, discusses their implications, and makes suggestions to the reader for self-improvement.

12. This is a good place for me to record my sincere thanks to my mentor, the late Frank H. George, a charismatic psychology professor at Bristol University, who showed me just how exciting a subject psychology could be, especially at the level of general theory, and in an interdisciplinary context. It was through his good offices that I was offered the graduate place at Princeton, and later he was my Ph.D supervisor at Bristol. I owe him a great deal.

13. This was noticed by other students too and became a kind of joking catchphrase among us. It did not surprise me when, many years later, I briefly met the then head of the department and her first question to me was: "How have you got on in the profession?" I made some kind of inane reply like "Very well, thank you." This is not to say that concern with a career is not perfectly legitimate and desirable. (Indeed, in recent years I have,

with colleagues, developed a reversal theory workshop on career development.) But surely in a great university like Princeton there should be considerable scope for encouraging learning for its own sake and for providing room for purely intellectual values and endeavours.

14. Twain, Mark (1959 edition) *The Adventures of Tom Sawyer.* New York: Signet Classics.

15. The original form of Behaviourism was due, early in the last century, to the animal psychologist John Watson, and was strongly influenced by Pavlov's famous observations on conditioning in dogs. See Watson, J.B. (1919) *Psychology from the Standpoint of a Behaviourist.* Philadelphia, PA: Lippincott. The later form of Behaviourism was promulgated in the second half of the century especially by B.F. Skinner, who focused more on what he called 'operant conditioning', which is about voluntary responses rather than the involuntary responses, like salivation, that Pavlov studied in his work. Skinner was highly prolific, but a good starting reference would be: Skinner, B.F. (1974) *About Behaviourism.* New York: Knopf. Interesting transcripts of a debate between Skinner and an 'intrinsic motivation' researcher will be found in Kohn (1993) op.cit. An excellent biography of Skinner is: Toates, Frederick M. (2009) *Burrhus F. Skinner.* London: Palgrave Macmillan.

16. Lewis, Gareth (2013) A portrait of disaffection with school mathematics: The case of Anna. *Journal of Research in Motivation, Emotion, and Personality,* 1, 36-43.

CHAPTER 7: IN THE GIVING VEIN

1. *Monty Python's Flying Circus,* Episode 30, "Blood, Devastation, Death, War and Horror." As everyone must

know, 'Monty Python' was a highly successful made-for-television comedy series created in the UK.

2. Actually, in a research study carried out with a colleague, we found that many different reasons for giving blood were reported by donors, even down to meeting girls and having free food! But the pleasure of giving was indeed the most prevalent reason provided. Other frequently given reasons were to do something meaningful and to do the right and moral thing. Apter, M.J. & Spirn, N. (1997) Motives for donating blood. In Svebak, S. & Apter, M.J. *Stress and Health: A Reversal Theory Perspective.* Washington D.C.: Taylor and Francis. Pages 145-156.

3. Titmuss, R.M. (1971) *The Gift Relationship: From Human Blood to Social Policy.* New York: Pantheon.

4. Upton, W.E. (1973) Altruism, attribution, and intrinsic motivation in the recruitment of blood donors. Unpublished Ph.D thesis, Cornell University.

5. Mellström, Carl & Johannesson, Magnus (2008) Crowding out in blood donation: Was Titmuss right? *European Economic Association, 6,* 4, 845-863.

6. Other research supports the general conclusion that payment can reduce volunteering. For further discussion and evidence, see: Le Grand, Julien (2003) *Motivation, Agency and Public Policy: Of Knights and Knaves, Pawns and Queens.* Oxford: Oxford University Press.

7. Frey, Bruno S., Oberholzer-Gee, Felix (1997) The cost of price incentives: An empirical analysis of motivation crowding-out. *The American Economic Review, 87,* 4, 746-755.

8. See: Evers, Adalbert (1994) Payment for care: A small but significant part of a wider debate. In Pijl, Maria & Ungerson, Claire (eds.) *Payment for Care: A Comparative Overview.* Aldershot, U.K.: Avebury.

9. Pearce, J.L. (1978) Something for nothing: An empirical

examination of the structures and norms of volunteer organisations. Unpublished dissertation, Yale University. Cited in: Pearce, J. L. (1985) Insufficient justification and volunteer motivation. In Larry F. Moore (Ed) *Motivating Volunteers: How the Rewards of Unpaid Work Can Meet People's Needs.* Vancouver Volunteer Centre.

10. *The Diane Rehm Show*, broadcast on National Public Radio, 14 November 2003.

11. Sidgwick, Henry (1874) *The Methods of Ethics.* London: Macmillan. See especially Pages 36-42.

12. Ibid, page 37.

13. Dorothy Kern, quoted in: Andrews, F.E. (1953) *Attitudes Toward Giving.* New York: Russell Sage.

14. Franklin, Benjamin. *The Autobiography of Benjamin Franklin.* As given in: J.A. Leo Lemay (ed.) *Benjamin Franklin's Writings,* New York: Library of America, 1987, page 1404.

15. Wiseman, Richard (2009) *59 Seconds: Think a Little, Change a Lot.* New York: Knopf. This study developed out of an earlier experiment: Hornstein, H.A., Fisch, E. & Holmes, M. (1958) Influence of a model's feeling about his behaviour and his relevance as a comparison on other observers' helping behaviour. *Journal of Personality and Social Psychology, 10,* 3, 222-226.

16. Harvey, Jerry B. (1988) *The Abilene Paradox, and Other Meditations on Management.* Washington, D.C.: Lexington Books.

17. Ibid., page 15.

18. There is an enormous literature here, but the classic Sociobiology reference is Edward O. Wilson (1975) *Sociobiology: The New Synthesis.* Cambridge, M.A.: Harvard University Press. In his most recent work he argues that natural selection occurs at both the individual and the group level. Selfish individuals beat altruists in the competition for individual survival, but groups of altruists beat groups

of selfish people: Edward O. Wilson (2012) *The Social Conquest of Earth*, New York: Liveright. For evolutionary psychology in general, a standard text is: Jerome Barkow, Leda Cosmides and John Tooby (Eds.) (1992) *The Adapted Mind: Evolutionary Psychology and the Generation of Culture.* Oxford: Oxford University Press. A recent entertainingly critical review of the whole area is: James Le Fanu (2009) *Why Us? How Science Rediscovered The Mystery of Ourselves.* New York: Pantheon Books.

19. Dawkins, Richard (1976) *The Selfish Gene,* Oxford: Oxford University Press.

20. Trivers, Robert (1971) The evolution of reciprocal altruism, *Quarterly Review of Biology, 46,* 35-57.

21. A detailed argument for the genuine quality of altruism will be found in: Samuel Bowles & Herbert Gintis (2011) *A Co-operative Species: Human Reciprocity and its Evolution.* Princeton: Princeton University Press.

22. Ridley, Matt (1998) *The Origins of Virtue,* Harmondsworth: Penguin. He argues that self-interest and mutual aid are not incompatible in evolutionary terms. See also: Oren Harman (2010) *The Price of Altruism: George Price and the Search for the Origins of Kindness.* New York: Norton. Michael Shermer investigates the evolutionary origins of morality, which is obviously related to unselfishness: Michael Shermer (2004) *The Science of Good and Evil.* New York: Holt. All these books are written for the general public and are highly readable.

CHAPTER 8: POSITIVE NEGATIVISM

1. In more technical works on reversal theory, rebelliousness is referred to as 'negativism.' The term 'negativism'

comes from two areas of psychology. In developmental psychology it refers to a phase that typically occurs at about the age of two – the 'terrible twos' – when the young child seems to take pleasure in disobeying parents and others. The other area is psychopathology, where the word is used to describe a symptom of catatonic schizophrenia in which the patient systematically does exactly the opposite of whatever he is requested to do. In reversal theory, as we have seen, the term is generalised to refer to the desire of people to escape from rules and expectations and to "be themselves." This is, however, not seen as inherently pathological but, as we shall see in this chapter, at times it can be healthy and desirable.

2. These can also of course be referred to as proactive and reactive negativism. These two forms of rebelliousness have been particularly researched by Mark McDermott, who has developed a Negativism Dominance Scale, also known as the Social Reactivity Scale, with subscales to measure these two different versions of rebelliousness. His research, much of it concerning health issues in connection with rebelliousness, is summarised in McDermott, M. (2001) Rebelliousness, In Apter, M.J. (ed.) *Motivational Styles in Everyday Life: A Guide to Reversal Theory.* Washington, D.C.: American Psychological Association, pp.167-185. A notable study using this scale and involving 4,500 subjects, is: Klabbers, G., Bosma, H., van den Akker, M, van Boxtel, M.P.J., Kempen, G.I.J.M., McDermott, M.R. & van Eijk, J. Th.M. (2009), Measuring rebelliousness and predicting health behaviour and outcomes: an investigation of the construct validity of the Social Reactivity Scale, *Journal of Health Psychology,* *14* (6), 771-779. See also: McDermott, Mark & Barik, Nilupa, B. (2014) Developmental antecedents of proactive and reactive rebelliousness: The role of parenting style,

childhood adversity, and attachment. *Journal of Motivation, Emotion and Personality, vol 2. 1*, 22-31.

3. Many others will be found in Dixon, Norman (1976) *On the Psychology of Military Incompetence.* London: Random House Pimlico. See also: Julian Spilsbury (2010) *Great Military Disasters: A History of Incompetence.* New York: Metro Books.

4. This example comes from: Chiles, James R. (2001), *Inviting Disaster: Lessons from the Edge of Technology.* New York: Harper Business. Many other examples of maladaptive conformity will be found in this book.

5. The original experiment was reported in: Latané, Bibb. & Darley, John M. (1968) Group inhibition of bystander intervention. *Journal of Personality and Social Psychology, 10,* 215-221. See also: Latané, Bibb & Darley, John M. (1970) *The Unresponsive Bystander: Why doesn't he help?* New York: Appleton-Century-Crofts. There is a hoary story that does the rounds of psychology laboratories, that an early experiment on fear involved the same kind of set up as this, but that a real fire started. Subjects had to be forcibly evicted from the laboratory by firemen, because none of them believed that the fire was real, thinking that it was all part of the experiment.

6. David Brown, Over-ruled. *Washington Post*, Outlook section, Sept 25, 2005.

7. A detailed documentation of the inadequate response to Katrina, due to bureaucratic interference among other things, will be found in: Heerden, Ivor van and Bryan, Mike (2007) *The Storm: What Went Wrong and Why During Hurricane Katrina – the Inside Story from one Louisiana Scientist.* London: Penguin. The President of Jefferson Parish is reported to have said (page 194 of this book): "Bureaucracy has committed murder here." See also: Michael D. Brown & Ted Schwartz (2011) *Deadly Indifference,* New York: Taylor.

8. There is now a literature documenting how easily ordinary people were turned by Hitler into concentration camp killers. A particularly disturbing study is: Browning, Christopher R. (1993) *Ordinary Men: Reserve Police Battalion 101 and the Final Solution in Poland.* New York: HarperPerennial. See also: Goldhagen, Daniel Jonah (1997) *Hitler's Willing Executioners: Ordinary Germans and the Holocaust.* New York: Vintage.

9. Much has been written about Milgram's experiment, which took place at Yale in the sixties. But to find out more it is best in the first instance to go to Milgram's own writing: Milgram, S. (1963) Behavioural study of obedience. *Journal of Abnormal and Social Psychology, 67,* 4, 371-378. Milgram, S. (1974) *Obedience to Authority: An Experimental View.* New York: HarperCollins. The set-up used by Milgram is reminiscent of the 'treatment' provided to soldiers suffering from shell shock in the First World War. They received increasingly strong electric shocks until they lost their symptoms (e.g. shaking, strange gait) and were able to return to the trenches. Many were permanently injured by the treatment, and some died. An interesting variant replication study was one which took place in a television studio, the 'authority' being the studio audience. In this case, as many as 81% of the subjects were willing to administer the strongest shocks. See report in *The Psychologist* (2012), No 6, page 410. At least one replication has shown subjects to be more conflicted than Milgram found: Shermer, Michael (2012) Shock and Awe, *Scientific American*, Nov. 2012, page 86. For a critique of Milgram's study, see: Perry, Gina (2012) *Behind the Shock Machine: The Untold Story of the Notorious Milgram Psychology Experiments,* New York: New Press.

10. The whole scandalous story was revealed to the public by the journalist Seymour Hersh, when he wrote about

his investigations for the Dispatch News Service. Subsequently he wrote a book about the massacre that won a Pulitzer prize: Hersh, S. (1970) *My Lai 4: A Report on the Massacre and its Aftermath.* New York: Random House. In his book *Kill Anything that Moves: The Real American War in Vietnam* (2013), New York: Metropolitan Books, Nick Turse showed that there was nothing exceptional about My Lai, but that such massacres were widespread.

11. Einstein, Albert (1979), *Autobiographical Notes,* La Salle and Chicago Illinois: Open Court Publishing (ed. Paul Arthur Schilpp), page 17.

12. This conception of Einstein as rule-breaker has been particularly developed by Scott Thorpe in his book: *How to think Like Einstein: Simple Ways to Break the Rules and Discover Your Hidden Genius.* New York: Barnes & Noble, 2000.

13. This phrase is reported by Walter Isaacson in his article "Patron saint of distracted students" that appeared in the *Los Angeles Times* on April 8, 2007.

14. Walter Isaacson (2007) *Einstein: His Life and Universe.* New York: Simon and Schuster, page 67. Another excellent biography is: Ronald W. Clark (2007) *Einstein: The Life and Times,* New York: Harper Perennial. (Originally published 1971.)

15. Isaacson, op.cit., page 317.

16. He still remained eccentric in his personal habits, however, famously wearing his shoes without socks, and leaving his iconic hair to grow wild.

17. Isaacson, op. cit., cited on page 317.

18. There is a huge literature on Gertrude Stein, and also on Alice B. Toklas. An excellent book on Stein is: Hobhouse, Janet (1975) *Everybody Who Was Anybody: A Biography of Gertrude Stein.* New York: Putnam.

19. Ibid, page 124.

20. A recent biography focuses on their charmed life during this period: Malcolm, Janet (2007) *Two Lives: Gertrude and Alice*. New Haven: Yale University Press. She refers to Stein as displaying "chronic contrariness" (p. 107) It is possible that they were protected by Bernard Fay, a Vichy official: See Barbara Will (2012) *Unlikely Collaboration: Gertrude Stein, Bernard Fay, and the Vichy Dilemma*. New York: Columbia University Press.

21. Op.cit., Malcolm, page 5.

22. *The Autobiography of Alice B. Toklas*. In, *Selected Writings of Gertrude Stein*, ed. Carl Van Vechten, New York: Vintage Books, Random House, 1972, p. 219.

23. *Composition as Explanation,* In, *Selected Writings of Gertrude Stein*, ed. Carl Van Vechten, New York: Vintage Books, Random House, 1972.

24. Much of this section on Wittgenstein is based on: Monk, Ray (1990) *Ludwig Wittgenstein: The Duty of Genius.* London and New York: Penguin Books. This is the most detailed and convincing of the many books that have been written about Wittgenstein the man and/or Wittgenstein the philosopher.

25. Ibid, page 65.

26. Monk, pages 265 and 493.

27. Ibid, page 486.

28. Ibid, page 493.

29. In this respect, the question arises of the part played by homosexuality in Wittgenstein's life. The truth is that he seems to have been bisexual, or, even more to the point, anti-sexual. As far as we know, he rarely actually practiced homosexuality, but into middle age many of his friendships, often intense, were with unmarried, sensitive, young men. It is possible to speculate that the homosexual urge may have been the source of at least some of his recurrent feelings of sinfulness and "lack of decency."

30. Page 277, Ray Monk.
31. Monk, page 365.
32. Osborn, Alex (1953) *Applied Imagination: Principles and Procedures of Creative Problem Solving.* New York: Scribner.
33. Nemeth, C.J. and Nemeth-Brown, B. (2003) Better than individuals? The potential benefits of dissent and diversity for group creativity. In P. Paulos & B. Nijstand (eds.) *Group Creativity*, Oxford: University Press. A readable critique of brainstorming is: Lehrer, Jonah (2012) Groupthink. In *The New Yorker*, Jan. 30, 2012, pp.22-27.
34. Kitzinger, Sheila (1983) *Woman's Experience of Sex*, New York: Putnam, page 79.
35. There is evidence for such token refusal. Muelhard, Charlene L. & Hollabaugh, Lisa C. (1988) Do women sometimes say no when they mean yes? The prevalence and correlates of women's token resistance to sex. *Journal of Personality and Social Psychology, 54*, 5, 872-879.
36. Louise May Alcott, *Little Women,* originally published 1868 and 1869. Quote on pages 351-2 in the 2004 edition published in New York as a Barnes and Noble Classic.

CHAPTER 9: THE POWER OF SYMPATHY

1. This pushback phenomenon against coercion, especially when it involves resisting a loss of freedom, is known in Social Psychology as 'reactance.' See Brehm, J.W. (1966) *A Theory of Psychological Reactance*, New York: Academic Press. Also: Wicklund, R.A. (1974) *Freedom and Reactance,* Potomac MD: Erlbaum. 'Reverse psychology' attempts to overcome reactance by encouraging the subject to do the opposite of what is really wanted. (I am reminded of a certain cartoon in which a policeman is standing on the ledge of a skyscraper, looking down, and saying "I knew

I shouldn't have used reverse psychology.") This rather unreliable technique, referred to more often in comedy than in serious psychiatry, is of course not to be confused with reversal theory.

2. By qualitative research is meant research that documents behaviour that is difficult to measure and quantify, but that can still be interpreted systematically. Particular attention is typically paid to the meaning to the respondent of what is said and done. For example a piece of qualitative research might involve the use of structured interview, followed by the coding of respondents' statements by independent judges.

3. *"Getting into the Minds of Motorists."* Report prepared by Apter International for the South Carolina Department of Public Safety, Office of Highway Safety, September 2007.

4. This is consistent with reversal theory-based research on adolescent and young adults' responses to a message designed to persuade them not to smoke cannabis. Message resistance was associated with frequency of both mastery and rebellious states. Ellen L. Boddington & Mark R. McDermott (2012), Predicting resistance to health education messages for cannabis use: The role of rebelliousness, autic mastery, health value and ethnicity. *Journal of Health Education,* DOI 10.1177/1359 1053 12438111.

5. The Marriage Project, Sponsored by the Human Rights Campaign, Washington DC, 2005. We obtained similar findings in a qualitative project that we carried out, with Grove Insight, for Third Way in Washington DC in 2010.

6. The master interrogator, who developed many of these techniques, was Hanns Scharff, who became an American citizen after the war. He never used torture or brutality, but is generally credited with always getting the information he needed. See: Tolivar, Raymond F. in

collaboration with Scharff, Hanns J. (1978*) The Interrogator: The Story of Hanns Scharff, Luftwaffe's Master Interrogator.* Self-published. This gives many case history examples of successful interrogation. The so-called "Reid technique," which is widely practiced today in police interrogation, is influenced by this, and, among other things, deliberately develops rapport with the prisoner. It was developed by John Reid in Chicago in the nineteen forties. See: Zulawswki, David E. & Wicklander, Douglas E. (1998) *Practical Aspects of Interview and Interrogation*, Ann Arbor: CRC Press. Among others who have systematically used these techniques were Chinese Communists on American airmen during the Korean war. Repatriated airmen, on debriefing, testified to their power: Albert D. Biderman (1960) Sociopsychological needs and "involuntary" behaviour as illustrated by compliance in interrogation. *Sociometry,* Vol. 23, pages 120-217.

7. A terrible indictment of the torture used in the Iraq war will be found in Tony Lagouranis (with Allen Mikaelian) (2007) *Fear Up Harsh: An Army Interrogator's Dark Journey Through Iraq*, New York: Caliber. This documents in harrowing detail not only the futility of torture but also what it does to those who have to practice it. The success of "newer" and more enlightened forms of interrogation is attested to by Matthew Alexander (with John R. Bruning) in: *How to Break a Terrorist: The US Interrogators who Used Brains not Brutality to Take Down the Deadliest Man in Iraq.* New York: St. Martin's Griffin (2011). This book describes how Al Zarqawi was tracked down using non-coercive interrogation techniques. The successful use of such techniques is also described in: Ali H. Soufan (with Daniel Freedman) (2011) *The Black Banners: The Inside Story of 9/11 and the War Against al-Qaeda,* New York: W.W. Norton.

8. Dylan Kurz, Dominance and submission: How the police use psychological manipulation to interrogate citizens. www.grayarea.com/police8tm

9. This was the Nigerian passenger who attempted unsuccessfully to detonate a bomb, on Christmas day, in a Northwestern Airlines flight to Detroit from Amsterdam. See *Wall Street Journal*, February 3, 2010, article entitled "Abdulmutallab Again Talking to FBI" by Evan Perez.

10. "How to Make Terrorists Talk" by Bobby Ghosh, *Time*, June 8, 2009, pages 41-43.

11. She has described her feelings and actions in detail in: Ashley Smith (with Stacy Mattingly) (2005) *Unlikely Angel: The Untold Story of the Atlanta Hostage Hero*. Grand Rapids, Michigan: Zondervan.

12. Ibid, page 33.

13. Brian Nichols was subsequently found guilty of murder and sentenced to life imprisonment after the jury deadlocked on the death penalty.

14. Tuff, Antoinette, with Tresniowski, Alex (2014) *Prepared for a Purpose,* Minneapolis: Bethany House. Page 141.

15. Associated Press, 2007. This account is based on: Bolman, Lee E. & Deal, Terence E. (2007) *Reframing Organisations: Artistry, Choice and Leadership.* New York: Jossey-Bass, pages 12-13.

16. Meir, Menahem (1983) *My Mother Golda Meir*. New York: Menahem House, page 227.

17. See for example, Peggy Mann (1971) *Golda: The Life of Israel's Prime Minister*, New York: Coward, McCann & Geoghegan, pages 265-6.

18. Meir, Golda (1975) *My Life,* New York: Dell, page 396.

19. Hayes, J., Schimel, J. & Williams, T.J. (2008) Fighting death with death: The buffering effects of learning that worldview violators have died. *Psychological Science,* vol.19, 5, 501-507.

CHAPTER 10: DEAR ENEMY

1. This is part of a larger question, which is that of why we ever allow people to control us. This is a puzzle in human behaviour that goes back a long time, and has its classic expression in a short book by the French philosopher Etienne de la Boétie entitled, in English, *An Essay on Voluntary Servitude:* Etienne de la Boetie, 1995, translated S. Auffret, Paris: Mille et un Nuits. Originally published in 1576. De la Boétie was a close friend of the essayist Montaigne who I have cited elsewhere in this book. Boétie asked the question: Why do we ever allow tyrants – Pharoes, Caesars, Kings, Emperors – to control us? He pointed out that if they have power over us, it is only because we give it to them – our servitude is voluntary. If everyone simply stopped obeying, then a tyrant would no longer be a tyrant. He was not able himself to go far in suggesting why people accept to be controlled in this way. But the ideas put forward in the present book may give us some insights, some possible reasons, for doing this with tyrants as well as other controllers such as captors, prison guards, and abusive husbands.

2. One of the best accounts of what actually happened in the Stockholm bank will be found in: Strentz, T. (1982) The Stockholm syndrome: Law enforcement policy and hostage behaviour. This is a chapter in: In F.M. Ochberg & D.A. Soskis, *Victims of Terrorism,* Boulder, CO: Westview Press. Pp.149-164.

3. So named by Nils Bejerot, a well-known psychiatrist and criminologist who advised the police during the stand-off.

4. Namnyak, M., Tufton, R., Szekeley, M., Toal, M., Worboys, S. & Sampson, E.L. (2008) 'Stockholm syndrome': psychiatric diagnosis or urban myth? *Acta Psychiatrica Scandinavica,* 117: 4-11. Other well-publicised

cases include: Patty Hearst who was abducted by the so-called Symbionese Liberation Army in 1974 and who took up their cause and helped them to rob banks; Elizabeth Smart, a 14 year old kidnapped in 2002 from her home in Salt Lake City and who remained captive for 9 months; and Natascha Kampusch who was held captive in Vienna for 8 years until 2006.

5. A detailed case study of the captive referred to, based on his troubling account of his ordeal, is in: Ochberg, F.M. (1982) A case study: Gerard Vaders. In F.M. Ochberg & D.A. Soskis, *Victims of Terrorism,* Boulder, CO: Westview Press. Pp. 9-36.

6. Franzini, Louis R. & Grossberg, John M. (1995) *Eccentric and Bizarre Behaviour.* New York: Wiley, page 84.

7. Ibid, page 79

8. Freud, Anna (1966) *The Ego and the Mechanisms of Defence.* New York: International Universities Press. (Originally published in German in 1936.)

9. The paper referred to is: Bettelheim, B. (1943) Individual behaviour in extreme situations. *Journal of Abnormal and Social Psychology, 38*: 417-452. The book reference is: Bettelheim, B. (1960) *The Informed Heart: Autonomy in a Mass Age.* New York: Knopf. Later in life he became the director of the Orthogenic School attached to the University of Chicago, whose pupils were emotionally disturbed children. After his suicide in 1990, former pupils came forward to denounce him as despotic. Ironically, some claimed that in running the school he recreated something like a concentration camp.

10. Bettelheim (1960) Op. cit. page 172.

11. Griffin, Susan (1992) *A Chorus of Stones: The Private Life of War.* New York: Doubleday. The quotation by Susan Griffin is on page 171. This is an amazing book that provides insights into the causes of violence and the ways

that we cover up and deny violence after it has occurred.

12. Zimbardo, Philip (2008) *The Lucifer Effect: Understanding How Good People Turn Evil*. New York: Random House.

13. In fact, Zimbardo was an expert witness in the case of one of the Abu Ghraib torturers, arguing that he was a decent young man who had been corrupted by the system. Despite this, the soldier was found guilty: Philip Zimbardo, You can't be a sweet cucumber in a vinegar barrel. In John Brockman (ed) (2011) *The Mind*. New York: Harper Perennial.

14. Zimbardo, Ibid. Page 205. It has been suggested, on the basis of a replication study, that the guards did what they did because they identified with Zimbardo rather than just following orders. This would mean that identification was playing an important part in the behaviour not just of the prisoners but also of the guards. This also provides another possible explanation for the behaviour of participants in Milgram's study of obedience. This view derives from the 'social identity' tradition in social psychology, associated with the name of Henri Tajfel, which emphasises what in Reversal Theory is referred to as the self-oriented to other-oriented dimension. The replication study referred to here, known as the "BBC Prison Study," broadcast in 2001 under the title "The Experiment," was carried out by Alex Haslam and Stephen Reicher.

15. Bettelheim (1960) Op. cit page 174.

16. Fifty four people were tried in total, and 47 sentenced to death. It has been estimated that in the purge as a whole, over two million people met their deaths, either through execution or through mistreatment in labour camps.

17. The most accessible and detailed account of this period will be found in: Conquest, Robert (1990) *The Great Terror: A Reassessment*. Oxford: Oxford University Press.

18. *Report of Court Proceedings in the Case of the Anti-Soviet Block*

of Rights and Trotskyites, Moscow, 1938, p. 777.

19. Koestler, Arthur (2005 edition), *Darkness at Noon.* London: Random House. (Originally published 1940.)
20. Krivitsky, W.G. (1939) Why did they confess? *The Saturday Evening Post,* June 17, *211,* no.51, page 98. This General in the Soviet army, who defected, also paints a horrendous picture of the torture methods used.
21. This view is reflected in the intriguing play, and film, "Who's Afraid of Virginia Woolf?" although the cruelty represented in this play is more psychological than physical.
22. Walker, Lenore E. (1979) *The Battered Woman.* New York: Harper and Row.
23. Ibid, pp. 64-65.
24. This is a different 'cycle of violence' from the passing on of aggressivity from one generation to another – a phenomenon for which this term is also used.
25. Ibid, p.73.
26. Barman, Tracy (2012) *Queen of the Conqueror: The Life of Matilda, Wife of William I.* New York: Random House. Gondoin, Stéphane William (2012) *Guillaume le Conquérant et les Femmes.* Paris: La Louve. Bisson, Alex & Erickson, Jean-Francois (2011) *Guillaume le Conquérant,* Rennes: Ouest France Press.

CHAPTER 11: ECONOMICS UNBOUND

1. I am referring here, and throughout this chapter, to microeconomics, the economics of individual people and institutions. This contrasts with macroeconomics, which deals with economy-wide phenomena such as business cycles, unemployment, inflation and the money supply.
2. The 'dismal science' epithet is attributed to the great

Scottish writer of the Victorian period, Thomas Carlyle. It seems to have been used as a cliché by practically every commentator on economics since then – including now, I regret to say, myself.

3. The most popular of the 'pop econ' books has been the best-seller *Freakonomics* by Steven Levitt and Stephen Dubner, published in 2006 by Penguin, London. This was followed in 2009 by *Super Freakonomics* by the same authors, New York: HarperCollins. Others include: Cowen, Tyler (2008) *Discover Your Inner Economist,* New York: Penguin. Frank, Robert H. (2007) *The Economic Naturalist*, New York: Basic Books, and (2009) *The Economic Naturalist's Field Guide*, New York: Basic Books. Harford, Tim (2007) *The Undercover Economist*, New York: Random House. Shermer, Michael (2008) *The Mind of the Market,* New York: Holt. Thaler, Robert H. & Cass, R. Sunstein (2008) *Nudge,* New York: Penguin. One of the characteristics these books have in common is their dealing with all kinds of offbeat topics, about which economics would not normally be thought to have anything much to say. Daniel Kahneman himself has added to this list with his 2011 book *Thinking Fast and Slow*, New York: Farrar, Straus & Giroux. See also: Dunn, Elizabeth & Norton, Michael (2013) *Happy Money: The Science of Smarter Spending*. Oxford: Oneworld.

4. Margolis, H. (1982) *Selfishness, Altruism and Rationality: A Theory of Social Choice.* Chicago: University of Chicago Press.

5. Veblen, T. (1934) *The Theory of the Leisure Class*. New York: Modern Library. This classic economic text was originally published in 1899.

6. Oscar Wilde. Chapter 8 in his novel *The Picture of Dorian Gray*, (1891) Ward, Lock and Co.

7. "A market for market psychology: Frank Murtha helps financial advisers understand why their clients sometimes make such illogical decisions about money." By Lea Winerman. *Monitor*

on Psychology, September 2011, pages 52-54.

8. This concept comes from Paul Ricoeur, the French philosopher, especially in his 1976 book *Interpretation Theory: Discourse and the Surplus of Meaning*, Fort Worth: Texas Christian University Press.

9. Kahneman, Daniel, Knetsch, Jack L. & Thaler, Richard H. (1990) Experimental tests of the Endowment Effect and the Coase theorem. *Journal of Political Economy, 98* (6), 1325-48.

10. The psychology of antique collecting has been explored further from the reversal theory perspective in: Smith, K.C.P. & Apter, M.J. (1997) Collecting antiques: A psychological interpretation. *Antique Collector,* 7, 64-66.

11. This perspective on organisations has been developed into a systematic reversal theory approach to leadership and to organisational change, this being an approach that can be used by management consultants. It is supported by two psychometric profiles, the Apter Leadership Profile System, and the Apter Work Impact System (see www.methode-apter.com).

12. A prime exponent of this 'irrationalist' view of economic behaviour is Dan Ariely. See his book *Predictably Irrational*, published by HarperCollins, New York, 2009. See also by Ariely: *The Upside of Irrationality: The Unexpected Benefits of Defying Logic at Work and at Home*, New York: HarperCollins, 2010. Another author who has explored human irrationality is Robyn Dawes. For example, see his 2001 book *Everyday Irrationality: How Pseudo-Scientists, Lunatics, and the Rest of Us Systematically Fail to Think Rationally*, Boulder, CO: Westview Press. Researchers in the new field of economic sociology also tend to take a more irrationalist view, such as: Viviana A. Zelizer (2011) *Economic Lives: How Culture Shapes the Economy*, Princeton University Press. The alternative traditional 'rational' view has been well put by Harford, Tim (2008) *The Logic of Life,*

New York: Random House. Ingeniously, Harford shows how peoples' rationality sometimes needs to be 'teased out' if it is to be understood as rational.

13. Gneezy, Uri & Rustichini, Aldo (2000) A fine is a price. *Journal of Legal Studies, 29,* no.1, 1-17.

14. See page 19 of: Levitt, S.D. & Dubner, S.J. cited above.

15. Read: Dan, Loewenstein, George & Kalyanaraman, S. (1999) Mixing virtue and vice: Combining the immediacy effect and the diversification heuristic. *Journal of Behavioural Decision Making, 12,* (4) 257-73.

16. Kahneman, Daniel & Tversky, Amos (1979) Prospect Theory: An analysis of decision under risk. *Econometrica 47* (2), 263-291

17. Easterbrook, Gregg (2003) *The Progress Paradox.* New York: Random House. It has also, confusingly, been called the Easterlin Paradox after the Californian economist, Richard Easterlin, who first argued for the lack of relation between economic development and level of happiness. Easterlin, Richard A. (1974) Does economic growth improve the human lot? In Paul A. David & Melvin W. Meder (eds.) *Nations and Households in Economic Growth: Essays in Honor of Moses Abramovitz.* New York: Academic Press.

18. Lane, Robert (2000) *Loss of Happiness in Market Democracies.* New Haven: Yale University Press.

19. In this respect see also: Schwartz, Barry (2004) *The Paradox of Choice: Why More is Less.* New York: Harper Perennial. Choice helps us to control our destiny, but also makes us anxious since we do not want to make bad decisions. Nowadays we have 'choice overload.'

20. Diener, Ed & Biswas-Diener, Robert (2008) *Happiness: Unlocking the Mysteries of Psychological Wealth.* Oxford: Blackwell.

21. Diener, Ed, Weiting, Ng, Harter, James & Raksha, Arora (2010) Wealth and happiness across the world: Material

prosperity predicts life evaluation, whereas psychosocial prosperity predicts positive feeling. *Journal of Personality and Social Psychology, 99* (1), 52-61. See also: Weiner, Eric (2008) *The Geography of Bliss.* New York: Twelve. This impressionistic account of happiness in different countries concludes that there is little relationship between wealth and happiness. The broad political implications are discussed by: David G. Myers (2000) *The American Paradox: Spiritual Hunger in an Age of Plenty.* New Haven: Yale University Press. See also: Skidelsky, Robert & Skidelsky, Edward (2012) *How Much is Enough? Money and the Good Life,* London: Allen Lane. Sandel also discusses materialism and economics: Sandel, Michael (2012) *What Money Can't Buy: The Moral Limits of Markets.* New York: Farrar, Straus & Giroux. A recent survey of this whole area is: Carol Graham (2011) *The Pursuit of Happiness: Toward an Economy of Well-being.* DC: Brookings Institution Press.

22. Kasser, Tim, Rosenblum, Katherine, Sameroff, Arnold J., Deci, Edward L. et al (2013) Changes in materialism, changes in psychological well-being: Evidence from three longitudinal studies and an intervention experiment. *Motivation and Emotion, 38,*1,1-22.

23. James, Oliver (2007) *Affluenza,* New York: Vermilion, Random House.

24. This was announced by British Prime Minister David Cameron in November 2010.

CHAPTER 12: GETTING TO HAPPINESS

1. In translation, Aristotle's question is: "How, then, is it that no one is continuously pleased?" This will be found in *The Nichomachean Ethics,* 1175, 3-6 in *The Basic Works of Aristotle,* Richard McKeon ed., New York: Random House,

1941. This was written about 350 BC.

2. This idea that happiness is a by-product of something else and cannot be aimed at directly, has been referred to as the paradox of happiness. See: Mike W. Martin (2008) Paradoxes of happiness, *Journal of Happiness Studies, 9,* 2, 171-184. In chapter six of the present book I referred to it as the 'hedonic paradox,' which is another of its names, and cited the Victorian philosopher Henry Sidgwick.

3. While we are on terminology, it is interesting to note that the word 'happiness' derives from Middle English 'happ,' meaning chance or fortune. We see this derivation in such words as 'haphazard,' 'perhaps,' and 'hapless.' Interestingly it starts as something that can be judged from outside – whether someone is fortunate or not – but in the course of centuries becomes a word depicting an internal state. See McMahon, Darran M. (2006) *Happiness: A History.* New York: Grove Press, pp.10-11. This book is a comprehensive intellectual history of the idea of happiness from the ancient Greeks to the present day. A highly readable recent discussion of the meaning of happiness will be found in Gilbert, Daniel (2007) *Stumbling on Happiness.* New York: Vintage. See also: Sissela Bok (2010) *Exploring Happiness: From Aristotle to Brain Science.* New Haven: Yale University Press.

4. Aldrin, Edwin E. "Buzz," with Wayne Wanga. *Return to Earth.* New York: Random House, 1973. Page 304.

5. Fox, Margalit (2013) *The Riddle of the Labyrinth: The Quest to Crack an Ancient Code.* London: Profile. Andrew Robinson (2002) *The Man Who Deciphered Linear B.* London: Thames & Hudson.

6. Lilly, Doris (1970) *Those Fabulous Greeks: Onassis, Niarchos and Livanos,* Spokane, WA: Cowles Book Co.

7. This point is developed in some detail in: B. Curtis Eaton & Mukesh Eswaran (2009) Well-being and affluence in

the presence of a Veblen good. *Economic Journal,* 119 (539) 1088-1104.

8. See for example: Smith, R. (2008) *Envy: Theory and Research.* New York: Oxford University Press.

9. Bhagwan Shree Rajneesh, known as "Osho," was an Indian guru who set up an ashram in Oregon. He let it be known that he liked Rolls Royce cars, and his American followers gave him a number of these over the years, eventually totalling ninety three. So much for the value of the spiritual over the material. He died in 1990. See Milne, Hugh (1986) *Bhagwan: The God that Failed.* London: Caliban Books. Also: Strelley, Kate. *The Ultimate Game: The Rise and Fall of Bhagwan Shree Rajneesh,* New York: Harper and Row. 1987.

10. Brickman, P., Coates, D. & Janoff-Bulman, R. (1978) Lottery winners and accident victims: Is happiness relative? *Journal of Personality and Social Psychology, 36,* 917-927.

11. Eysenck, Michael W. (1990) *Happiness: Facts and Myths.* New Jersey: Erlbaum.

12. Epicurus (1993) *The Essential Epicurus.* Translated by Eugene M. O'Connor. New York: Prometheus.

13. Gilbert, Daniel (2006) op.cit, footnote 3.

14. Gilbert (op.cit) cites scores of interesting studies that support his 'stumbling' theme. The two kinds of research mentioned here, on daydreaming and life expectations, are both dealt with in the first chapter of his best-selling book.

15. Geisler, Guide & Kerr, John H. (2005) Stress, emotions and metamotivational states in Canadian and Japanese Soccer. Paper presented at the 12th International Conference on Reversal Theory, Winnipeg, Canada, July 2005.

16. Hansen, James R. (2005) *First Man: The Life of Neil A. Armstrong.* New York: Simon and Schuster. Page 646.

17. Frankl, Viktor. *Man's Search for Meaning.* Originally published in German in 1946. First English translation

published in 1959. This quotation is from the 1984 edition published by Simon & Schuster, New York, page 57.

18. The American love of positive thinking goes back a long way in American history. The history of this characteristic is critically but entertainingly traced in: Barbara Ehrenreich (2009) *Bright-Sided: How the Relentless Promotion of Positive Thinking has Undermined America.* New York: Holt.

19. Positive Psychology can be seen as a development of the "Humanistic Psychology" of the forties, of which the father figure is Abraham Maslow. But it is only in more recent years that Positive Psychology has really taken off, both in its influence on mainstream psychology and on the general public. The founding text of Positive Psychology is Martin E.P. Seligman's book *Authentic Happiness: Using the New Positive Psychology to Realise your Potential for Lasting Fulfillment,* New York: Free Press, 2002. The relationship to happiness studies is particularly clear in Seligman's *Learned Optimism,* New York: Knopf, 1991. For more detail, consult: Snyder, C.R. & Lopez, Shane J. (Eds.) *Handbook of Positive Psychology.* Oxford: Oxford University Press, 2005. Also: Linley, P. Alex, Harrington, Susan & Garcia, Nicola (Eds.) *Handbook of Positive Psychology and Work.* Oxford: Oxford University Press, 2009. Carr, Alan (2004) *Positive Psychology: The Science of Happiness and Human Strengths*, Hove and New York: Brunner-Routledge.

20. The first major work on happiness in modern psychology was by Michael Argyle (1987), *The Psychology of Happiness*, London: Methuen. A good review of subsequent research on happiness, especially biological and neurological research, is: Klein, Stefan (2006) *The Science of Happiness.* Cambridge, M.A.: Da Capo Press. See also: Eid, Michael & Larsen, Randy J. (eds.) (2008) *The Science of Subjective Wellbeing.* New York: Guilford Press. 'Happiness studies' has now become such a major academic field that it has

its own journals, including: *Journal of Happiness Studies, The Journal of Positive Psychology*, and the *British Journal of Wellbeing*.

On the popularisation and self-help side, a whole cottage industry has arisen, with books too numerous to mention here. McMahon, op.cit. cites over thirty such books (page 472) with titles like *"101 Ways to Happiness," "Seven strategies for Wealth and Happiness," "Happiness is a Choice,"* and *"14,000 Things to be Happy About."* If the reader wants more titles or details, I would suggest that he or she visit any reasonable size bookstore and inspect the self-help section. They will not be disappointed. An unusual and interesting book that is neither science nor self-help properly speaking, is: Gretchen Rubin (2009) *The Happiness Project,* New York: Harper Collins. This is a 'diary' of the author's systematic attempt, over the period of a year, to become happier. (Some things worked, some didn't.) See also *Happier at Home,* by the same author.

CHAPTER 13: PATTERNS OF PARADOX

1. Value pluralism has been attributed to many thinkers of historical importance, including Niccolo Machiavelli, Giambattista Vico, Max Weber and William James.
2. These ideas appear throughout Berlin's voluminous writings. A clear and succinct statement comes in: Berlin, I. (1999) *The First and the Last.* New York: New York Review of Books.
3. Ibid. Curiously a fourth pair of opposites that he suggests is happiness versus knowledge. The rationale for this is that no one can be happy if they know too much about the suffering and cruelty of this world. Pages 76-78.

4. 'Multiple personality' is a term which is dropping out of favour in psychiatry, although it was popular for many years following the publication of two best-sellers: Firstly, *The Three Faces of Eve* (1957) by C.H. Thigpen and H.M. Cleckley, London: Secker & Warburg. Secondly, *Sybil* (1973), by Flora Rheta Schreiber, New York: Grand Central Publishing. By the way, it has now been argued that the famous case of Sybil referred to above was an elaborate fraud: Debbie Nathan (2011) *Sybil Exposed: The Extraordinary Story Behind the Famous Multiple Personality Case*. New York: Free Press.

   'Dissociative identity disorder' is the term which has taken over. In its psychiatric sense it refers to a person who not only displays very different personalities at different times, but for whom at least some of these personalities have independent memories making them just like independent people living separate lives within the same body. This is not the case with the motivational states described in the present book, so I am certainly not making what would be a bizarre claim that everyone suffers from this clinical syndrome. But in the non-clinical sense described in this book, it is possible to say that most people's personalities are multiple. It has been argued by some that dissociation involves a kind of 'splitting' of the personality, producing subpersonalities that can conflict with each other. This idea has a long and complex history. A good starting point to learn about this would be: Rowan, John (1990) *Subpersonalities: The People Inside Us*. London: Routledge. Also: Rowan, John & Cooper, Mick (eds.) (1999) *The Plural Self: Multiplicity in Everyday Life*. London: Sage.

5. Grange, Pippa & Kerr, John H. (2011) Do elite athletes renowned for their aggressive play transfer aggression to nonsport settings? A qualitative exploratory study. *Journal*

of Aggression, Maltreatment & Trauma, 20:4, 359-375, p.368.

6. If Man is created in the image of God, it is permissible to ask if this means that Man has the same emotions and motivations as God. Indeed, if God, as presented in the Old Testament, does have such contradictory emotions as love, anger, and jealousy, does God also have motivational states and does he move between them just as we do? Indeed, might the Devil be God on a bad day? Many Christian theologians have, over the centuries, tended to see God as emotionless, detached, and unchanging – 'immutable' – and for them these sorts of questions do not arise. However, in some religions the deity can actually take different forms over time. These religions, such as Hinduism, are referred to by theologians as 'henotheistic.' One is tempted to ask the intriguing, if disturbing question, of whether it would be possible to have a psychology of God to go along with the history of God presented by Jack Miles in his challenging book *"God: A Biography."* (New York: Knopf, 1995.) Interestingly, in early parts of the Old Testament Miles sees two opposing personalities in the Deity: God the creator and God the destroyer. This in turn reminds us of the Hindu deity Siva who is also both creator and destroyer. Either way we see recognition of a deity reversing.

7. Jones, R. (1981) Reversals, delinquency and fun. *Self and Society, 9,* 5, 237-40. This quotation is on page 239.

8. The way that sadomasochism is treated in law differs from country to country, and state to state within the United States. A compelling case for the exclusion from legal prosecution of all sadomasochistic practices between consenting adults is made by Bill Thompson in his book *Sadomasochism* (Published in London by Cassell, 1994). He particularly takes to task the way that the British legal system treats all SM behaviour as automatically a criminal

offence, whether it is playful or not (unlike, say, boxing, rugby, or other violent sports, whose playful nature is recognised).

9. This is known in reversal theory as the 'principle of behavioural indeterminacy.' What it says is that although certain objectively observable behaviours may tend to be associated with certain motivational states, we cannot be sure that they do so in particular instances because there is no indissoluble link between the two. It is reasonable to assume, for example, that someone playing tennis is doing so in the playful state. But we cannot be certain – his mind may not be on the game but on some serious decisions he has to take, or he is in pain through an injury and is about to give up, or he is losing so badly that his self-esteem is coming under threat. We might assume that someone in church is in the serious state, but they may be playfully enjoying the music and the colour and animation around them. They might even be engaged in sexual fantasy. This does not mean that we cannot find out in a given situation the motivational state that someone is experiencing, or at least make informed inferences. What it does mean is that we cannot assume that we know the state that someone is in just from knowing the activity in which they are engaged.

10. Baudelaire, Charles. Les yeux des pauvres. In, *Les Paradis Artificiel.* Paris: Bookking, 1995. (Originally published in 1860.)

11. As good an account as any will be found in: B.S. DeWitt (1970) Quantum mechanics and reality. In, *Physics Today, 23,* 9.

12. See for example: Soros, George (2006) *The Age of Fallibility: The Consequences of the War on Terror.* London: Weidenfeld & Nicolson.

13. The play nature of soccer hooliganism is brought out in a

book cited earlier, in chapter 4: Bill Buford (1993) *Among the Thugs*. New York: Vintage. The misunderstanding of hooligans by the police is documented in Marsh, P., Rosser, E. & Harré, R. *The Rules of Disorder*, London: Routledge and Kegan Paul, 1978. This misunderstanding is also explored in John H. Kerr (1994) *Understanding Soccer Hooliganism*, Buckingham, U.K.: Open University Press. This is, incidentally, a book which is written from the reversal theory perspective.

CHAPTER 14: CONTRARY DESIRES

1. It is interesting that this multifunctional view of human action has occurred at the same time as objects in our culture are becoming increasingly multifunctional: printers not only print, but can copy, scan and fax, coffee machines not only make coffee but any hot beverage, keyboards can simulate any musical instrument, cars are becoming hybrid, and so on. Of course the ultimate multifunctional machine (other than a human being) is the digital computer.

2. Anything that consists of parts that are connected and influence each other (especially through feedback loops) is called a system in Systems Theory. Various abstract mathematical principles may be brought to bear in order to analyze, design and build systems.

3. There is more to The Law of Requisite Variety than this, and the concept of variety is stated in precise mathematical terms, using a branch of Probability Theory called "Information Theory." But the essence of the law is as I have described it here. It was first formulated by W. Ross Ashby, and described in his ground-breaking 1956 book *Introduction to Cybernetics*, London: Chapman & Hall.

4. A similar analysis can be made for the ways in which an

individual employee can contribute to, and benefit from, his or her activity in the workplace. This is, in fact, the basis of personal development, team building, organisational development, and leadership workshops as offered by management consultants, counsellors and organisations using reversal theory. See: Carter, Steve & Kourdi, Jeremy (2003) *The Road to Audacity: Being Adventurous in Life and Work.* London: Palgrave Macmillan. (See also www.apterdevelopment.com, www.typetalk.com, www.methode-apter.com)

Quinn's influential organisational theory is in the same spirit of making positive use of contradictory tendencies and paradoxes in organisations: Quinn, R.E. (1988) *Beyond Rational Management,* San Francisco: Jossey-Bass. See also: Farson, Richard (1997) *Management of the Absurd: Paradoxes in Leadership.* New York: Touchstone. This is a delightful discussion of the absurdities and irrationalities that can enter into business organisations. For another approach to organisations, that sits well with the reversal theory approach, see: Johnson, Barry (1992) *Polarity Management.* Amherst, MA: HRD Press. On paradox in organisations and modern capitalist culture, see: Handy, Charles (1994) *The Age of Paradox,* Boston, M.A.: Harvard Business School Press.

5. Warren, Rick (2002) *The Purpose Driven Life: What on Earth Am I Here For?* Michigan: Zondervan.

6. Perls, Fritz (1951) *Gestalt Therapy: Excitement, and Growth in the Human Personality.* Gouldsboro, ME: The Gestalt Journal Press Inc. An example of emphasis on enjoying the present moment is: Rinpoche, Yongey Mingyur (2007) *The Joy of Living: Unlocking the Secret and Science of Happiness.* New York: Harmony.

7. For example: Robbins, Anthony (1991) *Awaken the Giant Within: How to Take Immediate Control of your Mental, Emotional, Physical and Financial Destiny.* New York: Free

Press. Another example would be: Reyes, Rudy (2009) *Hero Living: Seven Strides to Awaken your Infinite Power.* New York: Celebra.

8. For example: Williamson, Marianne. (1994) *A Return to Love: Reflections on the Principles of a Course in Miracles.* Nehring, Cristina (2009) *A Vindication of Love: Reclaiming Romance for the Twenty-First Century.* New York: HarperCollins. Buscaglia, Leo (1982) *Love: What Life is All About.* Thorofare NJ: Slack. (Originally published 1972.)

9. Her approach is bluntly presented in Rand, Ayn (1982) *Philosophy: Who Needs It?* London: Penguin. It is summarised by the statement: "If any civilisation is to survive, it is the morality of altruism that men have to reject." (p.61.)

10. A major French novelist and dramatist, Henri de Montherlant, has, in many of his writings, made the general point that the full life is a life of contrasts. A central idea is that of 'alternation,' which is not unlike the concept of reversal as presented here. He does not, however, develop a psychological theory to go with this or identify particular states that alternate. (On the other hand, he does write some great novels.)

11. Hamlet, Act 2, Scene 2, 250-251. The original line says: "There is nothing either good or bad, but thinking makes it so."

12. Dogor Di Nuzzo, Béatrice (2011) *Le Management de la Motivation: Améliorer les Services.* Paris: EMS. This book shows how reversal theory can be used in the hospitality industry. It would also serve as an excellent general introduction to reversal theory for French speakers.

13. It has been shown that people engaged in anxiety-causing activities, such as public speaking, perform better if they tell themselves that what they are feeling is excitement than they do if they tell themselves to relax. Brooks, A.W.

(2013) Get excited: Reappraising pre-performance anxiety as excitement. *Journal of Experimental Psychology,* advance online publication: doi:10.1037/a0035325. A similar result with people involved in carrying out negotiations has been found by Brown, A.D. & Curhan, J.R. (2013) The polarizing effects of arousal on negotiation. *Psychological Science, 24* (10) 1928-1935. This supports the ideas I have been putting here.

14. This is the central theme in a delightful French self-help book using reversal theory: Lunacek, Christophe & Rambaud, Jean (2014) *Le Petit Manuel Anti Prise de Tête*. Paris: Dunod.

15. This helpful twist on ways of describing the relationship between a motivational state and its concomitant possible emotions, is due to Hile Rutledge and Jennifer Tucker (2007) *Reversing Forward: A Practical Guide to Reversal Theory.* Fairfax, VA: Otto Kroeger Associates.

16. Blake, William (1790) *The Marriage of Heaven and Hell*, Plate 3. Blake was a British poet and artist, and something of a visionary.

17. I am indebted to my friend and former colleague Kurt Frey for this helpful, and previously unpublished, suggestion. The famous yin-yang symbol represents such interdependence very well: each half of the circle contains within it a smaller circle representing the opposite half.

18. Bloom, Paul (2008) First Person Plural. *The Atlantic,* November, pages 90-98.

19. For people trying to give up smoking, the most vulnerable time is when they are in either playful or rebellious states. For a review of the research showing this, see: O'Connell, Kathleen A. & Cook, Mary R.(1981) Smoking and smoking cessation. In Apter, M.J. (ed.)(1981) *Motivational Styles in Everyday Life: A Guide to Reversal Theory*. Washington, D.C.: American Psychological Association. Knowing this helps

people who are trying to give up to make sure that no cigarettes will be available at times they are likely to be in the playful or rebellious states.

20. Goleman, Daniel (1995) *Emotional Intelligence: Why it can Matter More than IQ.* New York: Bantam.
21. Hadow, Pen (2004) *Solo: The North Pole: Alone and Unsupported.* London: Michael Joseph. This is an enthralling true-life adventure book.
22. Lloyd, Juliette & Apter, Michael (2006) Motivation in extreme environments: The case of polar explorer Pen Hadow. *Journal of Human Performance in Extreme Environments*, 9, 1, 27-43.
23. Hadow, op.cit. pp 92-93.
24. This narrative is based on the following interviews: Ghosh, Aparisim (2005) Inside the mind of an Iraqi suicide bomber. *Time,* July 4, 2005, pp. 22-29. Jaber, Hala (2002) Inside the mind of a suicide cell. *The Sunday Times (U.K.)* March 24, 2002. Ambah, Faiza Saleh (2006) The would-be terrorist's explosive tell-all tale. *The Washington Post,* July 24, 2006. Applebaum, Anne (2005) The puzzle of the suicide bomber. *The Washington Post,* November 16, 2005.
25. The sequence given here is consistent with Moghaddam's evidenced-based 'staircase' model: Moghaddam, Fathali M. (2005) The staircase to terrorism: A psychological explanation, *American Psychologist, 60,* 2, 1611-169. A good review of the literature on the psychology of suicide bombers is: Gordon, Harvey (2002) The 'suicide' bomber: Is it a psychiatric phenomenon? *The Psychiatrist, 26,* 285-287. I can also recommend the following books: Jerrold M. Post (2007) *The Mind of the Terrorist,* New York: Palgrave Macmillan. Moghaddam, Fathali M. & Marsella, Anthony J. (eds.) (2004) *Understanding Terrorism: Psychosocial Roots, Consequences, and Interventions.* Washington, D.C.: American

Psychological Association. Gabriel, Mark A. (2006) *Journey Into the Mind of an Islamic Terrorist,* Florida: FrontLine. A reversal theory analysis will be found in: Baines, Paul R., O'Shaughnessy, Nicolas J., Maloney, Kevin, & Richards, Barry (2010) Islamist propaganda, Reversal Theory and British Muslims, *European Journal of Marketing,* 44: 3-4, 478-495.

CHAPTER 15: THE BIOLOGICAL ORIGINS OF OPPOSITION

1. I shall be using the words 'opposition' and 'polarity' more or less synonymously in this chapter. If there is a difference it is one of emphasis. 'Poles' are the extremities of an axis, 'polarisation' being the formation of such an axis. 'Oppositions,' as I shall use the term here, are more active and do things that have contrary effects. 'Alternations' are continuing 'reversals' over time. These and related words are examined rigorously in Ogden, C.K. (1967) *Opposition: A Linguistic and Psychological Analysis.* Indiana University Press.

2. If we continue to trace oppositionality 'upwards' from biology through psychology to sociology, we find that oppositions continue to proliferate, particularly as identified by 'structuralist' thinkers like the French anthropologist Claude Levi-Strauss. Levi-Strauss found 'binary oppositions' everywhere in the cultural systems he studied. He argued that binary oppositions structured such varied cultural phenomena as what is supposed to go with what in a meal, how myths are generated and spread, and who in a tribe is seen to be related by kinship to whom. A good introduction to his complex but brilliant work is his book *The Savage Mind* (1966) published in translation

by Weidenfeld & Nicolson, London. (Original French version: Plon, Paris, 1962.)

3. There are many kinds of circadian rhythm, i.e. rhythm following a roughly 24 hour cycle. I am here citing those systems that do not display gradual cyclic changes but definite switches at certain points in the cycle, in other words systems that are 'bistable.' I have discussed different kinds of bistability more technically and fully in Apter (1981) On the concept of bistability, *International Journal of General Systems, 6*, 225-232.

4. Some claims have been made, although, it seems, not well replicated at this point, that the alternating breathing between nostrils is correlated with alternations of the dominance of each of the two cerebral hemispheres. Shannahoff-Khalsa, David (1993) The ultradian rhythm of alternating cerebral hemispheric activity, *International Journal of Neuroscience, 3-4, 70*, 285-298. See also: Shannahoff-Khalsa, David (2007) *Psychophysiological States, Volume 80: The Ultradian Dynamics of Mind-Body Interactions (International Review of Neurobiology),* London and New York: Academic Press. If true, this would mean that there is an easy way of determining which cerebral hemisphere is dominant at a given time: stick your finger up your nose. Not too many biologists are taking this seriously at present. It should be added that, in any case, the whole concept of hemispheric dominance is itself somewhat problematic.

5. Li, Liang, Norrelykk, Simon F. & Cox, Edward C. (2008) Persistent cell motion in the absence of external signals: A search strategy for Eukaryotic cells. *PLoS ONE, 3(5)*.

6. Nakaoka, Yasuo, Imaji, Takafumi, Hara, Masahiro & Noboru Hashimoto (2009) Spontaneous fluctuation of the resting membrane potential in Paramecium: Amplification caused by intracellular $Ca2+$, *The Journal of Experimental Biology, 212*, 270-276.

7. Rudberg, Pia & Sand, Olav (2000) Bistable membrane potential of the ciliate Coleps Hirtus. *The Journal of Experimental Biology, 203,* 757-764.

8. Berg, Howard C. (2003) *E.Coli in Motion.* New York: Springer Verlag.

9. A classic expression of apoptosis is: Amiesen, Jean Claude (1999) *La Sculpture du Vivant: Le Suicide Cellulaire ou la Mort Creatrice,* Paris: Seuil. Just how important apoptosis is as a mechanism of biological development, does however remain a matter of some disagreement between biologists.

10. Melino, Gerry (2002) The meaning of death, *Cell Death and Differentiation, 9,* 347-348.

11. A visual animation of this process has been produced at the University of Chicago Centre for Cell Dynamics. It will be found at: munrolab.bsd.uchicago.edu/r1.html

12. I previously developed some models that show how this might work: Apter, M.J. (1966) *Cybernetics and Development.* Oxford: Pergamon Press. They presage the idea which now dominates the field of morphogenesis of 'positional information,' by means of which each cell knows precisely where it is in the growing organism. In my models this was achieved by means of opposing gradients (which I expressed in digital rather than analogue form). For this whole area, see Wolpert, Lewis (1989) Positional information revisited. *Development,* Supplement, 3-12.

13. Darwin, Charles (1872) *The Expression of the Emotions in Man and Animals.* London: Murray.

14. Darwin has two other principles of emotional expression: physiological change that produces emotional expression, as in trembling from fear, and learned habitual expression like shaking one's head from side to side in disagreement. Clearly neither of these methods of expression emerge through natural selection. The first would seem to be a

kind of byproduct generation, and the second would be nothing to do with evolution, but rather an effect of learned social custom.

15. A quick review of this field will be found in Marshall, Michael (2011) In the beginning was Pac-Man. *New Scientist*, 5 March 2011, pp.8-9. For more detail, see: Rasmussen, S., Bedau, M.A., Chen, L., Deamer, D., Krakauer, D.C., Packard, H., Standu, P.R. (eds.) *Protocells: Bridging Living and Nonliving Matter*, Cambridge, M.A.: MIT Press.

16. (My translation.) In: Le cerveau, capital du diable. *L'Express*, 17 December, 2010. This article is an interview with the well-known French biologist Jean-Didier Vincent. Among his works, in relation to this theme, see especially *La Chair et le Diable*. Paris: Editions Odile Jacob, 1996. His best-known work in English is: *The Biology of Emotions*, Oxford: Blackwell, 1990.